THE
C·O·M·P·L·E·T·E
BOOK OF
U.S. SNIPING

Peter R. Senich

The Complete Book of U.S. Sniping
by Peter R. Senich

Copyright © 1988 by Peter R. Senich

Printed in Mexico

Published by Paladin Press, a division of
Paladin Enterprises, Inc., P.O. Box 1307,
Boulder, Colorado 80306, USA.
(303) 443-7250

Direct inquiries to the above address.

Front cover photograph courtesy of the U.S. Marine Corps.
Back cover photographs, top to bottom, are courtesy of the
U.S. Army, the U.S. Marine Corps, and the U.S. Army,
respectively.

ISBN 0-87364-460-3

Contents

Other books by Peter R. Senich, available from Paladin Press:

The German Assault Rifle: 1935–1945
The German Sniper: 1914–1945

Preface and Acknowledgments

The United States military has been responsible for significant contributions to telescopic sight development and its combat application for over a century, but a comprehensive chronicle of these efforts has not been available prior to the release of this book. Since little official effort was directed toward preserving the minutiae associated with the development and fielding of American sniper equipment through the years, the obscurity surrounding this fascinating subject has been, for the most part, self-inflicted. Recognition of this fact prompted the decision to produce a thorough study devoted entirely to the chronological development of both United States Army and Marine Corps sniper arms and related optical sights from the Civil War era through the conflict in Vietnam, where first-class sniper training clearly demonstrated the value of precision marksmanship in combat.

In the interest of presenting fact, from the onset, the policy of utilizing only that material having accredited origins was responsible for what may seem to be incomplete segments. However, the material presented herein consists of documented information gleaned from original reports, documents, official correspondence, and the personal archives of knowledgeable individuals within or in close proximity to the military establishment. These individuals have had firsthand experience and the foresight to retain pertinent documents and records concerning American military sniping that would have otherwise been lost.

Were it not for the many friends made through the course of this endeavor, and their contributions over and above what any author has a right to expect, this book would not have been brought to fruition. Thus, for the first time, serious military students and martial arms collectors can trace American sniping materiel from its infancy to the sophisticated systems currently in use.

The following organizations rendered invaluable assistance in the form of original documents, technical information, photographs, and other archival material. For this help I wish to thank the staffs of: the Marine Corps Museum, U.S. Army Infantry Museum, West Point Museum, Rock Island and Frankford arsenals, Springfield Armory Museum, the Library of Congress, National Archives, Smithsonian Institution, Warner & Swasey Company, Night Vision Laboratory, the Winchester, Colt, and Remington firms, Excalibur Enterprises, U.S. Army Photographic Agency, U.S. Marine Corps Headquarters, Carlisle Barracks, Army Ordnance Museum, Aberdeen Proving Ground Museum, U.S. Army MTU, U.S. Marine Corps Scout-Sniper Instructor School, and the Gale McMillan Company.

In addition, the following gentlemen provided me with collection photographs, vital data, and in many cases, their encouragement: Sam Bases, Dick Boyd, Leo Champion, Stan Deka, John Edgar, Doug Edwards, Robert W. Fisch, Steve Fleischman, Myron Klein, William Lennox, Monty Lutz, Donald Stoehr, Thomas Swearengen, Larry Smith, J. David Truby, Ralph T. Walker, Thomas Wallace, Barry Zuckerman, Elroy Sanford, Bruce

Canfield, Morton Gray, John Slonaker, Hayes Otoupalik, Charles Leatherwood, Allan Cors, John Leach, John Minnery, Burch Eyberg, Gale Mc-Millan, John Mason, J. B. Anderhub, Thomas Shannon, John Amber, S. L. Walsh Capt. USMC, Ken Kogan, Bill Grube, Jim Shultz, Donald G. Thomas, James Alley, Steve Fuller, R. Blake Stevens, Tom Dunkin, Mike West, and John C. McPherson.

Special expressions of appreciation go to: Colonel William S. Brophy (Retired), an individual that many in the weapons field consider to be "Mr. Springfield," for graciously sharing rare Army Ordnance photographs that were uncovered only through his diligent research; and to Lieutenant Colonel Frank B. Conway (Retired), for offering his expertise and personal archives relevant to the development and fielding of the Army's XM21 sniping system.

In writing this book, I have purposely avoided fields of strategy, military movements, and "editorials" that have become synonymous with recent works dealing with United States involvement in Southeast Asia. This book is intended solely as an instrument of historical reference for the purpose of illustrating the activities and equipment of the American military sniper.

Peter R. Senich

A Federal sharpshooter with telescopic-sighted rifle selects a target from a lofty vantage point. Photo Credit: Smithsonian Institution.

Chapter 1 ◆◆

Sharpshooter— The Beginning

The concept of employing special shoulder weapons for sniping at extreme ranges originated during the American Civil War when select numbers of Union and Confederate sharpshooters recorded hits at distances so great they are considered remarkable even by contemporary standards. Their rifles, generally .50 to .58 caliber and originally intended for bench-rest match shooting, possessed long, exceptionally heavy one-and-one-half- to two-inch-thick octagonal barrels for safely containing the heavy powder charges required for such shooting.

Weighing in at twenty-five to thirty-five pounds, most rifles utilized special open sights, while a number were in fact fitted with telescopic-sight variants that found favor among match shooters in the years just prior to the War Between the States. The scopes, of high magnification with an extremely limited field of view, were virtually useless in anything but optimum light, but did permit uncanny accuracy when employed by a competent marksman.

Although such heavy weapon weight precluded off-hand shooting, in what has long since become accepted sniper practice, the Civil War sharpshooter made effective use of suitable rests when sighting his "mark." The accomplishments of the early snipers have become legendary with accounts of their prowess often cited in Civil War archives.

A measure of their long-range accuracy employing heavy caliber rifles can be judged by the frequency in which combatants in both armies were brought down silently behind their front lines at distances so great the report of the sharpshooter weapon could not be heard. The thought of being singled out and shot by an unseen, unheard enemy was as disconcerting in 1864 as it remains to this day.

While the vast majority of weapons employed for sharpshooting purposes were open sighted, it is significant to point out that the organized military use of telescopic-sighted rifles originated on American soil during this period. Despite their cumbersome nature, a surprising number of rather sophisticated telescope-sighted rifles were used throughout the war primarily for, as it was then stated, "special work." In addition to selecting targets of opportunity, that is, officers, artillery crews, and individual personnel, "special work" included bringing up a skilled marksman for the sole purpose of eliminating an opposing sharpshooter.

A particularly interesting example of early countersniping took place at Chancellorsville after a Confederate marksman had brought down an enemy colonel near an artillery position. A Union sharpshooter was summoned, and as members of the battery watched curiously:

First he took off his cap and shoved it over the earthwork. Of course, Johnnie Reb let go at it, thinking to kill the careless man under it. His bullet struck into the bank, and instantly our sharpshooter ran his ramrod down the hole made by the Johnnie's ball, then lay on his back and sighted along the ramrod. He accordingly perceived from the direction that his game was in the top of a thick bushy elm tree about

A heavy-barreled N. Lewis telescope-sighted, percussion muzzle-loader represents one of many variants used by Union marksmen in the Civil War. Photo Credit: Taylor Collection.

A close view of the N. Lewis rifle illustrates the simple device used for basic elevation adjustment and the double-set triggers employed on many precision rifles of this era. Photo Credit: Taylor Collection.

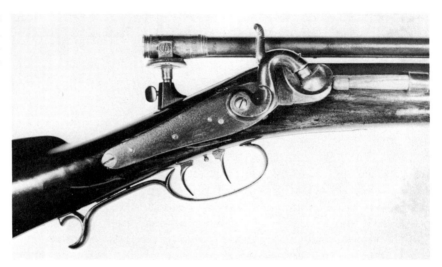

one hundred yards in front. It was then the work of less than a second to aim his long telescopic rifle at that tree and crack she went. Down tumbled Mr. Johnnie like a great crow out of his nest and we had no more trouble from that source.

By use of a long stick in place of a ramrod, the aforementioned method of locating an opposing sniper was later employed by the British to detect carefully concealed German snipers during the early stages of the First World War.

Although Confederate sharpshooters proved the equal of their Northern counterparts in every respect, their use of special telescope-sighted rifles was severely hampered by a lack of availability, and as a result their field use by the South did not reach the same proportions as in the Union Army.

The early rifle scopes, fashioned from sheet steel or brass, were rolled into a one-half- to three-quarter-inch diameter cylindrical tube with solder closing the seam. In most cases, a simple lens system consisting of a single-unit objective and

ocular lens with an erecting lens in-between provided a magnified upright image. Both reticle and lenses were carefully set, aligned, and held in place with threaded rings or fixed spacers.

The tubes, generally two to three feet in length, were either permanently attached to the barrel or held by simple clamping devices, which permitted their removal for repair or replacement. Although no provisions existed for internal adjustments, that is, elevation and windage, many sights could be raised or lowered for basic elevation settings by means of a threaded screw located near the rear of the tube.

While all were unique in their own right, perhaps the most noteworthy Civil War sharpshooter rifle was originally cited by Ned H. Roberts in his classic work, *The Muzzle-Loading Cap Lock Rifle:*

> During the Civil War, Morgan James made many heavy, muzzle-loading sharpshooter's rifles for Berdan's Sharpshooter Regiment and the U.S. Army, many of which were equipped with telescopic sights.

However, as far as can be ascertained, this is the only one of this type Morgan James ever made. The basis of this rifle was an E. Remington & Sons, "model 1864 contract musket" from which James removed the original Remington barrel and replaced it with a barrel of his own make using the Minnie bullet. James then made a full length telescope, having internal adjustment of the cross-hair, and soldered the telescope tube to the top of the rifle barrel. The reticle containing the cross-hair is, of course, in the eyepiece of the telescope and is raised or lowered to obtain elevations by means of a graduated brass dial affixed to the upper tang of the rifle and lower part of the rear of the telescope.

In addition to establishing a precedent by the adaptation of a telescopic sight to an existing military service rifle, Morgan James's effort, as experts contend, represents the first internally adjustable telescope sight to have been made in this country.

Oddly enough, even though the federal government had procured telescopic-sighted rifles from various civilian contractors for specific sharpshooter use, and the value of such weapons had been clearly demonstrated, no further consideration was given to the U.S. military use of telescopic rifle sights in the years following the Civil War.

Muzzle view of a Civil War percussion target/sharpshooter rifle depicting a false-muzzle used for loading, which with the help of a "starter," ensured accurate insertion of the bullet. Note the simple clamp for holding the objective end of the telescope to the barrel. Photo Credit: West Point Collection.

A telescope-sighted Edwin Wesson rifle, converted from a bench-rest type for Federal sharpshooter use by the addition of a ramrod under the barrel. Photo Credit: Smithsonian Institution.

TO THE
SHARP SHOOTERS
OF WINDHAM COUNTY!

Your Country Calls!!   Will you Respond?

CAPT. WESTON has been authorized to raise a Company of Green Mountain Boys for Col. Berdan's Regiment of Sharp Shooters which has been accepted by the War Department to serve for three years, or during the war. Capt. Weston desires to have Windham County represented in his Company.

The Sharp Shooters of Windham County and vicinity who are willing to serve their country in this time of need and peril, are requested to meet at the ISLAND HOUSE in Bellows Falls, on TUESDAY, the 27th inst., at 1 o'clock, P. M., for the purpose of testing their skill in TARGET SHOOTING. There are great inducements to join this celebrated Regiment, destined to be the most important and popular in the Service.

No person will be enlisted who cannot when firing at the distance of 200 yards, at a rest, put ten consecutive shots in a target, the average distance not to exceed five inches from the centre of the bull's eye to the centre of the ball.

GREEN MOUNTAIN BOYS!

"Rally for the support of the Stars and Stripes!"

YOU ARE INVITED TO BRING YOUR RIFLES.

F. F. STREETER, Supt. of Trial.

BELLOWS FALLS, VT., August 19, 1861.

Phenix Job Office, Bellows Falls.

An early Civil War broadside calling competent marksmen—note the marksmanship prerequisites—for service to the Union. Photo Credit: Peter R. Senich.

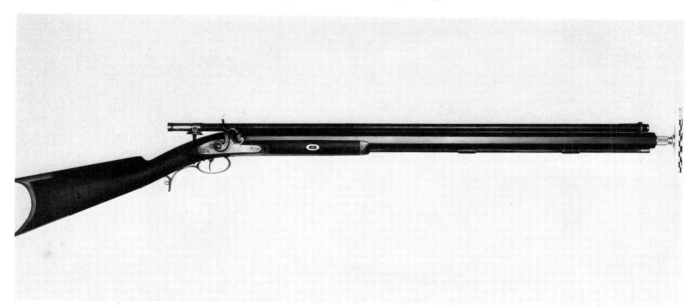

A Morgan James sharpshooter rifle and sight typical of those fielded by the Union Army during the Civil War. Photo Credit: Smithsonian Institution.

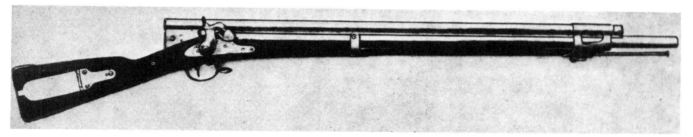

The unique Morgan James special telescope-sighted Civil War sharpshooter rifle based on a Remington model. Photo Credit: Stackpole Books.

Capable of precise long-range accuracy, special Whitworth hexagonal-bore rifles mounting Davidson telescopic sights were procured in England by the Confederate government for sharpshooter use. Photo Credit: Taylor Collection.

A Confederate marksman with an open-sighted rifle. Sharpshooters in both armies made frequent use of positions in trees while plying their trade. Photo Credit: Virginia State library.

Chapter 2 ◆◆

A Riflescope for Expert Riflemen

Even though telescopic rifle sights had proven their worth in a combat environment during the Civil War, with the exception of unsuccessful evaluations conducted with rifle scopes of unknown origin and configuration in 1896 and 1897, the application of such devices laid dormant until 1900 when the Ordnance Department conducted a feasibility study to determine the practicality of utilizing telescopic sights with the Model 1898 Krag Rifle.

The annual *Report of the Chief of Ordnance* for the year 1900 records Ordnance Department tests of three telescopic sights submitted by the Cataract Tool & Optical Company of Buffalo, New York. A board, appointed by Lieutenant Colonel F. H. Phippe, commander of Springfield Armory, was convened on 8 June 1900:

> The board met pursuant to the foregoing order. . . . Present, all the members. Mr. H. L. DeZeng, Jr., representing the Cataract Tool & Optical Company, was also present and explained the working of the telescopic sight submitted by his company for trial.
>
> The sight consists of a telescope which is attached by means of brackets to the left side of the rifle. The front bracket is secured to the lower band by two screws, and the ring through which the telescope passes has a horizontal motion to provide for drift and windage. A ball-and-socket joint in this ring allows the telescope to be moved in any direction, and it may be pushed forward or backward through this ring to bring it to the proper distance from the eye of the firer. The rear bracket is screwed to the side plate of the receiver, and the ring which holds

Model 1898 Krag Rifle with Cataract telescopic sight tested by the Ordnance Department in 1900 for use as a sharpshooter weapon. Photo Credit: Colonel William S. Brophy (Retired).

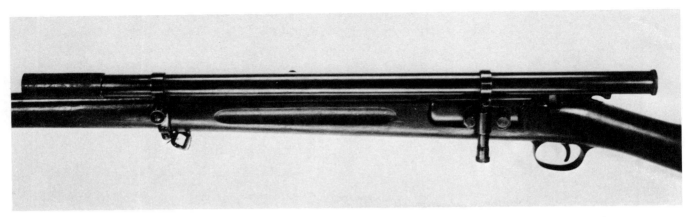

A close view of the Cataract sight as mounted to the left side of the Krag receiver. Photo Credit: Peter R. Senich.

the telescope has a vertical movement for changes of elevation. This ring is provided with a clamp screw for securing the telescope at the desired distance from the eye.

Telescopes of three different powers were submitted for trial, viz. 8 diameters, 12 diameters, and 20 diameters.

The medium power (12 diameters) gave the best results.

The telescope is of practically universal focus; that is, it does not require readjustment for different marksmen or for different ranges.

The eye can be placed close to the eyepiece or several inches away without any apparent difference in the focus. Danger of being struck in the eye when the piece recoils can therefore be avoided.

The lenses are large and are held in place by having the metal of the tubes in which they are mounted spun over their outer edges. The telescope is light, but at the same time strong. The brackets for attaching the telescope to the rifle are strong and durable and there appears to be no tendency to jar loose.

The sight was tested by actual firings up to a range of 2,000 yards, each member of the board participating in the firings. As a result of this test the board is of the opinion that the use of this telescopic sight appears to be of especial value in hazy or foggy weather and at long ranges. In either case the target can be seen with remarkable clearness, and the marksman can be absolutely sure that he is aiming at the proper object. This would be of especial importance to sharpshooters acting independently.

The firing conducted at the firing range showed that better targets were secured with the telescopic sight than with the regular sight; but the board is of the opinion that this does not indicate the full value of the telescopic sight.

The ordinary sight is useful for accurate firing at a regular target up to about 2,000 yards; but it is impossible to see a man or even a small body of men clearly at that range unless projected against the sky

or under other very favorable conditions. It is for this reason that volley firing is so largely resorted to at long ranges.

With a telescopic sight a man could be distinguished easily at 2,000 yards, even with an unfavorable background.

The board is of the opinion that this sight is suitable for use in the U.S. service, and recommends that a number of them be purchased for trial by troops in the field. If found to be satisfactory, a sufficient number should be purchased to supply such a number of the sharpshooters of each organization as experience in the field shall indicate to be desirable.

Despite the above recommendation for field trial, ordnance records make no further mention of Cataract sights or the consideration of any other rifle scopes for the Krag rifle. From a standpoint of the Cataract sights, however, in 1901 the J. Stevens Arms & Tool Company of Chicopee Falls, Massachusetts, acquired the assets of the Cataract Tool & Optical Company. Whether or not this event had a direct bearing on further military consideration of these sights remains open to speculation.

In 1903 the Krag was superseded by the Model 1903 rifle or the "'03 Springfield." Even though problems were experienced with the new service rifle in both manufacturing and use, ordnance efforts to adapt a telescopic sight to the infantry arm were to continue in earnest as cited in the *Report of the Chief of Ordnance* for the year 1904:

Telescopic sight—Different forms of telescopic sights have been tested during the year with a view to obtaining a suitable design for issue to expert riflemen. The only promising design so far is one made by the Warner & Swasey Company, of Cleveland, Ohio, which is now being tested.

Unfortunately, the "different forms of telescopic sights" mentioned along with the Warner & Swasey device have remained obscure.

As a point of interest, *Small Arms Firing Regulations* for 1904, paragraph 269, authorized a telescopic sight for the use of expert riflemen in advance of the actual acceptance of a specific sight design:

269. *Telescopic sight*—To encourage effort, to reward efficiency, and to properly equip a special class of shots who shall not only be designated as expert riflemen, but who, in action, shall be employed as such, the telescopic sight is adopted. These sights will be supplied by the Ordnance Department and assigned to enlisted men who have qualified under these regulations as expert riflemen. They will be issued to and accounted for by the company commander, and, in his discretion, may be carried by the men at inspections under arms.

However, by the end of fiscal year 1905 as noted in the *Report of the Chief of Ordnance* relevant to that period:

Telescopic sight for issue to expert riflemen—The telescopic sight referred to in my last report as being designed by the Warner & Swasey Company, of Cleveland, Ohio, proved satisfactory, and 25 are being procured for issue. The telescope can readily be detached from the rifle and carried in a leather case.

Patented by Ambrose Swasey and manufactured by the Warner & Swasey Company, a longtime, highly respected supplier of optical artillery fire-control equipment for the government, the new prismatic sight mounted to the left side of the '03 Springfield by means of a male dovetail receiver bracket (base), which permitted use of the standard rifle sights and clip (charger) loading in a conventional manner. Adjustment for both

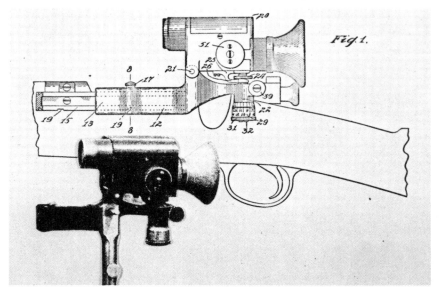

Design drawing and one of the twenty-five Warner & Swasey telescopic sights procured by the Ordnance Department in 1905. This sight served as a basis for the Telescopic Musket Sight, Model of 1908. Photo Credit: Peter R. Senich.

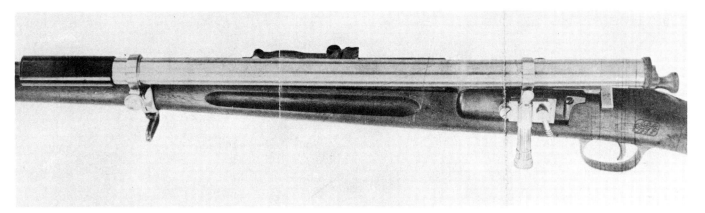

A Cataract Tool & Optical Company rifle scope—note that this sight is of shorter length—as originally illustrated in the Report of the Chief of Ordnance for 1900. Photo Credit: Peter R. Senich.

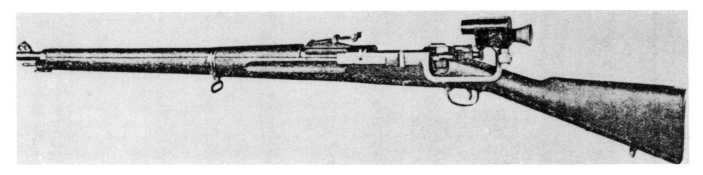

The Model 1903 Springfield rifle, an early variant, mounted with a Zeiss prismatic sight manufactured in Germany. It is believed to have been one of the "different forms of telescopic sights" tested by the Ordnance Department during 1904. The Zeiss instrument and the early Warner & Swasey prismatic sights were quite similar in appearance. Photo Credit: J. B. Anderhub.

windage and elevation was provided along with the fitting of a hard rubber eyecup to shield the ocular lens and protect the shooter.

While precious few details concerning the Army's subsequent application of this sight have survived, the mention of a "favorable report" by the Infantry Board was duly noted. However, with the cost of the new sight at approximately $80 per unit, it was considered almost prohibitive, particularly with a view toward procuring them in quantity.

As a result, early in 1907 it was officially recommended that a new sight be developed along the lines of the existing device, but with an eye toward a reduction in cost. This was accomplished by the Warner & Swasey firm with a reduction in price by means of "a simplification of the mechanical details," as it was then stated. A review of both American and British patents granted to Ambrose Swasey in 1906 for his prismatic telescopic sight, as referred to in the *Report of the Chief of Ordnance* for the years 1904 and 1905, indicates characteristics comparative to its direct successor, the Telescopic Musket Sight, Model of 1908.

Chapter 3 ◆━◆

Sniper Issue– An Army First

The improved telescopic rifle sight based on Ambrose Swasey's original military model was made available for Army evaluation in 1908, and as subsequently approved for regular issue bore the designation Telescopic Musket Sight, Model of 1908.

TELESCOPIC MUSKET SIGHT
MODEL OF 1908 No. 601
THE WARNER & SWASEY CO.
CLEVELAND OHIO U.S.A.
PAT. FEB. 13-06 MAY 22-06

The chronological progression of the Model 1908 Musket Sight can be followed best as originally documented in the *Report of the Chief of Ordnance* for the years 1908 and 1909:

Telescopic sight for the musket–A sight has been obtained for the use of expert riflemen, as provided for in paragraph 235, *Small Arms Firing Regulations for 1906*. These sights are now being delivered by the contractors, and each will be adjusted to a particular rifle and marked with the number of the rifle. The rifle will then be targeted with the telescopic sight. All rifles so used will be specially selected by star gauging.

The 6 power Telescopic Musket Sight, Model of 1908–the first rifle scope adopted for service by the U.S. Army. Photo Credit: Peter R. Senich.

Model 1903 Springfield Rifle and Warner & Swasey Model 1908 Musket Sight. Photo Credit: Canfield Collection.

As originally issued, Model 1908 sights were fitted to select M1903 rifles having star-gauged barrels. Photo Credit: Canfield Collection.

And as followed in the 1909 report:

> *Telescopic musket sight, model of 1908*—One thousand of the telescopic sights for muskets referred to in my last report were received from the contractors and issued to expert riflemen for trial and report. Above 90 percent of the reports received have been favorable to the sight. Recommendations were received that the sight be moved forward on the rifle to prevent the eyepiece striking the eye upon recoil; also that the rubber eyepiece be made of softer rubber. Steps have been taken to overcome these defects before procurement of the additional number of these sights necessary to equip the expert riflemen in the Army. A sufficient number of the sights will also be procured to meet the requirements of the militia.

The work of mating the Model 1908 sights as conducted at the Springfield Armory entailed careful inspection, fitting, and testing for each mounting after which the scope was stamped with the rifle serial number inside the mount dovetail, for example, "FOR RIFLE No. 352971." The reference to star-gauged barrels was a method of employing a device for measuring the gun-bore lands and grooves at one-inch intervals along the length of the bore to determine if they fell within prescribed tolerances deemed essential for precise shooting. This procedure had been in use since about 1905 and was not developed for, or limited to, the selection of sharpshooter rifles. Those barrels passing this test were stamped ☼ on the crowned portion of the muzzle.

A concise description of the Model 1908 Warner & Swasey sight was set forth in the original ordnance pamphlet Number 1957 under date of 14 December 1908:

> The telescopic sight consists of three essential parts, the telescope, the lever on which the telescope

A comparative view—the early experimental dovetail mounting base (top), used for evaluation purposes, was held to the '03 receiver by solder, and the final design adopted in 1910 (bottom) became the standard mounting bracket for the Model 1908 sight. Photo Credit: Peter R. Senich.

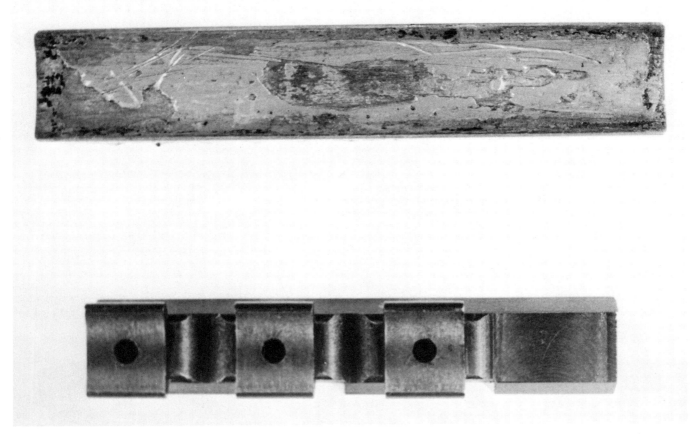

The receiver side of the early 1908 sight base (top) and the standard mounting bracket. Photo Credit: Peter R. Senich.

is mounted by a vertical axis, and the slide to which the lever is secured by a horizontal axis. Graduated dials provide means for turning the instrument on both of these axes.

The telescope: In the telescope body is mounted the objective cell for the objective, which has a clear aperture of thirteen-sixteenths inch, a focal length of 7 inches, and gives, with the eyepiece, a power of six diameters and a field of 4 1/2°. The telescope is provided with Porro erecting prisms, mounted in accurately milled recesses in the prism holder and held in place under constant pressure by the prism-cap springs of the prism caps, the caps being secured by the prism-cap screws. The telescope has a reticule holder, into which is spun the glass reticule, on which are etched vertical and horizontal cross lines and a stadia line, the latter being so placed that it spans the height (5 feet 8 inches) of an average man standing at a distance of 1,000 yards. The latest telescopic sights have three stadia lines for ranges of 1,000, 1,500, and 2,000 yards, respectively. [The mention of "latest" in this case constitutes specific reference to Ambrose Swasey's earlier 1906 sight, which had only vertical and horizontal cross hairs etched on the glass reticle. The word "latest" was deleted in subse-

quent revisions of this pamphlet.] The telescope has an eyelens holder for the Steinheil triple achromatic eyelens. The holder has a long threaded portion which screws into the body, and by which means for focusing is secured. The eyelens holder is locked in position by the focusing lock nut and is provided with an eye cap of soft rubber, fastened by the eye-cap ferrule. On each telescope is fastened, by means of table screws, the wind and range table and drift table, and on the rear face of the latest telescopes is fastened a range plate which shows the ranges corresponding to the three stadia lines.

The lever supports the telescope body by means of the adjusting screw. This screw forms a vertical axis for the telescope, and the segmental worm gear, together with the drift screw and its graduated drift dial, provide means for turning the telescope on this axis for drift and wind corrections.

The slide supports the lever on the horizontal axis. The pin of the lever engages with the internal hardened-steel cam of the range dial, and is kept in contact with it by the lever spring. The inner circumference of the range dial is conical and fits in a conical bearing, so that it can be clamped in any desired position by tightening the range-dial knob against

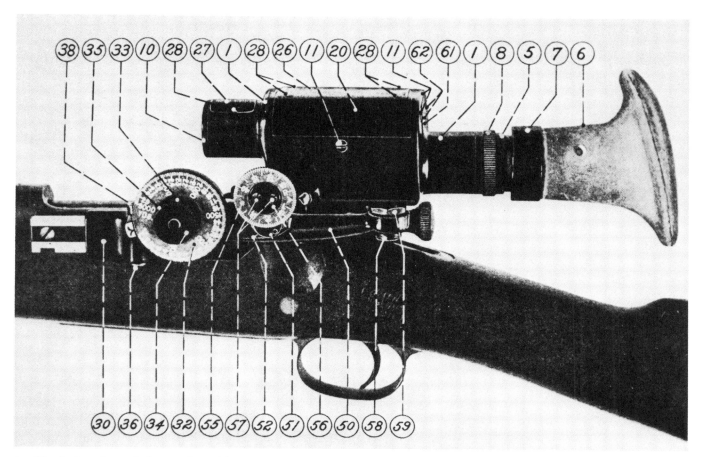

An illustration from Ordnance Pamphlet No. 1957 depicting the Model 1908 receiver base deemed unsatisfactory during initial field use, because the sight was positioned too far to the rear. Photo Credit: Peter R. Senich.

After adjustment to a particular '03 Springfield, the rifle serial number was stamped in the mount slide recess. In this case, sight no. 601 "FOR RIFLE No. 352971." Photo Credit: Peter R. Senich.

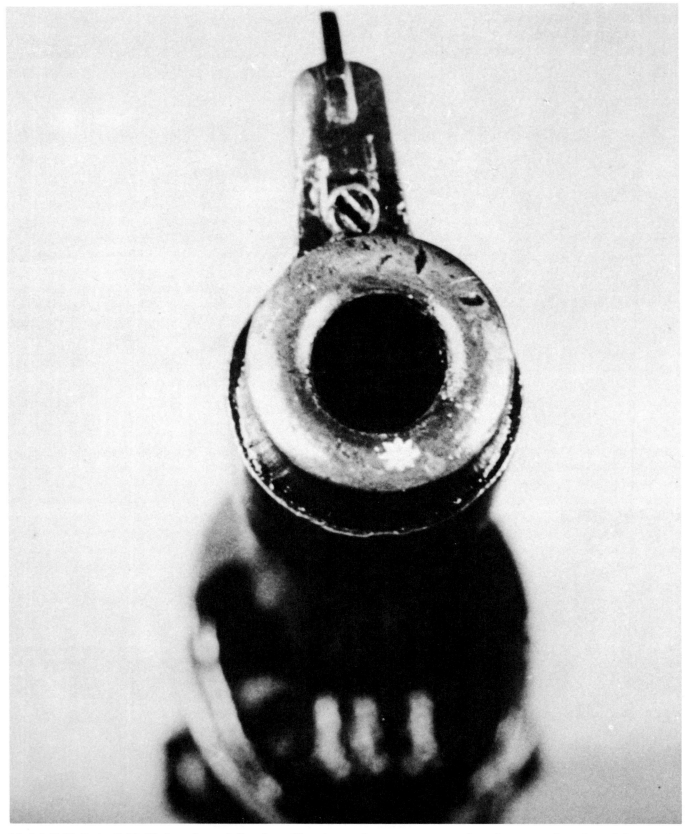

Model 1903 Springfield rifle barrels specially selected by star-gauging were so stamped on the crowned portion of the muzzle. Photo Credit: Peter R. Senich.

the keyed range-dial washer. By turning the dial the telescope is rotated on the horizontal axis, giving the proper depression angle for range correction.

The telescopic sight bracket is assembled to the receiver of the rifle by means of screws. The sight is mounted on the bracket by means of the dovetail in the slide and is held in position by means of the catch which engages the notch in the bracket. The catch can be released by pressing the knob.

An early male dovetail receiver bracket (base) used for evaluation purposes was affixed to the '03 Springfield receiver by means of solder rather than screws. While this base permitted greater fore and aft positioning of the sight, the separations between the locking notches proved entirely too fragile for the heavy Model 1908 sight.

A second base design, fastened to the receiver by three screws, and provided with two deeply recessed locking notches approximately one inch apart, while equal to the task, required an awkward

position by the shooter, which proved to be quite uncomfortable during sustained firing.

The third and final design developed in 1910 was found acceptable in all respects, and thus became the standard receiver base for both the Model 1908 sight and its eventual successor, the Model 1913 Musket Sight.

By virtue of the use of erecting prisms in the Model 1908 sight, as opposed to direct vision erecting lenses found in conventional telescopic sights, an extremely short eye-relief of approximately one and one-half inches was necessary. Because of this, a rubber eyecup was provided to both position and protect the shooter's eye. Nonetheless, the force of recoil drove the eyecup into the shooter's face creating an unpleasant vacuum effect.

A candid summation of this problem was recorded by Edward C. Crossman in his classic work, *The Book of the Springfield:*

Original issue russet leather carrying case and shoulder strap for the Model 1908 Musket Sight. Both this and the 1911 variant case were provided with a stud, to hold the case lid closed, and with hooks for the cartridge belt. Most, but not all, cases were fitted with a small pouch under the lid for an adjustment tool furnished with each sight. Photo Credit: Peter R. Senich.

Right and left view of the Model 1908 sight. Early ordnance efforts to keep the heavy scope in place on the receiver base at recoil saw the addition of one, and in some cases, two mount locking screws. Not all sights were so modified, however. Photo Credit: Peter R. Senich.

The first ones didn't have any [air holes] and if the thing happened to fit your face neatly and you shot the rifle, setting the cup firmly back into your face from recoil, it took three strong men to pull you loose from the fool telescope.

To rectify this, holes were punched through the rubber eyecups to permit the escape of air on recoil, thereby preventing suction on counter recoil. Although most ordnance documents cite the addition of three air escape holes, four were variously mentioned as well. At this point, however, only three holes have been noted in surviving specimens.

Air holes notwithstanding, the cumbersome eyecup made shooting this equipment rather unpleasant, as E. C. Crossman further related that "it had a rubber eyecup that would make a flincher out of a cigar store Indian."

Concurrent with the adoption of the Model 1908 Musket Sight, in 1909 the Army School of Musketry and Springfield Armory's Department of Experiment commenced test and evaluation of

rifle silencers manufactured by the Maxim Silent Firearms Company of Hartford, Connecticut. Whereas: "Extensive tests of the Maxim silencer have been conducted at different periods throughout the year."

Acting on recommendations of the review board responsible for silencer evaluation, in 1910 an unspecified number of telescopic-sighted, star-gauged Model 1903 Springfield sharpshooter rifles, prepared at Springfield Armory and fitted with Maxim Model J silencers, were issued to Regular Army and Guard units. The issuance of silencers ostensibly for sniping purposes—to allow sharpshooters to fire without being located by the sound of their firing—during an era of ultraconservative ordnance development, provided the Army with a bold concept in infantry weapons.

Not only did the U.S. Army become the first military power to adopt telescopic rifle sights and silencers, it also was the first to employ their simultaneous use as well. In search of more efficient silencers, devices made by Corumboef and Moore, competitors of Maxim, were procured and

Select Model 1903 Springfield rifles with Warner & Swasey telescopic sights and Maxim Model J silencers were prepared at Springfield Armory for regular Army and National Guard units in 1910. Photo Credit: Donald G. Thomas.

M1903 Springfield rifle mounting the Maxim Model J Silencer. Although issued for sharpshooter use, most silencers were fitted to rifles with conventional sights. Photo Credit: Donald G. Thomas.

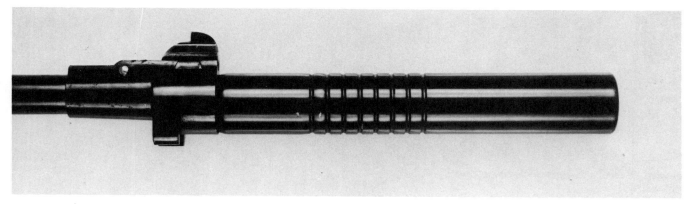

A close view of the Maxim Model J silencer. Photo Credit: Smithsonian Institution.

Side and rear view of the soft-rubber eyecup, which proved bothersome during extended use, furnished with Warner & Swasey sights. Photo Credit: Peter R. Senich.

tested in 1912 with one hundred of the Moore design evaluated under field conditions.

Research conducted with the assistance of the Warner & Swasey Company indicates that a total of 2,075 Model 1908 Musket sights were manufactured and sold to the government as follows:

YEAR	TOTAL MANUFACTURED
1908	1,000
1910	10
1912	1,065

Serial numbering for the original twenty-five musket sights noted in the 1905 *Report of the Chief of Ordnance* were numbers 1 to 25 inclusive, as cited in Warner & Swasey records.

While not clearly defined, evidence and the study of surviving sights strongly suggests that subsequent numbering of the Model 1908 variant was simply a continuance of the practice that commenced with the original twenty-five furnished to the Army for test and evaluation. When the design for the Model 1908 sight was finally established, serial numbering for regular production began where the last number of the original twenty-five government sights had left off. The earliest Model 1908 sight noted thus far bears the serial number 33, with the legend "FOR RIFLE No. 352839" stamped in the mount slide recess.

With the exception of prototype and tool room variants, musket sights were numbered consecutively, but they were not issued with the Model

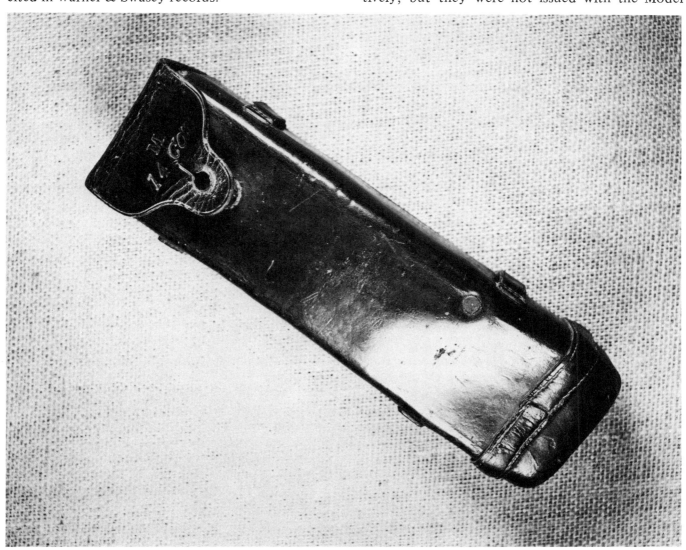

A model 1911 leather carrying case issued for use with Warner & Swasey musket sights. Note the unit markings impressed in the flap. Photo Credit: Otoupalik Collection.

Automatic Machine Rifle, Caliber .30, Model of 1909 mounting a Model 1908 telescopic sight as issued for service use. Photo Credit: Smithsonian Institution.

1903 Springfield in a specific rifle serial number sequence, as the following random sampling of various Model 1908 sights indicates:

TELESCOPE NUMBER	FOR RIFLE NUMBER
33	352839
275	353159
296	353009
461	352645
601	352971
728	353326
798	353262

Model 1908 sights having only three-digit serial numbers stamped in the mount slide recess, for example, "FOR RIFLE No. 116," represent those telescopic sights that were mated with the Automatic Machine Rifle. In any case, all sights issued with either the '03 Springfield or the automatic rifle will bear weapon serial numbers as indicated. All but a few Model 1908 Musket sights were issued, with virtually all nonissue sights found in the last lot that was procured in 1912.

In addition to acceptance for sharpshooter use with the service rifle, in 1909 Warner & Swasey telescopic sights were tested and eventually adapted for use with the Benet-Mercie automatic rifle, or as it was officially designated, the Automatic Machine Rifle, Caliber .30, Model of 1909. By no stretch of the imagination was this application intended to produce precision shooting with

an automatic weapon. As it was then stated:

> This instrument, if properly used, is a great aid to the effectiveness of the Benet Gun, as by its use the line of sight is removed from above the hot barrel and the heat mirage is avoided. The telescopic sight is also an aid to target recognition, and very often allows the gunner to observe strikes of his gun shots.

The Model 1908 sight was mounted to the left side of the machine rifle receiver by means of a male dovetail bracket (base) in much the same manner as on the service rifle. Although no difference is apparent in the sights used on either weapon, the machine rifle receiver brackets were not the same as those intended for the service rifle. Despite the fact that a moderate number of automatic weapons were issued with telescopic sights, it must be emphasized that all machine rifles were not fitted with receiver brackets to mount the Model 1908 scope. Surviving musket sights stamped with three-digit automatic machine rifle serial numbers are far from common.

In early use the Warner & Swasey sight was well received and was considered reasonably effective. However, it was hardly the best telescopic sight available. As compared with conventional iron sights, it proved to be a revelation to those who had never used a telescopic rifle sight before. But as time progressed, and the capabilities of marksmen increased, the real defects of this sight became obvious and as a result the need for an improved sight again became a serious consideration of the Ordnance Department.

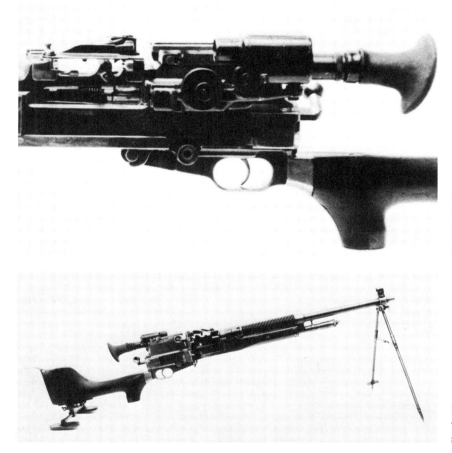

Close view of the Automatic Machine Rifle and Warner & Swasey sight, with telescope mounted to the left side of the receiver in the same manner as the service rifle. Photo Credit: Smithsonian Institution.

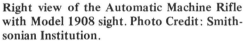

Right view of the Automatic Machine Rifle with Model 1908 sight. Photo Credit: Smithsonian Institution.

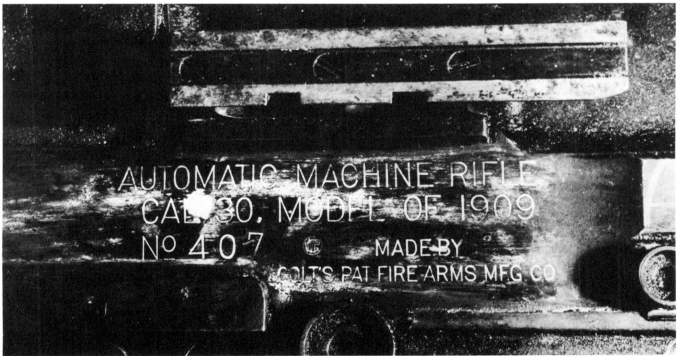

Receiver bracket (base) used for mounting the Model 1908 sight to the .30 caliber automatic rifle. At least two types of bases were used for this purpose. Photo Credit: Donald G. Thomas.

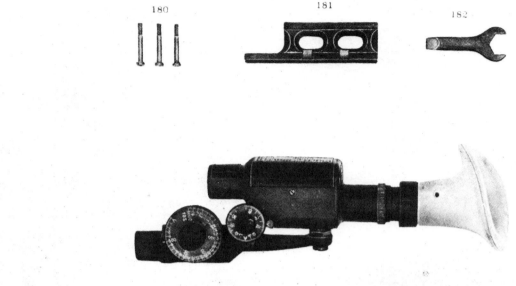

TELESCOPIC SIGHT MODEL OF 1908

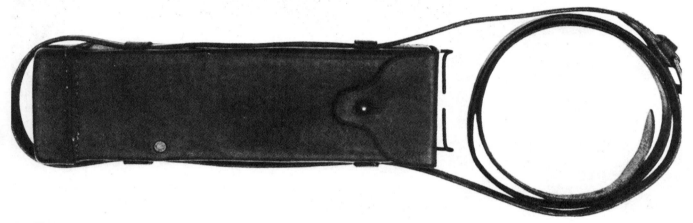

An illustration from the Automatic Machine Rifle Handbook showing sight, receiver base, Model 1911 carrying case, and the first issue combination tool used for scope adjustment. Photo Credit: Peter R. Senich.

Chapter 4 ◆◆

Musket Sight— Model of 1913

Acting on the request of the Ordnance Department, efforts by the Warner & Swasey firm to improve upon the limitations of the Model 1908 sight resulted in the introduction of the Telescopic Musket Sight, Model of 1913.

The principal changes, other than the exterior configuration, were a lowering of the magnification from 6 power to 5.2 power, the substitution of a cruciform locking nut for the elevation dial in place of the round type used with the Model 1908 sight, and the addition of a clamping screw to secure the eyepiece adjustment. Otherwise the new sight was essentially the same as the 1908 variant.

Modifications notwithstanding, the new sight proved to be far from adequate. Following limited initial procurement, objections to the Model 1913 sight were as follows:

(1) With the eyepiece offset 1.75 inches left of the rifle center, the shooter was forced to assume an uncomfortable position for shooting. (Cheek rests or pads were not an official consideration at this point.)
(2) Insufficient eye relief made the shooter liable to injury in spite of the rubber shield.

The 5.2 power Warner & Swasey Telescopic Musket Sight, Model of 1913, designed to replace the Model 1908 service sight. Photo Credit: Peter R. Senich.

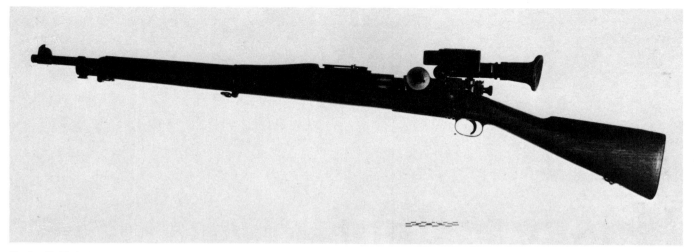

Springfield Armory M1903 sniper rifle with the Model 1913 Musket Sight. Photo Credit: Donald G. Thomas.

An early Warner & Swasey Company photo depicting one of the first Model 1913 sights (No. 2132) made for the government. Note the round range dial, as used with Model 1908 sights. Minor variations were characteristic of Model 1913 sight production and were not consistent with progressive scope (serial number) manufacture. Photo Credit: Warner & Swasey Company.

(3) The power (magnification) was higher than necessary and the field of view correspondingly smaller than desirable.

(4) Too small an exit pupil limited the sight's effectiveness at night.

(5) Excessive weight and bulk made the sight awkward.

(6) The glass reticle was easily obscured by film and moisture in spite of efforts to prevent this.

(7) Lost motion in the windage and elevation adjustments made them subject to error.

The new Warner & Swasey device had in fact offered little improvement over the Model 1908 variant, and thus by 1914 efforts to find or develop a satisfactory telescopic sight for service use commenced again in earnest.

Concurrent with the Army's quest for a suitable rifle scope, early in 1915 the British and Canadians, without the benefit of even an unsatisfactory telescopic sight, were desperately attempting to catch up with the German sniping effort during the initial stages of World War I. Consequently, in addition to procuring an unspecified quantity of commercial Winchester A5 telescopic sights for sniping purposes, the Canadian government urgently requested that the Warner & Swasey firm adjust its Model 1913 Musket sight for use with the Ross Mark III service rifle.

Accordingly, the first of two lots were ordered by the Canadian government on 11 March 1915 with delivery taking place between April and July of the same year. The second purchase, placed on 19 February 1916, was completed and shipped during the following October. The initial order called for the manufacture of 250 sights, consecutively serial numbered 1 through 250. The second and final lot, for an additional 250, continued the numbering up to and including 500. No more than five hundred Model 1913 sights were made by Warner & Swasey for the Canadian government.

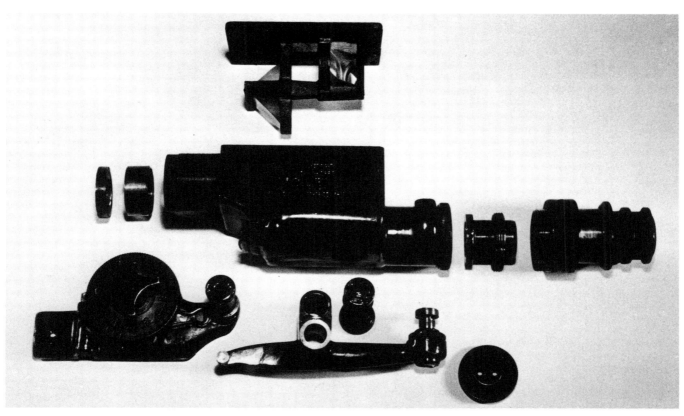

A disassembled Model 1913 telescope reveals its major components. Complex and highly susceptible to moisture, its sight picture was easily obscured by film forming on the internal optics. Photo Credit: Peter R. Senich.

Issue Model 1913 sights were stamped with the rifle serial number in the same manner as 1908 sights. Note the spring-loaded mount catch which engaged either of the two receiver base notches. Photo Credit: Peter R. Senich.

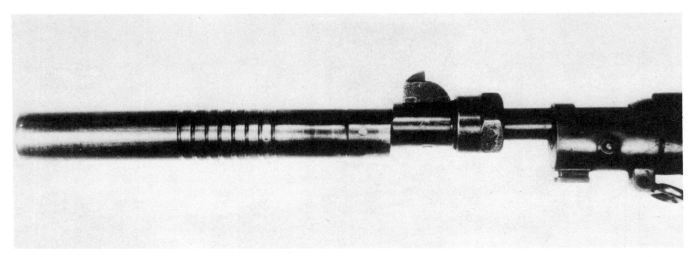

Maxim Model 15 silencer fitted to an '03 Springfield as first used in combat during the Punitive Expedition into Mexico. Photo Credit: Donald G. Thomas.

A comparative view of a standard brass eyepiece (top) with an internally threaded ferrule to retain the rubber eyecup, and a simplified, knurled aluminum eyepiece on which the rubber eyecup could be readily slipped on and off. The aluminum design appears on various sights throughout the entire serial number range. Photo Credit: Peter R. Senich.

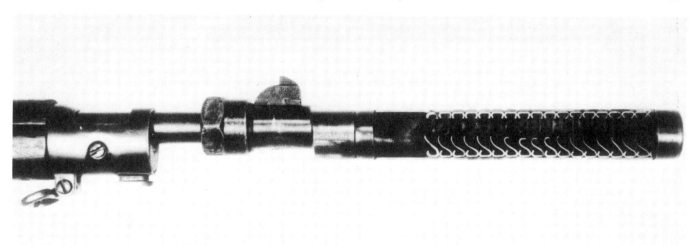

A cutaway view of the Model 15 silencer illustrates the heart of Hiram Maxim's device: a series of baffles which controlled the powder gases, thereby reducing the sound of the report. The one-inch-diameter tube extended seven inches past the muzzle. A .375-inch opening in line with the bore provided clearance for the .30 caliber bullet to pass through the silencer. Photo Credit: Donald G. Thomas.

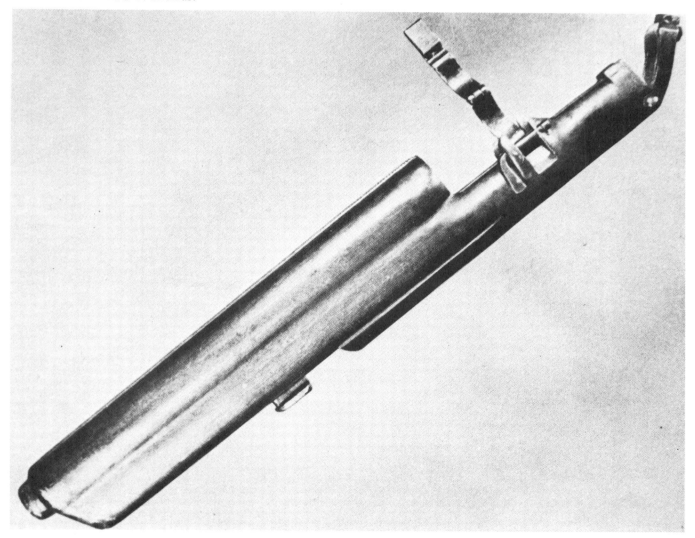

The Moore silencer, while no match for Hiram Maxim's device, reportedly saw limited use by Army snipers against the Germans in 1918. Photo Credit: John Amber.

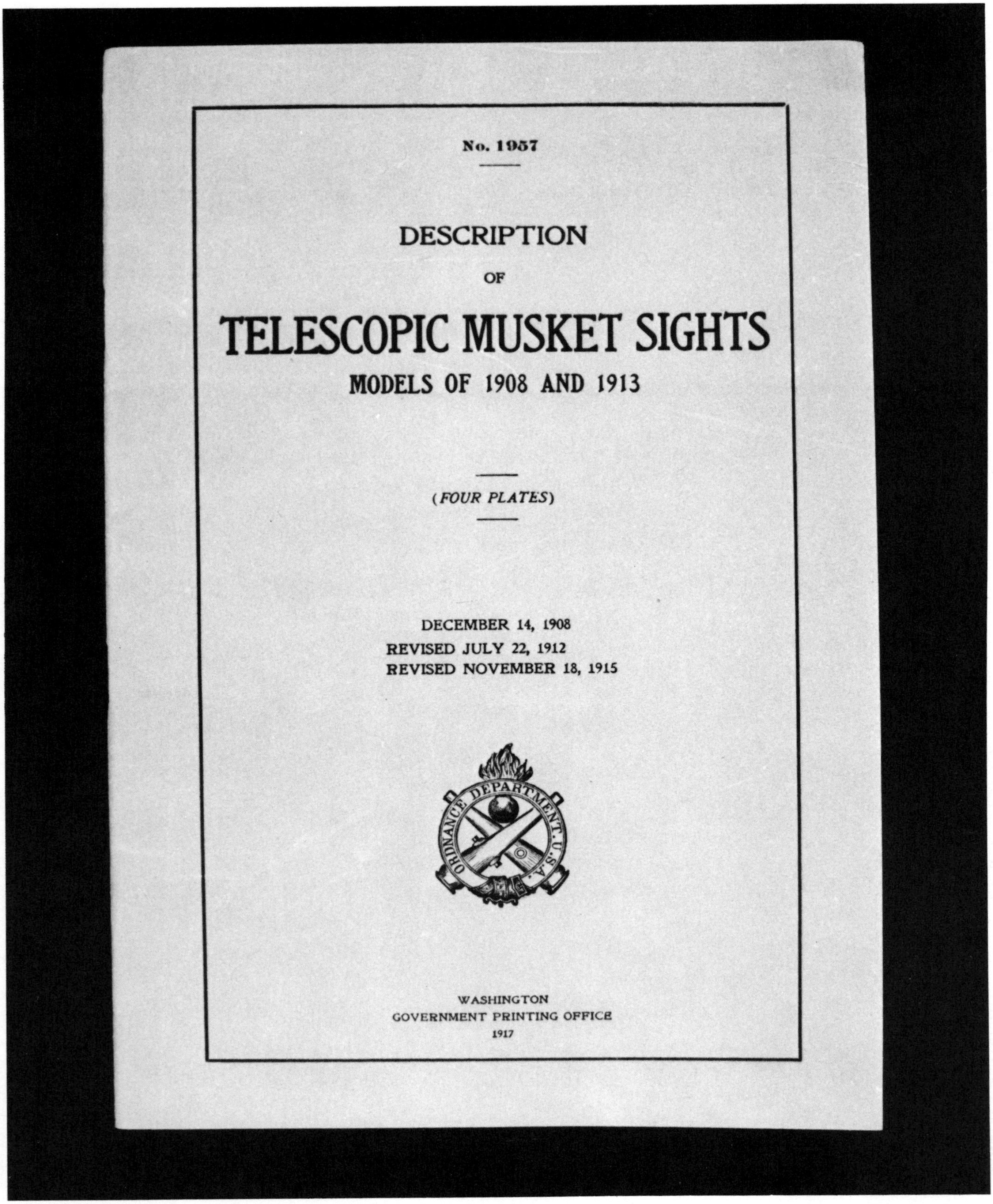

No. 1957
———

DESCRIPTION

OF

TELESCOPIC MUSKET SIGHTS

MODELS OF 1908 AND 1913

———

(FOUR PLATES)

———

DECEMBER 14, 1908
REVISED JULY 22, 1912
REVISED NOVEMBER 18, 1915

WASHINGTON
GOVERNMENT PRINTING OFFICE
1917

Ordnance Pamphlet No. 1957 explained the "care and feeding" of both Warner & Swasey sights. Original pamphlets bear an official copy number in the upper right-hand corner. Photo Credit: Peter R. Senich.

While virtually identical in most respects, including overall appearance, the principal differences between the Canadian pattern and U.S. sights were two-fold. The elevation range dial on the U.S. model was graduated from 0 to 3,000 yards by 20-yard divisions; the Canadian, from 200 to 2,400 yards by 100-yard divisions to 1,000 yards, followed by 50-yard divisions to maximum adjustment. In addition, the wind and range table plate was omitted from the top of the Canadian sight with the four mounting holes left open. The reason for both modifications was to allow for correct adjustments with Mark VII .303 caliber Canadian service ammunition that was used with the Ross rifle.

The receiver bracket (base) utilized with the Canadian variation differed from those used to mount the United States Model 1913 sight to the '03 Springfield. The steel brackets intended for the Ross rifle were furnished by Warner & Swasey in a semifinished state, with final machine work and heat treatment performed at the Ross facilities to ensure a perfect fit with each weapon.

Both U.S. and Canadian Model 1913 Musket

Sights bear the same manufacturer's legend on the left side of the scope body:

TELESCOPIC MUSKET SIGHT
MODEL OF 1913 No. 2454
THE WARNER & SWASEY CO.
CLEVELAND OHIO U.S.A.
PAT. FEB. 13-06 MAY 22-06 DEC. 15-08

Since the Warner & Swasey firm continued its practice of consecutive numbering, serial numbers of regular production U.S. Model 1913 sights began where the last regular production Model 1908 sight had left off, and therefore the sights were manufactured with only four-digit serial numbers through final production in 1918. The Canadian pattern, on the other hand, bears only three-digit numbers as cited earlier.

Made from bronze, brass, and steel, Model 1913 sights weighed a hefty two pounds, four ounces, or more than double that of any other rifle scope available during this period. Adding to its unwieldy nature, the great weight also increased the tendency for the scope to jar itself loose at recoil.

Efforts by Warner & Swasey to prevent moisture entering the Model 1913 sight included recessing and sealing the screws used to fasten the lid to the scope body. Note the scope (top) with protruding screws and those recessed on a later variant. Of further interest was the addition of a prism-holder screw (upper-rear section of lid, bottom sight) noted on miscellaneous sights throughout the entire serial number range. This recess was also sealed as originally manufactured. Photo Credit: Peter R. Senich.

A side view of the Model 1913 sights clearly illustrates the different methods used to fasten the lid to the main case. Photo Credit: Peter R. Senich.

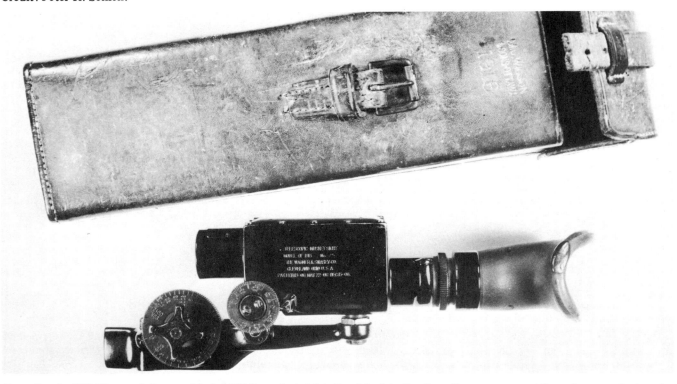

One of only 500 Warner & Swasey Model 1913 musket sights furnished to the Canadian government for sniper use during the initial stages of WWI. The russet leather scope case—made by M. J. Wilson & Son of Ottawa—although similar to U.S. cases, has no pouch for the combination tool and no shoulder strap. The lid-closing strap forms a belt loop in the rear of the case. Photo Credit: Peter R. Senich.

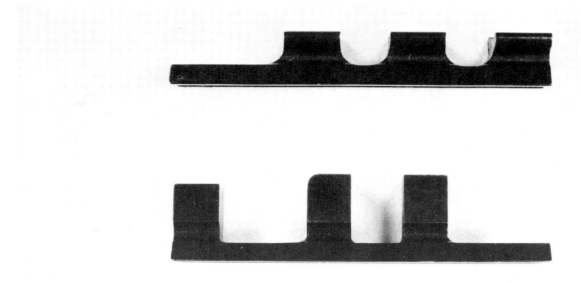

A comparative view of the standard M1903 receiver bracket (top) and the variant used to mount the Model 1913 sight to the Canadian Ross sniper rifle. Photo Credit: Peter R. Senich.

The spring-loaded locking lug provided on the mount was not equal to the task.

Alluding to this problem in his excellent work, *A Rifleman Went to War,* Captain Herbert W. McBride relates his method of keeping the Model 1913 sight in place on his Ross rifle while serving as a sniper with the Canadian Army in Europe:

> I had a little trouble in getting it securely mounted so that it would not jar loose but finally, by using a wedge—made of a piece of safety-razor blade—and salt water, got her on so tight that I came near being court martialled when I finally turned it in. The armourer could not get it off.

Efforts to overcome this difficulty with U.S. sights resulted in modifications to the mount, which simply entailed the addition of one, and in some cases, two locking screws that were turned in tightly against the receiver base after the scope was in place. Not all Model 1913 sights were so modified, however.

Although developed specifically for United States service use, it remained the task of the Canadian Army to introduce the Model 1913 sight to combat, and despite its inherent deficiencies, on an overall basis the Warner & Swasey Musket Sight was considered both effective and dependable by the Canadian snipers, who brought it to bear against the German Army on the Western Front. Of further interest is that even after some relatively good sniping equipment was made available by the British, the vast majority of Canadian

snipers who were originally issued Model 1913-sighted Ross rifles chose to retain this equipment through to the end of the war.

The Model 1913 sights saw action in yet another campaign. In March 1916, as a result of continued border raiding by Pancho Villa and his irregular Mexican cavalry, President Woodrow Wilson ordered Brigadier General John J. Pershing into Mexico to assist the Mexican government in taking Villa. On 16 March the punitive expedition entered Mexico in "hot pursuit" in what became the first constrained use of American military force. Included among Pershing's command were a number of expert riflemen (Lingler's Sharpshooters) equipped with '03 Springfields fitted with Model 1913 telescopic sights, and in some cases, Maxim silencers. It was intended that these weapons be used to quietly eliminate sentries so that surprise attacks could be mounted against Villa's forces.

With involvement in the European war imminent, a residual benefit of this campaign provided conditions under which it was possible to evaluate the effectiveness of sniping and silencers, as well as to study their combined use. Pershing failed to capture Villa, and in January 1917, as conditions between the United States and Germany approached the critical stage, the expedition was withdrawn.

In retrospect, as a direct result of the Army's disfavor with the Model 1913 sight, extremely few were procured between 1913 and 1916. According to Warner & Swasey records, a total of only thirty

Model 1913 telescopic-sight, standard receiver base used for both model 1908 and 1913 sight mounting and the late-issue leather carrying case with front pouch for holding the stamped combination tool. Photo Credit: Peter R. Senich.

Right view—Model 1913 sight and receiver side of the standard base. As originally fitted under ordnance auspices, all receiver bases were mounted in the same precise place and manner. Photo credit: Peter R. Senich.

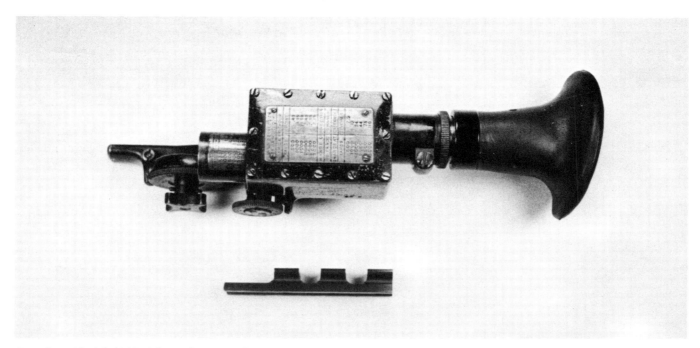

Top view—Model 1913 sight and receiver base. Note the drift-table (front) and range-table located on top of the scope body. Photo Credit: Peter R. Senich.

A 1918 Springfield manufacture '03 sniper rifle with an extremely late Model 1913 sight (no. 7671). Note the aluminum eye-piece and single mount locking screw. Photo Credit: Peter R. Senich.

The practice of camouflaging sniping equipment originated among German snipers during World War I. The American sharp-shooter, circa 1918, is depicted with a "pattern painted" M1903 Springfield rifle mounting the Model 1913 sight. Photo Credit: Peter R. Senich.

Model 1903 sniper rifle with the twenty-round capacity magazine made for the '03 Springfield during WWI. Considered "exotic" by some, ordnance records make no mention of this combination having been sniper issue during that period. Photo Credit: Gray Collection.

sights were delivered during those years. However, when it became apparent that sharpshooting equipment would be a benefit for the campaign in Mexico, the procurement and fitting of Model 1913 sights commenced again in earnest with a total of 1,500 obtained by the Ordnance Department during 1916.

Despite the fact that the Ordnance Department had been seeking a suitable alternate to the Model 1913 sight since 1914, when the armed forces of the United States were finally committed to the European conflict by declaration of war on 6 April 1917, the Model 1913 Musket Sight was for all intent regular issue for sharpshooting purposes. As the conflict progressed, a telescopic sight deemed satisfactory in all respects was selected somewhat prematurely and officially designated the Telescopic Musket Sight, Model of 1918. Although thousands of these sights were to be manufactured, none were delivered to the Army for combat use before the war ended on 11 November 1918. At no point during the development or subsequent placement of orders for the Model 1918

device was production of the Warner & Swasey sight discontinued. The Model 1913 was to remain the issue telescopic sight throughout World War I with 4,000 sights ordered late in 1917 and the final order for 200 placed in 1918.

Adequate as U.S. sharpshooting weapons were for the task at hand, by no stretch of the imagination were American personnel ready to do combat with the Germans in this capacity. Consequently, specialized training attuned to combat conditions on the Western Front was conducted at various "Schools of Sniping" by experienced British and Canadian instructors in order to thoroughly prepare American sniper candidates prior to their actual involvement in the trenches. As the British and Canadians had learned painfully early in the war, there was a great deal more to mastering the extremely efficient German snipers than pointing telescopic-sighted rifles in their direction.

Unprepared as they were initially, by the summer of 1918 when the total weight of the American Expeditionary Force was finally brought to bear, American snipers, while employed only in

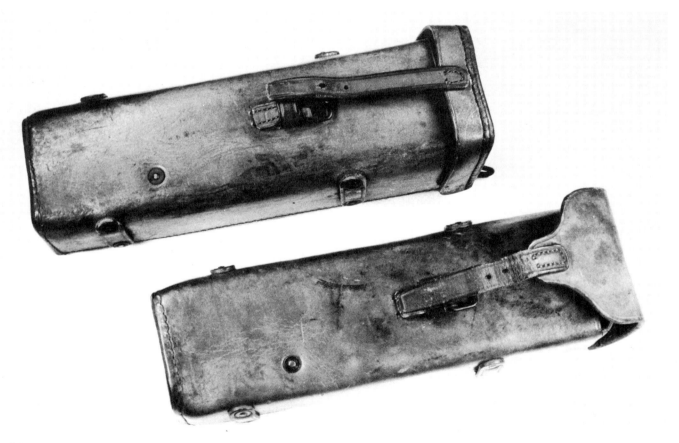

Model 1913 scope case variations included those depicted with Rock Island Arsenal markings and 1917 or 1918 dates. Both cases have small tool pouches under each flap. Photo Credit: Peter R. Senich.

In addition to telescope-sight use by American marksmen against German combat personnel, many expert riflemen did their share of sharpshooting with standard open sights. Photo Credit: U.S. Army.

limited numbers, proved to be as effective as their British and Canadian counterparts. Following their active combat involvement, American forces were provided with rifle silencers for sniping purposes, in spite of the fact that the punitive expedition in Mexico had determined that these devices would not sufficiently reduce the report to the extent that the source could not be located.

Nevertheless, as noted by silencer expert J. David Truby in *Silencers, Snipers & Assassins:*

> In 1917, select Army snipers were issued Maxim equipped Springfield rifles. Other troops were issued Springfields equipped with the Moore silencer—a not very effective competitor of Maxim. By the time U.S. snipers got into action, German soldiers had already nicknamed silenced British sniper weapons as "Whispering Death." The British weapons used Maxim silencers.

Although U.S. snipers employed silencers with marginal success during the "Great War," such use was extremely limited. Judicious shooting and effective camouflage proved far more effective than silencers for preventing a sniper's detection.

From their introduction through 1918, when the Warner & Swasey Company ceased regular production of Model 1913 Musket Sights, a total of 5,730 were furnished to the United States government. Included in this figure were the last 4,200 sights, which were ordered and delivered so late in the war that few were ever issued. The difference in these two figures amounts to 1,530 and represents the bulk of Model 1913 sights actually issued for sharpshooting purposes. From this last total, as a careful study of surviving issue sights indicates, the vast majority were fitted to '03 Springfields manufactured during 1916 and 1917.

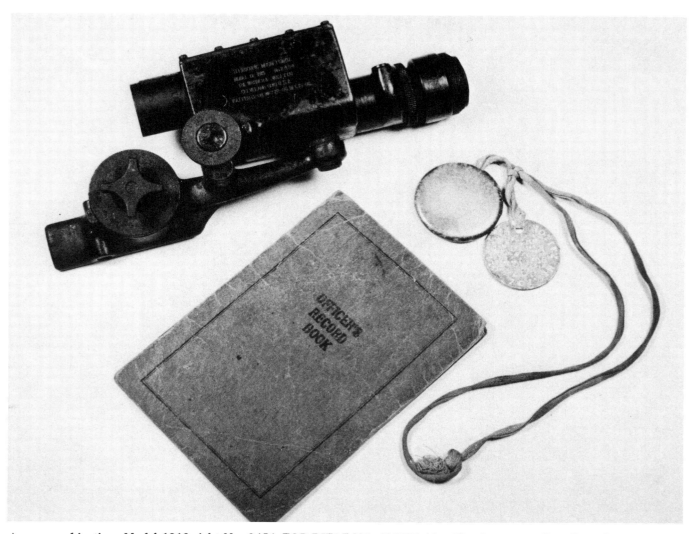

A rare combination: Model 1913 sight No. 2454, FOR RIFLE NO. 625537, identification tag, sterling silver photo case, and Officer's Record Book belonging to an Army lieutenant having seen action with the 37th Division during the Meuse-Argonne Offensive. The record book cites his sniper training at Clamecy, France, in July 1918. Photo Credit: Peter R. Senich.

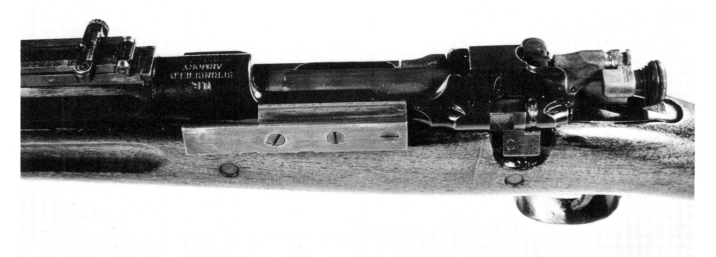

A unique 6-18 barrel date M1903 sniper rifle manufactured at Springfield Armory has both a star-gauged barrel and the late, "flat-sided" receiver base for mounting the Model 1913 sight. Photo Credit: Peter R. Senich.

The second and final issue Warner & Swasey combination tool (screwdriver-wrench) for the Model 1913 sight. Unlike the smaller, original machined tool furnished with the Model 1908 and some Model 1913 sights, the 1 1/4-inch-by-3 3/4-inch variant was stamped from sheet steel approximately 1/16-inch thick. Photo Credit: Peter R. Senich.

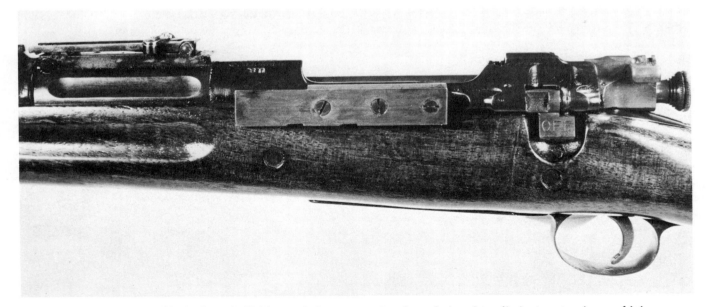

A late manufacture, simplified "flat-sided" Warner & Swasey receiver base designed to eliminate extensive machining operations necessary with the standard base. Photo Credit: Peter R. Senich.

The first issue Warner & Swasey combination tool (screwdriver/wrench) for the Model 1908 sight, an accessory item furnished with the Model 1908 and some early Model 1913 sights, the 2.235-inch-by-.970-inch tool was machined from steel. Produced in limited quantity, original tools are considered rare. Photo Credit: Butch Eyberg.

An Army sharpshooter operating from a trench in the Alsace Sector, France, 1918. The M1903 Springfield mounts a Model 1913 sight. Note the abbreviated eyecup. Photo Credit: U.S. Army.

Members of the U.S. Army, 167th Infantry, 42nd Division, American Expeditionary Force (A.E.F.) following action in France (13 May 1918). The Springfield rifles are fitted with Model 1913 Warner & Swasey sights. Photo Credit: U.S. Army.

The Army combat personnel are shown examining their sharpshooter issue. According to the original caption, the men were photographed following a raid on German positions. Photo Credit: U.S. Army.

The earliest known surviving Model 1913 Musket Sight, number 2130, "FOR RIFLE No. 586004" (1914 manufacture) and one from the last production run, number 7813, "FOR RIFLE No. 937139" (1918 manufacture), represent both serial number extremes for issue sights thus far recorded. Although sights having serial numbers higher than number 7813 have been noted, as mentioned earlier, few from the last 4,200 sights, and especially those in the 7800 number range, were issued under Ordnance Department auspices. While the Model 1913 Musket Sight was considered to be of marginal value even before its use in the Mexican Campaign and in the First World War, an indeterminate number remained in service with various Army and National Guard units until the mid-1920s, when the last were finally sold by the government as surplus.

Chapter 5 ◆◆

The Marine Corps Choice — A Target Scope

The A5 telescopic sight (style A-5 power) manufactured by the Winchester Repeating Arms Company at its New Haven, Connecticut, works, when introduced in 1910 was considered to be one of the best commercial sights available in the United States. Despite its efficiency for target shooting under controlled conditions, and its rather extensive use by British and Canadian snipers during the early stages of the First World War, the A5 rifle scope proved entirely too fragile for sustained combat use. Nevertheless, the Winchester device was the only rifle scope to see unilateral use by British, Canadian, and to a limited extent, American snipers following their involvement in the European war.

As discussed in early Winchester technical data, the A5 scope was unique in that the tube was not drawn, but bored and turned from a solid piece of steel. Although a variety of reticle patterns were available and interchangeable, the standard, single cross-hair pattern appears to have seen the most use in sights employed by the military.

The nickel-steel front mount, designed to prevent indentation of the tube, has a spring-loaded, bevel-nosed plunger engaging in a long corresponding groove in the underside of the tube to keep it from rotating, and to permit longitudinal movement. This ensured that the axis of the tube remained constant once adjusted.

The standard commercial rear mount, shaped to

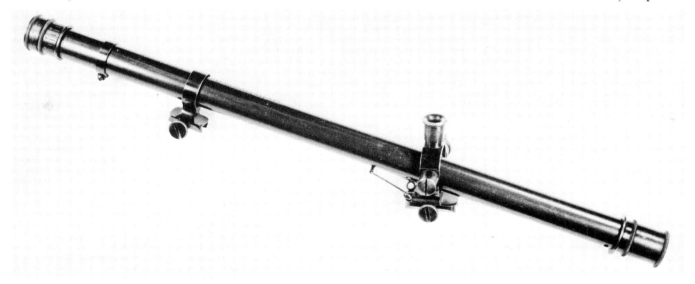

Winchester A5 telescopic rifle sight (Style A-5 power) in standard commercial form as introduced to the American market in 1910. Photo Credit: Peter R. Senich.

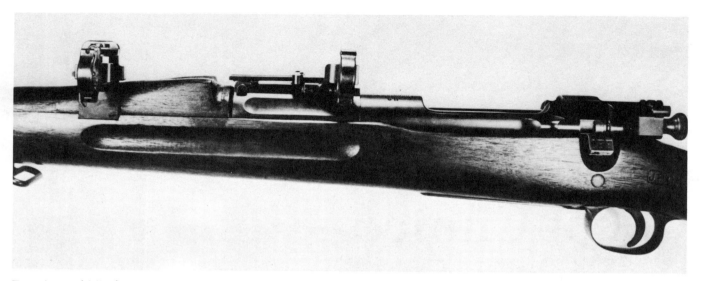

Experimental Winchester A5 side-mounting as evaluated by the Ordnance Department for use with the M1903 service rifle. Photo Credit: Colonel William S. Brophy (Retired).

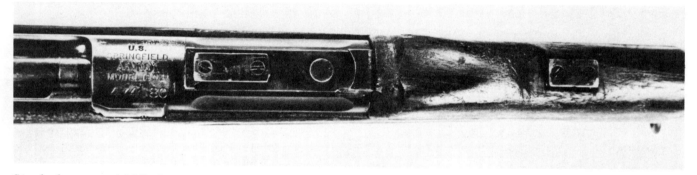

Standard commercial Winchester A5 sight bases as mounted to an M1903 Springfield. In this case, the rear scope base was attached to the standard sight base in order to place both scope bases on the barrel as deemed desirable in some quarters for this type of rifle scope. Photo Credit: Colonel William S. Brophy (Retired).

allow clearance for elevation and windage adjustments, has two springs to hold the tube in contact with the elevation and windage adjustment screws (drums). The tube is constantly thrust upward toward the top of the mount by a "grasshopper" type of flat-wire spring with a coil or turn in it near its lower end. Lateral thrust is provided by a spring-loaded plunger located in a housing in the left side of the mount. Elevation and windage adjustment, set by micrometer dials with divisions (markings) enameled in red at the factory, were near impossible to read in anything but optimum light. The vast majority of A5 sights that saw military use have the division markings redone in white for obvious reasons.

Both the ocular and objective lenses were fully adjustable. The eyepiece was adjusted by loosening the locking sleeve and rotating the eyepiece until proper focus was obtained. Micrometer adjustment of the objective lens provided a simple means for

minute adjustment of the lenses and reticle for accurate focusing of the image at the reticle for various ranges.

A locking stop ring located between the front mount and the objective end of the scope positioned the sight for correct eye-relief (approximately two inches) when pulled back into battery after firing.

Placing the scope on the weapon entailed turning out both the front and rear mount clamping screws as far as necessary, slipping the mounts over the steel dovetail bases, and firmly tightening the screws to lock the telescope in place. In addition to military use of the commercial pattern mounts and bases, a "special A5 mounting," developed for the Marine Corps, made use of "Mann-type" taper dovetail bases, special click adjustment elevation and windage drums, and a spring-loaded plunger directly beneath the tube in place of the regular "grasshopper" spring.

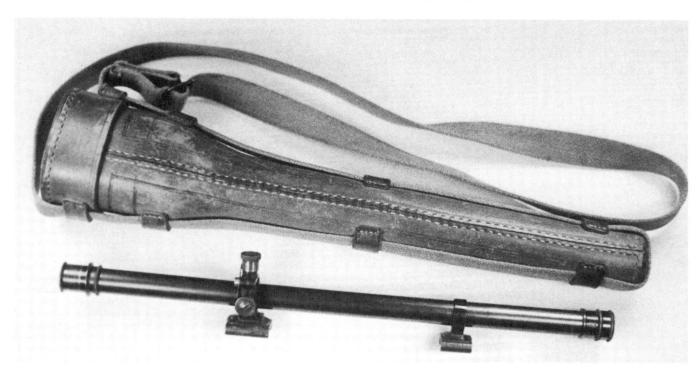

Winchester A5 telescopic sight with "special USMC mounting" and commercial carrying case adapted for military use by the addition of a shoulder strap and loops for same. With the exception of the mounts, the 15 7/8-inch-long, 10-oz. sights were standard commercial models. Photo Credit: Peter R. Senich—Smith Collection.

Special Winchester A5 sight mounting developed for the Marine Corps made use of Mann-type tapered dovetail bases, special click adjustment elevation and windage drums, and a spring-loaded plunger directly beneath the tube. Photo Credit: Peter R. Senich—Smith Collection.

Top view of the Smith Collection Marine Corps issue Winchester A5 scope carrying-case lid with rifle number, marksman's name, and USMC in ink faded with the passing of years. Photo Credit: Peter R. Senich—Smith Collection.

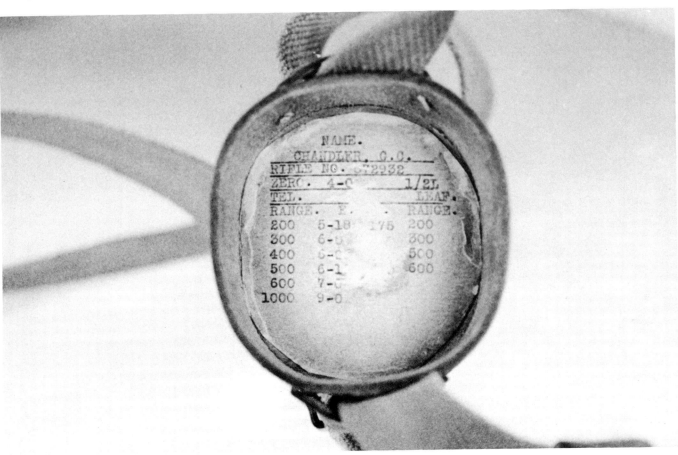

The underside of the USMC A5 scope case lid with marksman's name, G. C. Chandler, M1903 rifle serial number originally paired with this sight (No. 672932), and range table. Photo Credit: Peter R. Senich—Smith Collection.

Comparative view of a standard commercial Winchester A5, No. 2 rear mount (right) and the same type of mount as modified for USMC service. Photo Credit: Peter R. Senich.

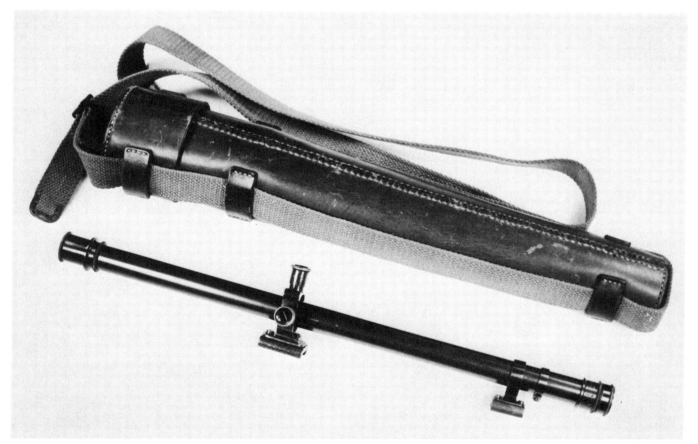

A modified commercial mount Winchester A5 sight and russet leather carrying case with web shoulder strap represents one of the two A5 sight/mount variations utilized by Marine Corps marksmen. Photo Credit: Peter R. Senich.

A Marine Corps sergeant, circa World War I, sighting a Winchester A5-equipped M1903 sharpshooter rifle. Photo Credit: National Archives.

Model 1903 rifle and modified mount Winchester A5 sight with bases attached to the barrel and receiver ring for 7 3/16-inch spacing between mount centers as an alternate to 6-inch spacing. Either of which (spacing) provided different adjustment values at the target at various ranges with a given mount. Photo Credit: Peter R. Senich.

A soldier demonstrates an experimental camo pattern during World War I, the era when military camouflage became indispensable. Photo Credit: Peter R. Senich.

Although camouflage uniforms did not see general issue during World War I, special camo-suits were made available for sharpshooters and observers. This was especially necessary in the later stages of the war when more and more sniping activity was conducted in the open. Photo Credit: U.S. Army.

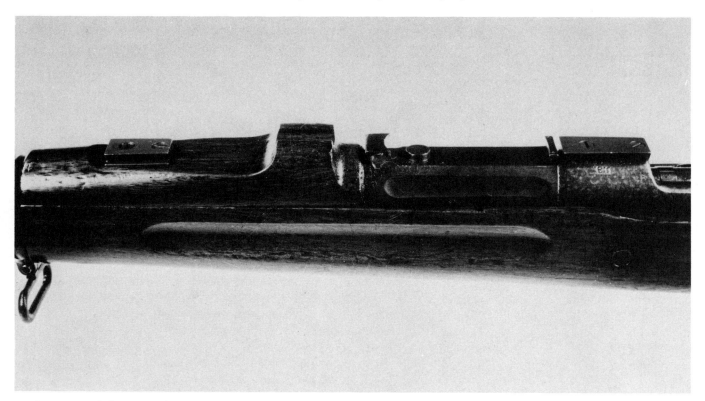

A close view of the tapered sight bases as employed with the M1903 Springfield rifle for Marine Corps A5 scope mountings. **Photo Credit: Peter R. Senich.**

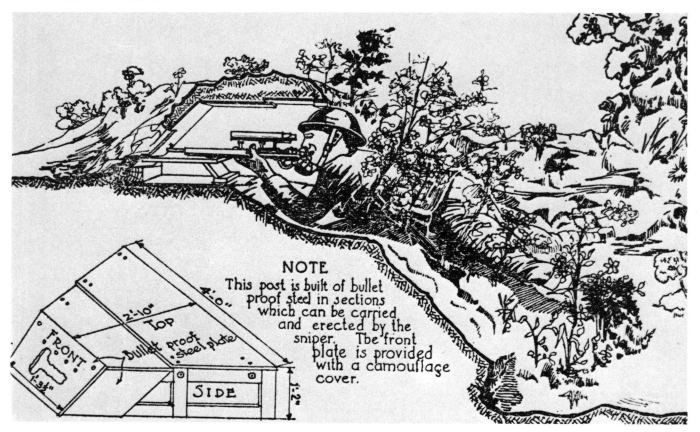

An excerpt from a 1918 A.E.F. training pamphlet illustrates a "sniper post" of the type used along the Western Front on both sides of the trenches. **Photo Credit: Peter R. Senich.**

A Winchester B5 telescopic rifle sight (Style B-5 power) mounted to an '03 Springfield with early Marine Corps service to its credit. According to early Winchester data, "The Style B-5 power telescope has the same magnification as the Style A-5 power, but a smaller field of view." A limited number of B5 sights were procured for training purposes during World War I. Photo Credit: Gray Collection.

A combat sketch by W. J. Aylward depicts a Marine Corps sniper sighting his mark from a rooftop at Chateau Thierry, 1918. According to various accounts, many Army and USMC marksmen preferred using conventional sights for sniping purposes during World War I. Photo Credit: National Archives.

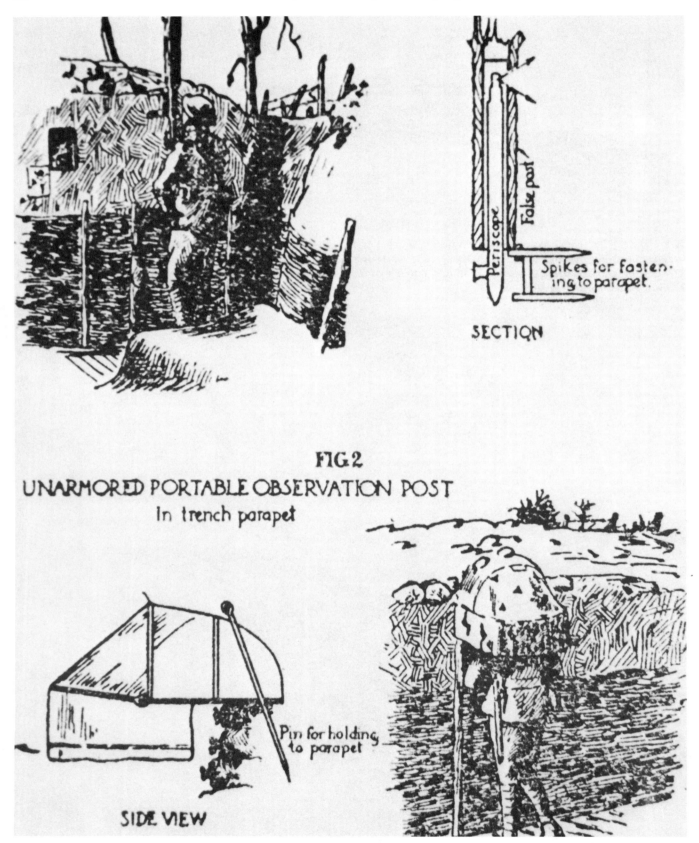

FIG 2
UNARMORED PORTABLE OBSERVATION POST
In trench parapet

With enemy sharpshooters continuously scanning the trench lines for a suitable "mark," undetected observation required the imaginative use of cover. A World War I training illustration depicts portable observation posts. Photo Credit: Peter R. Senich.

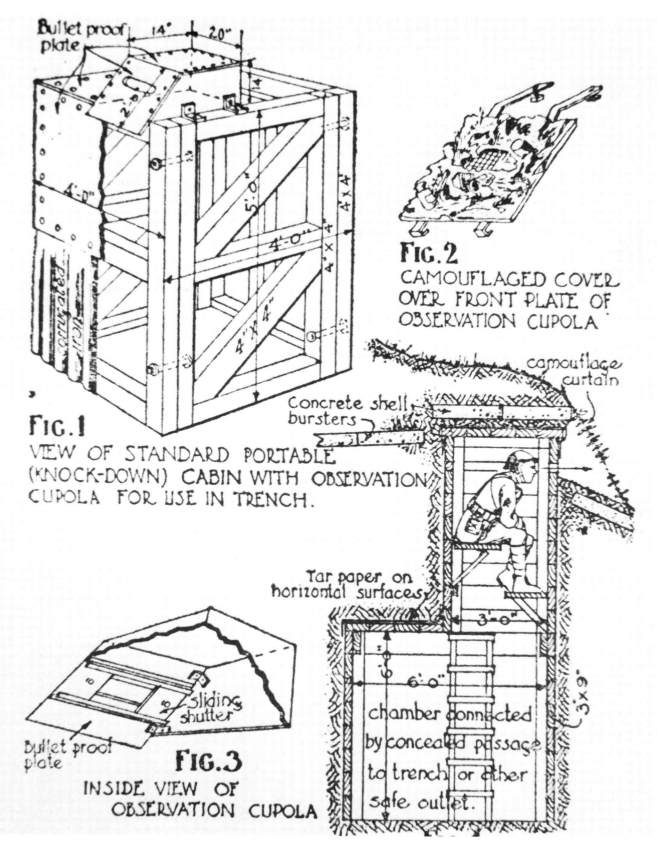

Bullet proof plate

14" 20"

4'-0"

5'-0"

4'-0"

4"x4"

4"x4"

FIG. 1
VIEW OF STANDARD PORTABLE (KNOCK-DOWN) CABIN WITH OBSERVATION CUPOLA FOR USE IN TRENCH.

FIG. 2
CAMOUFLAGED COVER OVER FRONT PLATE OF OBSERVATION CUPOLA

camouflage curtain

Concrete shell bursters

Tar paper on horizontal surfaces

3'-0"

6'-0"

3'x9'

chamber connected by concealed passage to trench or other safe outlet.

Sliding shutter

Bullet proof plate

FIG. 3
INSIDE VIEW OF OBSERVATION CUPOLA

A part of the unique measures used to protect observers from sniper and machine-gun fire during World War I. An excerpt from a training manual illustrates an "Observation Cupola." Photo Credit: Peter R. Senich.

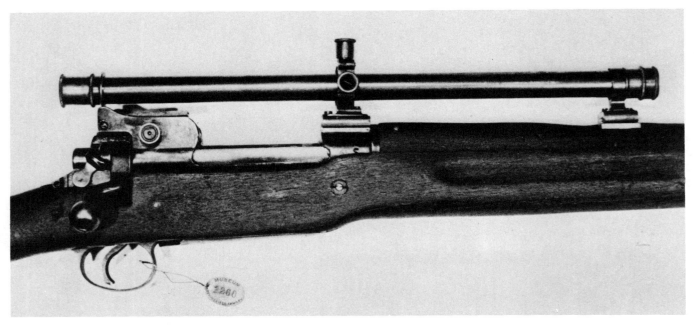

A unique Model 1917 (Enfield) rifle with a modified mount (tapered bases), Winchester A5 telescopic sight, and experimental Marine Corps rear sight. Photo Credit: Colonel William S. Brophy (Retired).

The mounts in this case, without clamping screws and corresponding to the configuration of the taper dovetail bases, were firmly pushed into place with subsequent weapon recoil tightly wedging the mounts on the bases. As such, removing the scope necessitated carefully tapping the mounts in a manner that proved somewhat difficult. The primary purpose of this system was to ensure that removing and replacing the sight would not change the point of impact. However, as experts of the day concluded, the end difference between this and the standard A5 mounts was not enough to justify the increased cost and trouble.

Although Winchester mounts with regular elevation and windage drums were also modified for use with "Mann-type" bases, the A5 telescopic sights employed by the military were standard commercial scopes. Unlike those issued by the British and Canadians, which were stamped with a Crown property proof mark and the rifle serial number to which they were paired, those used by the Army and Marine Corps bear only the manufacturer's legend.

MANUFACTURED BY THE
WINCHESTER REPEATING ARMS CO.
—A5
NEW HAVEN, CONN. U.S.A.
PATENTED FEBRUARY 9, 1909

A method of mounting the Winchester scope on the Model 1903 Springfield service rifle had been devised and noted in the *Report of the Chief of Ordnance* as early as 1912. In 1915, however, comprehensive evaluations of various telescopic sights by the Army School of Musketry, including both top- and side-mounted A5 sights, found the following objections to the Winchester sight as recorded in a report dated 18 December 1915:

(A) The field of view is so small on account of the excessive power as to seriously affect its usefulness, except for slow fire at fixed targets for which work it was considered excellent.
(B) The spacing of the brackets only 6 inches apart on such a long telescope is considered a source of weakness.
(C) The bolt of the rifle cannot be operated unless the telescope is pushed forward about 2 1/2 inches from its firing position. This fact and the necessity of drawing the sight back to the firing position after each shot materially increases the time of firing.
(D) The exit pupil is so small that the sight is of no use in poor light.

For these reasons, the Army School of Musketry reports that the Winchester A5 sight is not suitable for general military use.

Concurrent with Army rejection of the A5 rifle scope, the British and Canadians, desperately attempting to match the German sniping effort, obtained a considerable number of readily available A5 sights, adapting them to both specially

Garbed in camo suits fashioned from burlap sacking, A.E.F. personnel display pattern-painted Springfield rifles while undergoing sniper training in France, 1918. Photo Credit: U.S. Army.

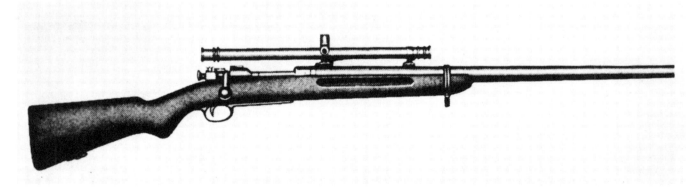

Winchester heavy barrel (26 inches long; 1 1/8-inch diameter at receiver; 7/8-inch diameter at muzzle) target rifle with M1903 Springfield action, as made for the commercial market in 1922, was available with only the A5 telescopic sight and no metallic sights. As such, this weapon came quite close to being an "off the shelf" military sniping arm. Photo Credit: Donald G. Thomas.

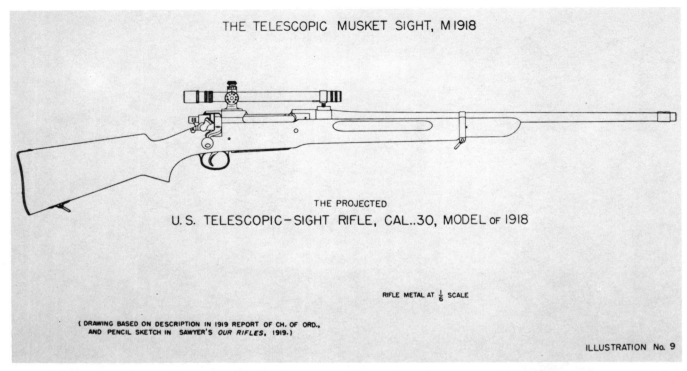

THE TELESCOPIC MUSKET SIGHT, M 1918

THE PROJECTED
U. S. TELESCOPIC–SIGHT RIFLE, CAL..30, MODEL of 1918

RIFLE METAL AT ⅙ SCALE

(DRAWING BASED ON DESCRIPTION IN 1919 REPORT OF CH. OF ORD.,
AND PENCIL SKETCH IN SAWYER'S *OUR RIFLES*, 1919.)

ILLUSTRATION No. 9

An illustration of the Model 1918 Winchester Telescopic Musket Sight and special, modified M1917 rifle as intended, but never fielded, for Army sniper use during World War I. Photo Credit: Copyright by Clark S. Campbell from The '03 Spring-fields.

modified Ross sporting rifles and to the British S.M.L.E., Mark III service arm for sniping purposes.

After the United States was drawn into the European conflict, as an expediency, the A5 sight was pressed into service as cited by the *Handbook of Ordnance Data,* dated 15 November 1918: "Five hundred of these sights were puchased by the United States Army, Ordnance Department, for emergency training use."

While serving primarily in a supplementary capacity with the Army, the Marine Corps adopted the Winchester A5 scope as its sniper standard: "The Winchester telescopic sight, model A5, produced by the Winchester Repeating Arms Co., with a special Marine Corps mounting, was found satis-

factory in use by the Marine Corps and adopted as Marine Corps standard." In either case of the Army or the USMC, however, extremely few A5 sights were employed by American snipers in European combat zones during the First World War.

Production of A5 sights continued until the telescope operations and manufacturing rights were purchased from Winchester by the Lyman Gunsight Corporation in 1928, thus marking the end of the A5 scope as such. Nevertheless, this rifle scope remained in quasimilitary use with Army and Marine Corps rifle teams, and it was retained on USMC sniping arms until its replacement with the improved Lyman 5A telescopic sight in the years prior to World War II.

World War I vintage Winchester A5, USMC special mount sight in use by a Marine Corps sniper on Guadalcanal early in World War II. Photo Credit: National Archives.

Chapter 6 ◆◆

Sight Development— The Golden Era

Efforts by the Ordnance Department in the years between 1915 and 1925 to select and/or to develop an efficient telescopic sight for the service rifle, when compared to subsequent endeavors of similar intent, represent a truly significant period of American military sniping.

Even though the Army considered the Winchester A5 and Warner & Swasey M1913 telescopic sights unsatisfactory for general service use, in 1915 the School of Musketry at Fort Sill, Oklahoma, conducted comparative evaluations of both sights along with a C.P. Goerz sight of German manufacture, with their conclusions cited in a report dated 18 December 1915:

The report of the School of Musketry states that in its opinion, the C.P. Goerz sight possesses all the essential requirements of such an instrument, viz., power, definition, field, ready adjustment, simplicity, strength, rigidity, and convenience to the user, and that for military use it is as such superior to the Warner & Swasey type as the latter is to the Winchester A5 model.

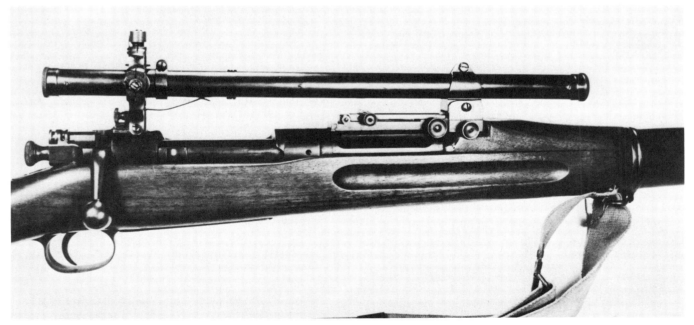

J. Stevens Arms & Tool Company target-type telescopic sight mounted to M1903 Springfield rifle No. 460634 (5-11 barrel date). The 5 power, fixed-tube (nonsliding) 15 3/4-inch x .750 diameter sight has a cross-hair reticle pattern and sufficient clearance in the rear mounting for elevation and windage adjustments. Photo Credit: Colonel William S. Brophy (Retired).

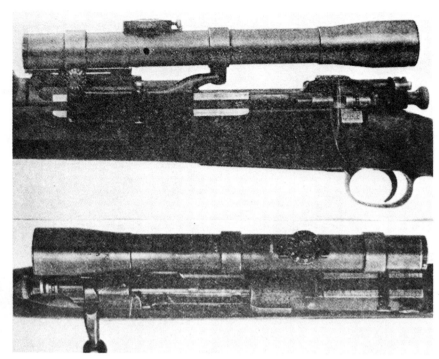

A C.P. Goerz rifle scope of German manufacture mounted on a U.S. Model 1903 rifle as tested by the Army School of Musketry prior to World War I. Photo Credit: Copyright by the Army Ordnance Association.

Frankford Arsenal telescopic sight No. 7 with modified M1903 service rifle. Photo Credit: Donald G. Thomas.

The recommendations of the School of Musketry were:

(A) That the Goerz Telescopic Sight be adopted for issue, replacing the Warner & Swasey sight.

(B) That they be issued at the rate of two to each organization of the mobile army armed with the rifle.

The Goerz sight exemplified the type being used so effectively by German snipers in Europe, so it came as no surprise that it was judged superior, since it was in fact a better telescopic sight than any of the others tested by the Ordnance Department up until that point.

Were it not for a series of comprehensive articles by H. K. Rutherford that appeared in the July-August 1921 and January-February 1924 issues of *Ordnance* magazine, the details of the sight tests would have been relegated to certain obscurity. With the permission of the Army Ordnance Association, Washington, D.C., the most significant portions of Rutherford's articles are presented in this chapter.

According to Rutherford's 1921 article:

The C. P. Goerz Musket Sight . . . mounted on a U.S. Model 1903 Rifle was obtained from C.P. Goerz Company, of Berlin, in August, 1913, and after a preliminary test and a relocating of the sight on the rifle, was submitted to the School of Musketry for competitive test.

It consists of a straight telescope 10 7/8 inches long, 1 inch in diameter for 8 inches from the objective, then expanding to 1 1/2 inches to accommodate an eyepiece of 1 5/8 inches in diameter. The focus is universal. The following are the chief characteristics of the optical system:

Aperture	inches	.80
Power	diameters	3.2
Field of view	degrees	8.45
Diameter exit pupil	inches	.25
Longitudinal eye relief	inches	2.76
Erecting system	lenses	2

The telescope is of the moving reticule type. Ranges are set on a graduated knob on top of the tube, which, by means of a screw, gives a corresponding movement to the reticule. Deflections are set by moving the entire telescope under the action of the deflection screw located in the front support of the telescope.

The telescope is attached to the rifle by means of a steel slide with beveled edges, secured to the left side of the receiver in a manner similar to that of the Warner & Swasey sight. The lower edge of this slide has three notches, permitting three positions of the telescope.

The sight itself is firmly attached by a front and rear bearing to a bronze support which dovetails over

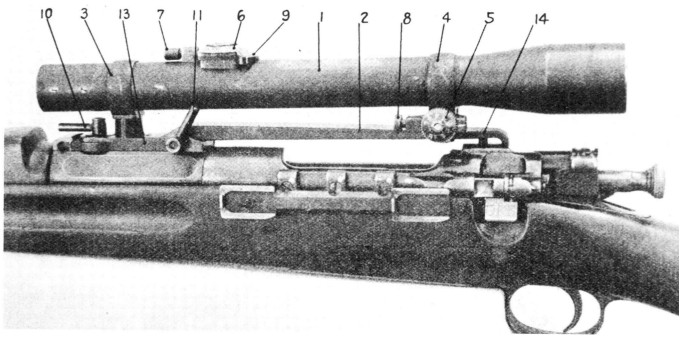

Model 1903 rifle with Frankford Arsenal telescopic rifle sight No. 9 as cited in H. K. Rutherford's 1924 article. Photo Credit: Copyright by the Army Ordnance Association.

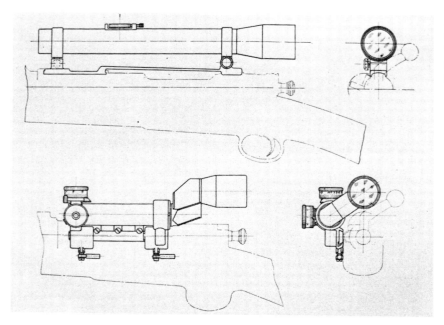

Frankford Arsenal design proposals for a Goerz pattern musket sight (top) and a "Casey type" prismatic sight. Photo Credit: Copyright by the Army Ordnance Association.

the steel slide above referred to and is locked to the same by a spring catch. The front bearing of the telescope carries the deflection worm and knob, and the rear bearing consists of a vertical pivot about which the deflection movement is made. The location of the parts is such that the line of sight is .89 inch to the left of the center of the bore, so that the telescope clears the well and the bolt handle, and does not obstruct or interfere with the iron sights.

The reticule consists of a heavy vertical pointed stud extending from the bottom of the field to the center, and of two heavy horizontal wires and a vertical one extending from the edges to within a short distance of the center. This arrangement leaves the center of the field clear and gives a sharply defined point on which to bring the target.

Acting on the recommendations of the School of Musketry, the Chief of Ordnance, in February, 1916, communicated with the representative of the C.P. Goerz Company in this country relative to the conditions under which that firm would permit the manufacture of the sight in the United States. The communication was acknowledged, but no further reply was received.

In retrospect, with the United States an avowed ally of the British and the Canadians, who were then locked in combat with German forces in Europe, it is not difficult to understand why the Goerz firm was not overly anxious to cooperate with the United States Army.

Even so, as Rutherford pointed out:

To determine if there was any reason why the Goerz sight could not be manufactured with the facilities and materials available in the United States, drawings were prepared at Frankford Arsenal, from the sample sight, and one sight was manufactured and called Telescopic Musket Sight, Model 1916, No. 1. This sight was proved in limited tests to be as satisfactory as the original Goerz sight, although in a report by the School of Musketry under date of June 26, 1917, objection is made to the fact that the telescope is offset too far to the left of the center line of the rifle.

On account of the pressure of more essential work, and the apparent lack of further demand on the part of the service for musket sights, little action toward producing the Goerz type was taken until March, 1917. At this time a representative of the Winchester Company stated that he believed his concern to be in a position to develop an improved sight which would equal the Goerz optically and would be an improvement on the Goerz in certain respects, and which could be produced more readily in quantity. The drawings of the Goerz sight prepared at Frankford Arsenal, also the general specifications of the same, were turned over to the Winchester Company in April, 1917, and permission was given to proceed with the experimental work.

Subsequently, in a manner characteristic of the armed forces to this date, that is, defying all logic, Army marksmen were not furnished with a comparatively good sight at this point in time. Produc-

Frankford Arsenal telescope sight No. 10 as mounted on the '03 Springfield. Photo Credit: Copyright by the Army Ordnance Association.

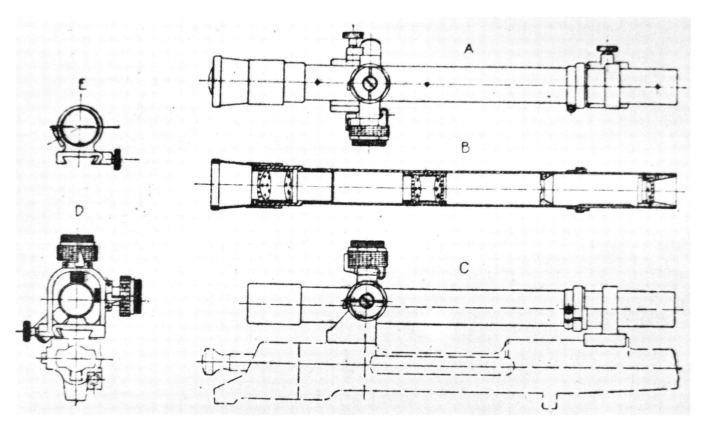

Frankford Arsenal experimental musket sight with nonadjustable eyepiece and objective. Photo Credit: Copyright by the Army Ordnance Association.

tion of the Goerz/Telescopic Musket Sight, Model of 1916, did not transpire, and efforts to develop a better sight were to prove fruitless once again.

As Rutherford further related:

A sample of the improved sight was tested by a Board of Officers convened at Camp Meade, Maryland, and report submitted under date of April 20, 1918. The improved, or Model 1918 Sight, is very similar in construction and method of mounting to the Winchester Model A5, but is only 10 7/8 inches long. The main optical characteristics are as follows:

Aperture objective . . . . inches		.56
Magnification . . . . diameters		2.6
Field of view		8°22'
Diameter exit pupil . . . . inches		.2
Longitudinal eye relief . . . . inches		2.25
Erecting system . . . . lenses		2

The sight is permitted a longitudinal movement of about one inch in its brackets under the action of recoil. The method of mounting is such that the rear sight of the rifle must be removed, the bolt handle modified, a modified form of lock furnished, the bridge of the receiver changed, and the cutoff modified slightly to clear the rear bracket.

The Board at Camp Meade had also before it the C.P. Goerz Sight, the Winchester Model A5, the Warner & Swasey, Model of 1913, and a new model of Warner & Swasey Sight identical to the 1913 model except in power, which was decreased to 3 diameters with a consequent increase in field. There was also considered the Casey-Czegka Sight, which will be described more in detail later under the name of Casey Sight.

The Board reported that the 2.6 Winchester Sight was in its opinion superior to the Goerz model in all essentials, such as the following:
(A) Size.
(B) Optical qualities.
(C) Position on the rifle.
(D) Rigidity of mounting.
(E) Method of setting range and deflection.
(F) Lateral and longitudinal eye relief.
(G) Adjustability of objective and eyepiece.
(H) Maintenance of accuracy under test.

The Board also commented on the undesirable features of the Winchester Sight:
(A) Necessity of modifying the rifle.
(B) Necessity for discarding the iron sights.
(C) Impossibility to load by clip.

The recommendations of the Board were that the Winchester 2.6 Power Telescope be adopted for issue in place of the Warner & Swasey Model 1913 Sight, and that none of the other sights tested be adopted.

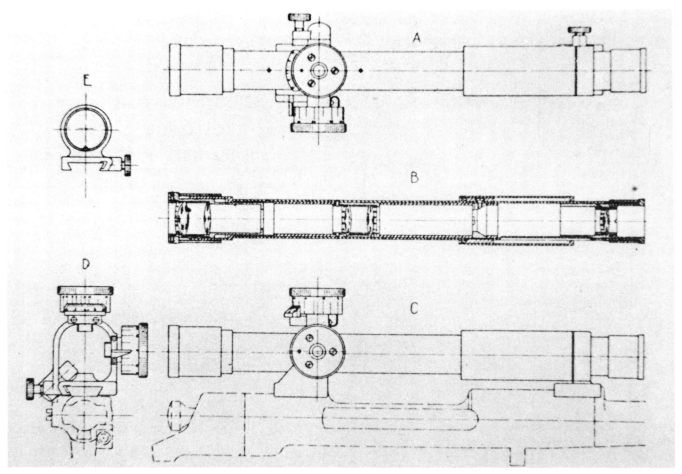

A Frankford Arsenal sight variant with adjustable eyepiece and objective. Photo Credit: Copyright by the Army Ordnance Association.

Although preliminary testing of Model 1918 sights was reportedly conducted on "modified Model 1903 rifles," it was later decided that the new scope would be best mounted on the Model 1917 (Enfield) rifle. Whether this decision was based on the contention that the M1917 rifle would require minimal rework, as variously cited, or that it represented a logical choice since many of the military considered it to be the eventual successor to the '03 Springfield, stands unconfirmed.

Despite the fact that the Ordnance Department originally intended to issue a substantial quantity of M1917 rifles in sniper trim, few were ever completed. The time of origin, specific number, and the source performing the rifle modification and sight mounting, remains undetermined at present. According to an article in the 13 April 1918 issue of *Arms and the Man,* one of these special rifles mounting an M1918 Winchester sight appeared in civilian hands at an impromptu 1,000-yard shooting match held at the Congress Heights range near

Washington, D.C., on 4 April 1918. Officially, the Model 1917 rifle was designated the U.S. Telescopic Sight Rifle, Caliber .30, Model of 1918 as noted in the *Handbook of Ordnance Data* published by the Office of the Chief of Ordnance under date of 15 November 1918:

This rifle, which is derived from the United States rifle, model 1917, is adopted for the telescopic musket sight, model of 1918. It is intended primarily for sniping and most of its parts are interchangeable with the parts of the 1917 rifle. The exceptions are as follows:

Receiver—There is no rear sight base and no rear sight. A dovetail for the telescope mount takes the place of these.

Barrel—There is no front sight, the barrel being adapted to receive screws for the front telescopic parts. The rifling is right-hand twist with one turn in 10 inches and the standard tolerances and type of land on the Springfield are employed. The stock is of special construction with no barrel guard, nor upper bands, while the lower band is of special design.

Reading from top to bottom: A Casey prismatic sight variant, Frankford Arsenal musket sight No. 7, Zeiss musket sight on a Frankford Arsenal mount, Zeiss sight with original mounting as used by German snipers on the Gew. 98, and the Knoble mount as used for various sight evaluations. Photo Credit: Copyright by the Army Ordnance Association.

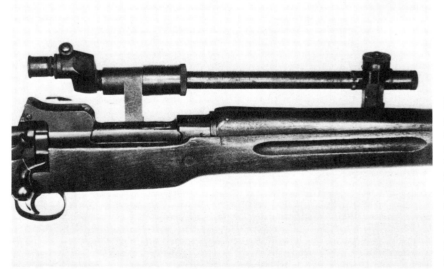

Model 1917 rifle No. 68336 (10-17 barrel date) with a variation of the Casey/Czegka side-mounted 2.8 power prismatic rifle scope. Elevation adjustments were made with a graduated drum (readings in minutes) located at the objective end of the sight, with windage corrections by means of an adjusting screw located between the eyepiece and the rear mount, which moved the vertical cross hair in the reticle as required. Photo Credit: Colonel William S. Brophy (Retired).

Orders for 32,000 of the Model 1918 sight were placed with the Winchester firm during the summer of 1918, with the Eastman-Kodak Company of Rochester, New York, acting as subcontractor for the optical elements, of which 42,607 sets were ordered. Unfortunately, manufacturing difficulties held up scope production to the extent that except for the few which were furnished for testing early in the year, none were delivered to the government before the war ended on 11 November 1918. A large portion of the order was then cancelled, and work continued slowly until October 1919 when three sights were forwarded to the Infantry School (Department of Experiment) at Camp Benning, Georgia, for further evaluation.

Additional testing revealed a number of deficiencies in the Winchester design, which prompted the Infantry School to recommend against adoption until corrections were effected. E. C. Crossman commented on this turn of events in his classic work, *The Book of the Springfield:*

> The 1918 telescope was never a good glass and proved it promptly when subjected to use. . . . I was one—the Department of Experiment, without bowels of compassion, respect for tradition, reverence for the selection of boards, or any other redeeming feature. Their idea of how to find out about a telescope sight was to put it on a rifle, give the rifle and a lot of "hulls" to some of the rifle shooting sergeants attached to the department and tell them to shoot the thing daily until something let go.

This they did, and defects in the Model 1918 sight were thus noted by Crossman:

(A) The optical lens shot loose and the lens became uncemented rendering it impossible to use the sight.
(B) The rear mounting bracket fractured from recoil.

George W. Chesley, a Winchester representative, with the Model 1918 telescopic musket-sight-equipped U.S. telescopic-sight rifle, caliber .30, Model of 1918 (modified M1917 rifle) in competition with Victor Czegka at Congress Heights, 4 April 1918. Photo Credit: Copyright by the National Rifle Association.

Victor H. Czegka firing the M1917 rifle with the 2.8 power prismatic rifle scope that he designed in collaboration with Major K. K. V. Casey on the Congress Heights range near Washington, D.C., on 4 April 1918.

(C) If the sight was not drawn back into firing position each time, the shooter was liable to injury from the rebound of the telescope.

In lieu of these difficulties, Rutherford continued:

Steps were then taken by Frankford Arsenal to manufacture sample sights which would overcome the above defects, and four telescopes were produced, each having the same optical system as the Model 1918 Winchester. Two of these telescopes were provided with adjustable eyepiece and objective and two were nonadjustable. Two of the telescopes were provided with a spring recuperator, just in rear of the front brackets, so designed as to return the sight automatically to the firing position after each shot; in the other two this operation had to be performed by hand, leather buffers being provided to limit the forward movement of the telescope.

The mountings for the lenses in all four telescopes were redesigned to hold these parts more securely, and this necessitated the use of a larger tube for the telescope body.

The front and rear brackets were redesigned to increase their strength, and more reliable clamps for securing them to the rifle were provided. Two types of rear brackets were furnished, the first which is practically the same as the Winchester, Model 1918, except that the range and deflection indices are made separate and a spring detent is provided to prevent the accidental movement of the knobs; and second in which a different type of range and deflection knob is furnished. It will be noted that a range index on this type, instead of being a simple pointer, consists of a strip graduated in minutes of elevation to 10 on each side of the normal. This idea is one patented by Maj. S. A. S. Hammar, and was included in the design at the request of the Infantry School. The advantage claimed for it is that it gives a convenient means for adjusting the range in terms of minutes of elevation.

The clamping screws on both types of rear bracket were moved to the left side, where more room was available.

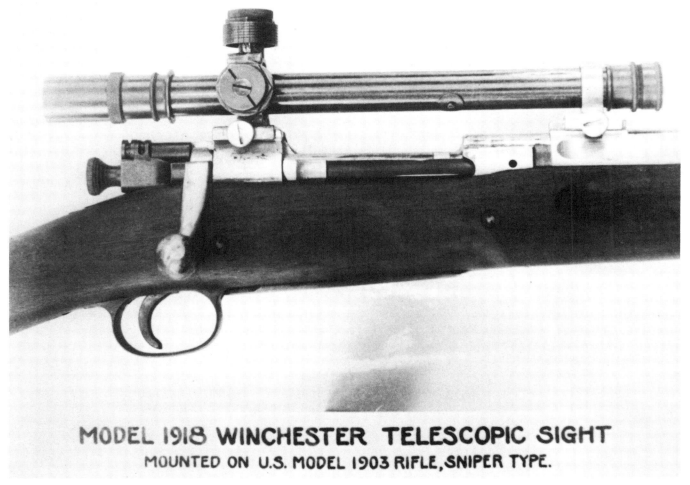

MODEL 1918 WINCHESTER TELESCOPIC SIGHT
MOUNTED ON U.S. MODEL 1903 RIFLE, SNIPER TYPE.

Preliminary Ordnance Department evaluations of the Model 1918 Winchester sight were conducted with modified M1903 Springfield rifles. Note the altered bolt-handle and integral dovetail receiver bases. Photo Credit: Colonel William S. Brophy (Retired).

The Casey Sight—This model was developed at the same time as the four sights above referred to, but due to difficulties in design and manufacture was not completed for some weeks after Nos. 1, 2, 3, and 4 had been sent to Camp Benning for test. Credit for the method of mounting involved is due to Major K. K. V. Casey of the Du Pont Company. The main feature of this sight is that the body of the telescope is mounted on the side of the rifle by means of a bracket similar to that used with the Warner & Swasey Sight and the eye-piece is brought up to a position as nearly as possible over the center of the piece by means of an offset prism in the optical system. The telescope slides forward in its bearings under the force of recoil and is brought back to the firing position by a coil spring in the housing on the rear bracket. The sight has the additional feature that the eye-piece may be rotated outward and downward to the left side of the rifle where it is out of the way. The optical system is the same as that of the Winchester Model 1918 Sight, except that the offset prism is added. Range and deflection are set by moving the telescope as a whole about its rear bracket as a pivot.

The sample sight was completed and shipped to Camp Benning for test in August, 1920. Many difficulties were encountered in its construction and when finished it was not as good optically as the preceding four telescopes. Since its completion, however, an improved optical system has been worked out which, when mounted in the Casey Sight, will make it the equal, optically, of the No. 7 Sight described below,

and considerably superior to designs Nos. 1, 2, 3, and 4.

A preliminary report dated June 8, 1920, on the four Frankford Arsenal Sights, above referred to, outlined certain defects and recommended that another sight be constructed to eliminate them. These defects were:
(A) Too short longitudinal eye relief.
(B) The spring recuperator brought the sight back to the firing position too violently.
(C) Reticule not satisfactory.
(D) A rear mounting with deflection knob on the left was desired for test.

As a result of the above recommendations, the Frankford Arsenal No. 7 Sight was developed. The optical system was entirely redesigned so as to obtain the following characteristics:

Aperture of objective		.50
Magnification	diameters	2.5
Field	sharp to edges	7°
Exit pupil	inches	.20
Aperture of eye-piece	inches	.95
Longitudinal eye relief	inches	2.87

Its chief superiority over the Winchester Telescope is in increased longitudinal eye relief and in the extent of the clear field.

The objection to the shock of counter recoil was overcome by placing a leather buffer on the telescope in front of the rear bracket. A rear bracket with deflection knob on the left was furnished and an im-

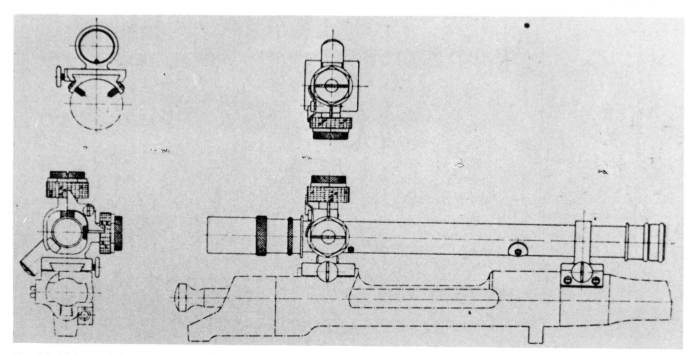

Frankford Arsenal design drawing of the 2.6 power Winchester telescopic musket sight, Model of 1918. Photo Credit: Copyright by the Army Ordnance Association.

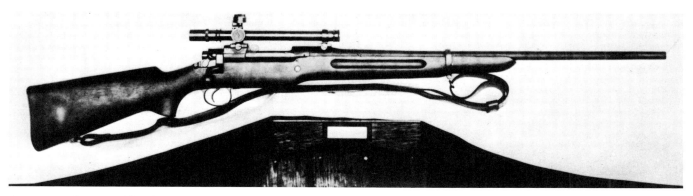

An extremely rare official Ordnance Department photograph of the Model 1918 Winchester telescopic musket sight and Model 1918 sniper rifle uncovered through the diligent efforts of William Brophy. Photo Credit: William S. Brophy (Retired).

proved reticule was inserted, but otherwise the sight is the same as the recuperator types Nos. 3 and 4, above described. This sight was shipped to Camp Benning in September, 1920, together with the Zeiss Prism Sight described below. This sight is still undergoing test.

Zeiss Prism Sight—This telescope was received from overseas with a shipment of captured material. Its optical qualities were so excellent that it was considered advisable to mount it on a rifle so that it could be tested with the other types.

It differs from the other types previously described chiefly in that it utilizes a special roof-edge prism as an erector in place of the usual lenses, and has an unusually large, adjustable eyepiece. The optical characteristics are as follows:

Aperture of objective 59
Magnification . . . . diameters 2.03
Field . . . . clear to edge 12.2°
Longitudinal eye relief . . . . inches 2.8
Diameter exit pupil . . . . inches .29
Diameter eye lens . . . . inches 1.20

The eye-piece of this sight is manufactured of special glass, not available in this country in quantity, and this makes possible a somewhat greater eye relief than is obtainable with domestic glass in the F.A. No. 7 with an eye-piece of the same diameter.

On the original sight, range was set by moving the objective by means of a knurled collar which carried the range graduations. No means for setting deflections was provided. As originally used abroad the sight was apparently mounted rigidly on the rifle by one point of support.

On the sight as mounted for test at Camp Benning, a front and rear bracket are provided, through which the sight slides during recoil. The usual spring recuperator brings it back to the firing position. Range and deflection are set by the usual knobs on the front bracket by means of which the telescope is moved as a whole about the rear bracket as a pivot.

The Modified Casey Sight—As stated above, the optical system mounted in the original Casey Sight was not equal to that developed for the Frankford Arsenal No. 7 Sight which was produced after the completion of the Casey model. To improve it in this respect, the sight has been returned to Frankford, where it will be given the same optical system as No. 7 telescope and have certain minor changes made in the mounting, preparatory to a final test at Camp Benning. A leather buffer is also being assembled to the tube to reduce the force of counter recoil, and an improved type of reticule will be assembled.

Neither the Frankford Arsenal Number 7 nor the Casey Sight proved satisfactory in subsequent tests, however. Frankford Arsenal was directed to continue the development of these sights, which resulted in the introduction of numbers 9 and 10 as recorded in H. K. Rutherford's 1924 article relevant to the subject of "New Telescopic Musket Sights."

These sights have now been completed and tested by the Ordnance Dept. and forwarded to the Infantry Board for further consideration. The present article is written with a view to describing in detail the characteristics of the two new sights and indicating wherein improvement may be made in the designs in case of future manufacture.

The No. 9 telescope is of the straight type permanently attached by bearings at either end to a rigid bar, this bar being arranged at one end to clamp into the rear sight fixed base of the rifle and at the other end to make contact with the bridge of the receiver without clamping.

The telescope of the new sight has the following optical characteristics:

Power 2.5
True field . . . . 9 degrees
Exit pupil .27 inch
Eye relief . . . . 2.9 inches

It is of the universal focus type, no provisions being made for focussing either the objective or the eyepiece by the user.

The telescope tube 1 is attached to the bracket 2 by means of two collars, viz., a front one 3, the lower end of which is pivoted in the bracket 2, and a rear one 4, the lower end of which passes through a transverse slot in the bracket 4, thus permitting the windage screw 5 to rotate in the whole tube about the pivot at 3 when setting deflections. Spring washers are placed at the lower ends of both bearings 3 and 4, between them and the bracket 2, to compensate for any lost motion or wear that may occur. A coil spring is provided to oppose the motion of the windage screw 5, and removes all lost motion from this mechanism.

The range knob for moving the reticule of the telescope in the vertical direction is shown at 6. Combination counting and locking devices for the range and windage knobs are shown at 7 and 8 respectively. When these locks are screwed home, no movement of the knobs is possible. When they are released, the passage of the serrations of the knobs over a spring detent in the housings of 7 and 8 indicates by sound the amount of movement of the knobs.

Since the serrations on range and windage knobs are accurately spaced at one minute increments as measured by the corresponding movement of the telescope, this affords a ready means of adjusting the aim without looking at the telescope.

The range dial 6 is graduated in yards from 0 to 1400. A correction scale 9 is provided for use in conjunction with the range dial and is graduated so that each division corresponds to one minute of change in range. Corrections in range may thus be made in terms of minutes of elevation either visually by use of the scale 9 or audibly by use of the counting device above referred to.

The deflection knob 5 is graduated so that each division corresponds to one minute of angular movement of the telescope.

The telescope bracket 2 consists of a bar as rigid as practicable for the weight of metal contained in it. At its forward end, it is adapted to fit in the recess provided in the rifle for the rear sight movable base and carries the two clamping levers 10 and 11, locking it in place on the rifle. The clamping device 10 is adapted to engage with the rear sight pivot on the rifle and, regardless of slight variations in diameter of this pivot, to make firm connection to it. The clamping device 11 serves to grip the rear lug of the rear sight fixed base firmly between corresponding parts on the bracket 2 and thus to lock the bracket rigidly to the rifle against any possibility of lateral movement.

A strong leaf spring is located in a recess underneath the portion 13 of bracket, for the purpose of taking up any lost motion between bracket and recess on the rifle.

The rear end 14 of the bracket 21 is provided with a lug or lugs which are designed to make loose contact with the bridge of the receiver on the rifle. These lugs are not essential to the locating of the sight on the rifle and may, in fact, be omitted, but were added as a safety feature to prevent any accidental blow at the rear end of the telescope from being transmitted to the fastenings at the front end, where it might disturb the adjustment of the sight or damage the connecting parts.

It will be evident therefore, that the sight is held to the rifle by the attachment at the forward end of the bracket only, the body of the bar 2 being sufficiently rigid to give the required support to the rear end of the telescope without assistance from the lugs at 14. While this construction would seem to place too much dependence on the clamping mechanism provided, it has been found in practice that the method is entirely reliable.

Some thousands of rounds have been fired with this sight using a full service charge and no weakness, loss of adjustment, or change in position of the sight on the rifle has been apparent. The sight has been removed repeatedly from the rifle in the midst of a string of shots and then replaced with no perceptible change in the location of the center of impact. The sight may be placed on any caliber .30 Springfield rifle, after the iron sight is removed, without any modification or fitting whatever in rifle or sight. This sight apparently comes very near to fulfilling all the conditions for an ideal telescopic musket sight for our service.

The Number 10 offset sight, on the other hand, while proving reasonably efficient, was ultimately rejected for the following reasons:

The positive disadvantages of greater cost, less reliability, lack of interchangeability on different rifles without modification of the same, the absence of any compensating advantages, condemn this type of sight for service use in comparison with the straight type.

Although basic refinements were made to the Number 9 Frankford Arsenal sight through 1925, for reasons that remain obscure, further telescopic sight development was suspended at the official level and remained in this state until the Second World War.

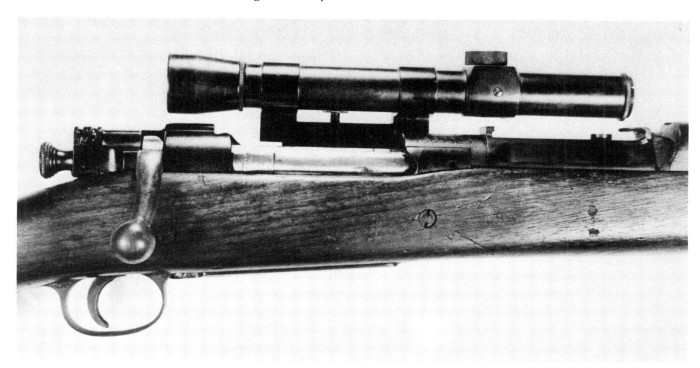

M1903 National Match Springfield rifle No. 1369025 (11-30 barrel date) and 1.5 power Noske telescope and mount. The 8 5/8-inch by .870 diameter sight has a tapered post reticle with threaded caps covering the elevation and windage adjustment dials. Although mounted to the left side of the receiver (dovetail base and mount), the scope was centered on the rifle. Sights by Rudolph Noske were highly regarded and received consideration for sniper use prior to World War II. Photo Credit: Colonel William S. Brophy (Retired).

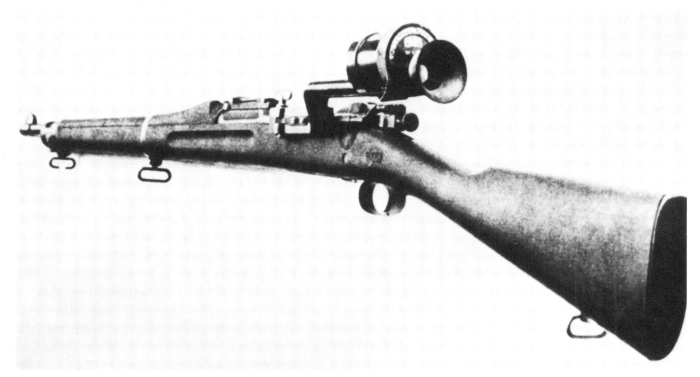

A Model 1903 Springfield rifle with a Zeiss prismatic sight and mounting of unknown origin. Extremely popular in Germany prior to World War I, Zeiss prismatic sights were noted for their exceptionally clear definition and extensive field of view. Photo Credit: J. B. Anderhub.

Chapter 7 ◆◆

The USMC Springfield Sniper

When the first units of the Marine Corps landed on Guadalcanal in August 1942, included among them were qualified marksmen armed with the then-standard USMC sniper rifle, the Model 1903 Springfield mounting Lyman 5A telescopic sights. Unlike the Army, which did not possess an issue sniping arm when the war began, the Marine Corps had retained the modified-mount Winchester A5 sight as its sniper standard following World War I and had made a transition to the improved Lyman 5A sight in the years prior to World War II.

While essentially the same as the Winchester A5 device, the Lyman Number 5A (5 power) rifle scope improved on the fundamental defects of its predecessor by the addition of enlarged and strengthened lens mountings as well as a revision of Winchester's practice of using fine screws, which turned out against the tube from within to lock the various parts, in favor of considerably stronger screws passing through spring washers from outside

the tube to hold the works of the scope together under continuous use on a high-power rifle.

The Lyman sight had proven satisfactory in Marine Corps service, but recognizing that continued use had passed the point of practicality, in 1941, as a result of recommendations that certain sniper materiel be standardized for Marine Corps use, a Marine Corps Equipment Board made an exhaustive study of various telescopes under field conditions. The board arrived at the conclusion that "a scope of about 8x, with an object lens of about one and one-half inches, medium fine cross-hair reticle, and double micrometer quarter minute click mounts, was decidedly the best under all conditions."

A target telescope furnished by John Unertl and cited as the best they had found, was recommended for adoption, with 8 power or 10 power Lyman and Fecker scopes designated as alternate equipment. The board recommended further that

A USMC M1903-A1 (Springfield) Sniper Rifle with 8 power Unertl target telescope and mounts as issued for Scout Sniper use in World War II and the Korean War. Photo Credit: Peter R. Senich.

A photograph taken immediately after a Marine sniper has fired his rifle shows the Unertl scope in the forward or recoil position. Saipan, July 1944. Photo Credit: U.S. Marine Corps.

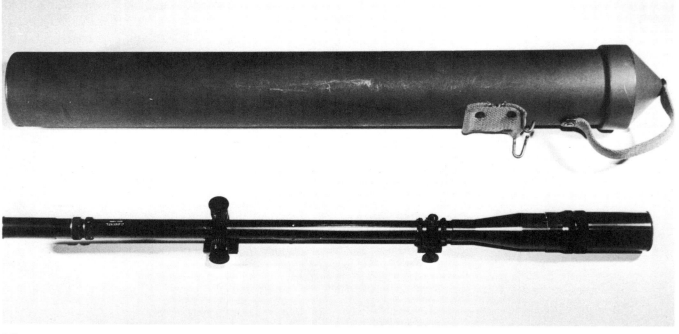

Micarta carrying case and Unertl telescopic sight as furnished to the Marine Corps during World War II. Photo Credit: Peter R. Senich.

A camouflage suit or cape typical of those employed by Japanese snipers in the Solomon Islands (1942). Photo Credit: U.S. Army.

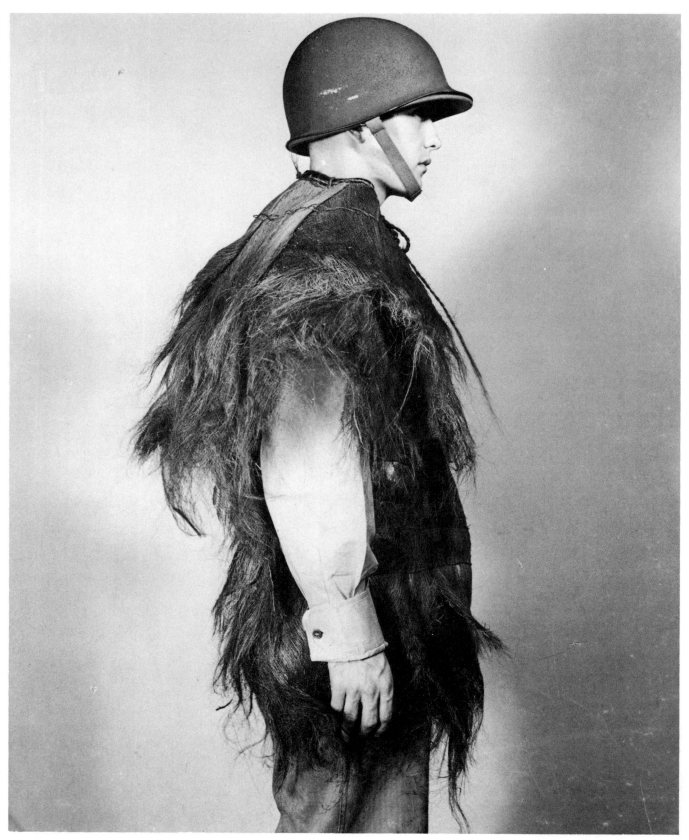

According to Army Intelligence reports, Japanese sniper training placed considerable emphasis on individual camouflage. An example of these efforts, the camo suit is shown ready for use. Photo Credit: U.S. Army.

A close view illustrating the Unertl target-type duraluminum rear mount. Even though the telescope was easily removed, according to Marine snipers in the Pacific and Korea, "the telescope was rarely taken off the rifle." Photo Credit: Peter R. Senich.

the Unertl sight be placed, preferably, on a .30-06 Winchester Model 70 Target Grade Rifle, or as an alternate, on a Springfield or Enfield rifle with an equally heavy barrel and similar stock.

However, the Model 70 Winchester was not adopted in lieu of favorable accuracy comparisons between it and specially selected M1903-A1 rifles. An additional point of consideration in this case centered on the impracticality of injecting another rifle into the supply system. Consequently, the U.S. Rifle, Caliber .30, M1903-A1 (Springfield), mounting the 8 power Unertl telescope, was adopted for use by the Marine Corps as its sniper standard.

Despite this acceptance of the Unertl, a considerable number of Lyman 5A-equipped Springfields were to see combat as well. Receipt and field distribution of both types of equipment reached such a state of confusion that a Marine Corps directive dated 29 October 1943 stipulated that the 1st, 2nd, and 3rd Marine Division base depots make "special reference" to rifles with Unertl telescopes as distinguished from those with Lyman 5A sights.

Unertl scopes were made for the Marine Corps

beginning about 1942 and were used primarily to fill the equipment requirements of newly organized Sniper-Observer-Scout Teams (Scout Snipers) destined for action against the Japanese in the Pacific. While most of the Unertl scopes were installed on Springfields, a number were also used with Model 54 and Model 70 Winchester rifles. These were not official issue, however.

Through the course of the war between five thousand and six thousand sights were furnished by the Unertl firm to various Marine Corps depots, where installation and basic targeting were effected by qualified armorers. Regardless of their 8 power reference, all sights were actually 7.8 power and were supplied without a recoil absorber, a spring that brings the tube back into firing position after each shot. It was thought that sand from the beaches working between the spring would score the tube. A ring located in front of the forward mount clamped to a rib affixed on top and in line with the tube, the combination of which served to prevent the telescope from rotating in its mounts. A second ring behind the front mount was simply a "spare" rather than an effort to limit the recoil of the tube, as some experts contend.

A Marine sniper team armed with the ever-effective 03-A1/Unertl combination in action on Okinawa, May 1945. Photo Credit: U.S. Marine Corps.

An early form of the "camouflage suit" tested by the Army (April 1942). The camo pattern was intended for island warfare in the South Pacific. Photo Credit: U.S. Army.

Considered to be indispensable for eliminating hidden enemy snipers, the .45 caliber Thompson submachine gun emerged as a favorite weapon among Army and Marine Corps combat personnel in the South Pacific. Photo Credit: U.S. Marine Corps.

A rib located on top of the Unertl tube prevented the scope from rotating in its mounts. The front clamping ring was used to position the sight. Photo Credit: Peter R. Senich.

When the rifle was fired, the scope slid forward in the mounts and was pulled back into firing position by hand. Some rather ingenious recoil systems were used by Marine snipers in place of a regular recoil absorber. The simplest was a slice of rubber taken from a truck inner tube which, stretched between the front clamping ring and the rear mount, brought the scope back into battery automatically.

The rear mount provided an adjustment of approximately two hundred minutes, with each division on the graduated thimble representing one-half minute and each click a one-quarter minute adjustment. Later scopes were modified for one-half minute adjustments for each click.

A micarta carrying case, also manufactured by Unertl, was supplied with every sight assembly. The cases were fitted with hooks for attaching to the cartridge belt, but they were considered too bulky and were rarely used in the field.

Marine Corps sights, furnished by the Unertl firm under World War II contracts, bore the fol-

lowing legend on the tube directly in front of the eyepiece:

J. Unertl
USMC–Sniper
2774

Not much need be said for the shooting capability of a select Springfield. In response to the question, "Was the Unertl satisfactory?" Stan Deka, a Scout-Sniper veteran of the Pacific Campaign who survived Tarawa and the action on Saipan and Tinian with the 2nd Marine Division, simply replied, "We found it quite adequate. We found no faults with the scope."

Regardless of the combat use of Lyman 5A and other scopes, the M1903-A1/Unertl combination remained as the principal issue for Marine Corps sniping specialists throughout the war. Although the Springfield had outlived its usefulness as a basic infantry arm, it continued to serve as a sniping weapon in Korea, too.

Long before the end of hostilities in the Pacific, Japanese combat personnel had developed a healthy respect for the marksmanship of Marine Corps snipers. Photo Credit: U.S. Marine Corps.

A Marine Corps scout sniper candidate receives instruction prior to "firing the combat range" (July 1943). The Model 1903 Springfield is fitted with a Lyman Number 5A (5 power) telescopic sight, an improved version of the early Winchester A5 target model. Photo Credit: U.S. Marine Corps.

Among the first Scout-Snipers trained by the Marine Corps during World War II, the marksmen are equipped with Springfield rifles and Lyman telescopic sights. Note the improvised supports for the spotting scopes (July 1943). Photo Credit: U.S. Marine Corps.

A close view of the USMC 03-A1 sniping arm depicting the manner in which Unertl bases were attached to the barrel and receiver ring. Photo Credit: Peter R. Senich.

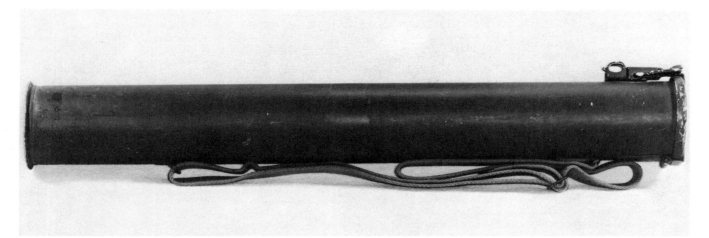

An extremely rare tubular metal carrying can produced by the Marine Corps in limited numbers for use with Unertl telescopes. The bottom of the tube was fitted with a wood disc having a recess in its center for the objective end of the sight, while the rear mount was held by a formed sheet metal rail located inside the tube toward the opening. Photo Credit: Peter R. Senich.

The front cover of Ordnance Maintenance Bulletin No. F-(Telescope)-1, 15 December 1943. The operation and maintenance instructions for the USMC Unertl 8x Snipers' Telescope. Photo Credit: Peter R. Senich.

NAVM(OMB F-(Telescope)-1

ORDNANCE MAINTENANCE   U. S. MARINE CORPS HDQRS.
BULLETIN No. F-(Telescope)-1   Washington, D. C., 15 Dec. 1943.

OPERATION AND MAINTENANCE
UNERTL 8X SNIPERS' TELESCOPE

	Paragraph
Introduction	1
Operation	2
Maintenance	3

1. INTRODUCTION—The Unertl telescope is an eight power telescope for use on the U. S. Rifle cal. .30, M1903A1. (Fig. 1.) It is constructed to withstand the recoil of the rifle without necessitating a change in adjustment.

General Data:

Magnification-8X
Objective size (effective) 1¼"
Exit pupil-4.2mm
Field of view at 100 yds.-11'
Luminosity-17.6
Eye relief-2¼" to 2¾"
Length-24"
Resolution-3/32"
Reticle angle-¼ minute
Medium size cross wire with center dot
Weight-24 oz.
Maximum O. D.-1½"
Main tube diameter-¾"
Eye piece adjustable for individual eye
*Target type ¼ minute click anodized,
    Duraluminum mounts with hardened steel
    bases and screws.

2. OPERATION—**a.** Focus the eyepiece against the sky until cross-wire or aiming mark appears black and distinct. Then leave the eyepiece undisturbed for all ranges.

b. Focusing for ranges under 200 yards is accomplished by moving the objective focusing sleeve as follows: Loosen sunshade about one turn, follow with the graduated focusing sleeve to the indicated range markings on the objective cell, tighten sunshade again.

c. The rear mount provides an adjustment of approximately 200 minutes, each division on the graduated thimble representing ½ minute, each

A Marine Corps sniper team during action on Okinawa. Trained as snipers and observers, while one scans the area with field glasses, the other stands by ready to fire on sighted targets of opportunity. Photo Credit: U.S. Marine Corps.

A seasoned Scout Sniper of the 1st Marine Division during the Korean War. Photo Credit: U.S. Marine Corps.

A 1st Marine Division scout sniper instructor is shown making an adjustment to the Unertl scope (June 1952). According to official reports, the long-range capability of the M1903-A1/Unertl combination accounted for some rather impressive kills in Korea. Photo Credit: U.S. Marine Corps.

Even though target scopes provide a limited field of view at extreme ranges, Marine snipers registered a number of 1000-yard kills with the Unertl sight. Many considered the 03-A1/Unertl combo to be the most effective sniping arm employed in Korea. Photo Credit: U.S. Marine Corps.

A Marine sniper directing machine-gun fire, Korea, May 1951. Photo Credit: U.S. Marine Corps.

In late 1951, however, as a result of studies to determine long-term requirements for a telescopic-sighted weapon, the Marine Corps Equipment Board recommended that:

(1) The U.S. Rifle, Caliber .30, M1903-A1 now in use and in stock as sniper's rifles be declared limited standard.
(2) The Unertl 8x Telescope be declared obsolete.
(3) The Unertl Mounts for the Unertl Telescopes be declared obsolete.
(4) The U.S. Rifle, Caliber .30, M1C, with telescope, cheek-pad and flash-hider, be standardized for the Marine Corps.

In use until the cease-fire ended combat in Korea, the venerable "Springfield Snipers" gradually disappeared from Marine Corps service.

The Browning Automatic Rifle (BAR) and the 03-A1/Unertl provided an effective combination for the Marine Corps in Korea. The BAR was a favorite support weapon of the Scout-Sniper teams. Photo Credit: U.S. Marine Corps.

A member of the 82nd Airborne Division
in North Africa, June 1943, with an M1903-
A4 rifle. U.S. parachute forces were among
the first to be equipped with the early A4
sniping issue. Photo Credit: U.S. Army.

Chapter 8 ◆◆

Sniper Rifle – Mass Production

As a result of initial U.S. combat involvement in the Pacific (Guadalcanal Campaign), efforts to meet urgent requirements for telescopic-sighted rifles required tests and evaluations conducted by the Infantry Board and the Ordnance Department for the purpose of adapting a commercial telescope to the Springfield rifle. In late 1942, Headquarters, Army Ground Forces, recommended that the readily available Weaver 2.5 power 330-C hunting telescopes be adopted for use with M1903 or M1903-A1 rifles. The rifles were to be "especially selected for accuracy and smoothness of operation; type 'C' stocks were to be used; and the bolt handles remodeled to eliminate interference with the sight." According to ordnance records: "The rifle adopted in December, 1942 met established requisites through the use of a modified Redfield 'Junior' type of mount fastened to the receiver of the M1903-A1 Rifle, less iron sights, utilizing the 2 1/2x Weaver Telescope."

While acceptance of the new sniping arm had been predicated on tests conducted with the Model 1903-A1 Springfield Rifle, in lieu of its status at that point, the War Department directed Remington Arms of Ilion, New York, to divert 20,000 of the new simplified M1903-A3 variant from regular production for conversion to sniping weapons. Remington then commenced manufacture of a sniping variant officially designated as the U.S. Rifle, Caliber .30, M1903-A4 (Sniper's) in February 1943. According to government production figures, a total of 28,365 M1903-A4 rifles were produced through completion of the project in June 1944.

Although the 03-A3 and the A4 were essentially the same, the primary difference rested with the

U.S. Rifle, Caliber .30, M1903-A4 (Sniper's) with Telescope M73B1 and "scant" grip stock fitted with the enlarged trigger guard introduced in mid-1943 to provide clearance for a gloved trigger finger. Photo Credit: Peter R. Senich.

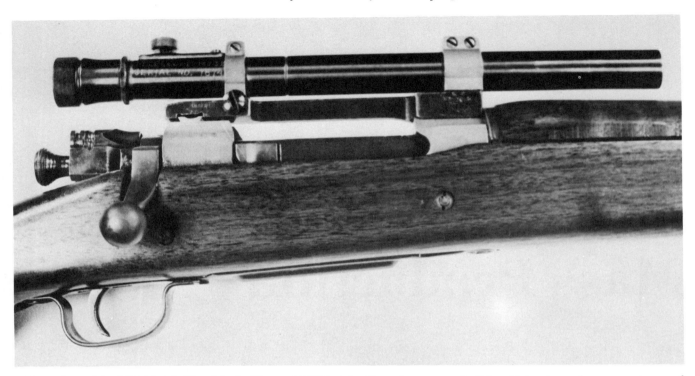

A close view of the M1903-A4 rifle with the Weaver M73B1 sight. Note the concave bolt-handle having a clearance cut ground in it to clear the scope, and the corresponding notch cut into the stock. In most cases, issue scopes were engraved with a serial number on the right side below the adjustment plate as exemplified by this sight. Photo Credit: Peter R. Senich.

An example of World War II jungle camouflage (1943). "A jungle-pattern suit issued by the Army to troops engaged in jungle warfare. Its mottled pattern blends with the green foliage, and the outline of the soldier and his equipment melt into the background." Photo Credit: U.S. Army.

A Marine Corps rifleman displays his M1903-A4 rifle at Russell Island, May 1944. The A4 was utilized by both Army and USMC marksmen in virtually every combat theater during World War II. Photo Credit: U.S. Marine Corps.

A4 having a concavely forged bolt handle with a considerable amount of metal machined from the outside to allow for a low telescope mounting. As such, the Weaver 330 or the Lyman Alaskan, with its larger tube diameter, could be fitted to this rifle. A point of interest centers on the "03-A3" marking on the A4 receivers to the lower left of the scope mount to allow "insufficiently accurate A4s to be reconverted to A3s."

The first block of A4s were reportedly assembled using select, cut-rifled, two-groove barrels. However, a transition to four-groove, draw-rifled barrels was later effected, but the exact point of the conversion in terms of serial number range or date remains obscure.

Initially, full grip M1903-A1 type "C" stocks were produced at Springfield Armory and eventually by Keystone Manufacturing with quality in both cases frequently rivaling "sporter-grade." When the expediencies of wartime production took hold, though, flat-sided, rather crudely finished "scant-grip," or as they were field-designated,

"warthog" stocks became regular issue with the A4. Stocks were stamped "S" or "K" in the cut-off recess to denote their point of manufacture.

The receiver mount secured the scope over the bore by means of a recess which engaged a corresponding lug located below the front ring. The lug was inserted into the mount, eyepiece to the right, and rotated ninety degrees clockwise to bring it into battery. Two slotted-screws threaded into the mount clamped the rear scope ring from both sides. After basic lateral zero had been established by adjusting the left screw, the right screw was tightened, locking the telescope in place.

While comparatively simple, once in the field the "windage-screws" were easily broken and virtually impossible to obtain through supply channels. Basic vertical zero was obtained by placing shims between the base and the receiver. This was necessary even though the base was made for this specific rifle. By design, the mount allowed the scope to be readily removed for carrying in a canvas bag attached to the rifleman's cartridge belt.

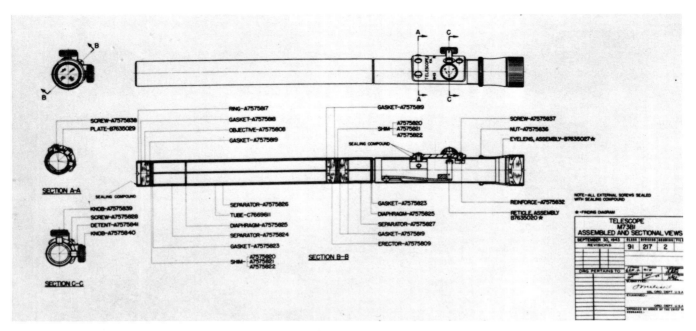

An illustration of an early Ordnance Department design drawing of the M73B1 telescopic sight. Photo Credit: Peter R. Senich.

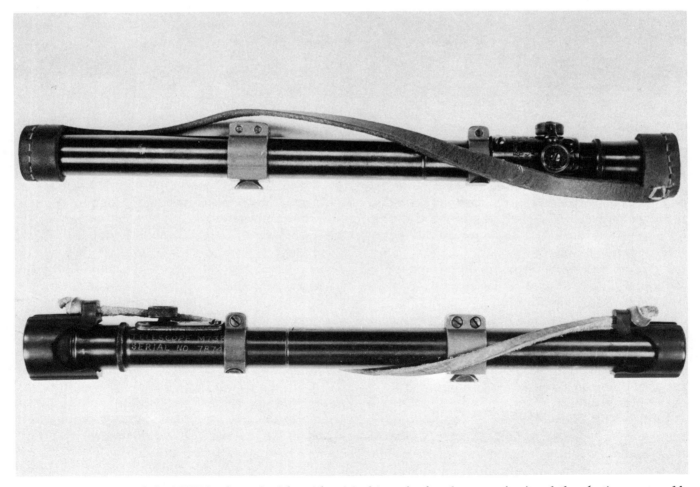

Right and left views of the M73B1 telescopic sight with original issue leather dust caps (top) and the plastic-cap assembly introduced following World War II. The M-65 web case was used for carrying this sight when removed from the rifle. Photo Credit: Peter R. Senich.

TM9-270

WAR DEPARTMENT TECHNICAL MANUAL

U. S. RIFLE

CAL. 30, M1903A4 (SNIPER'S)

CHARACTERISTICS
AND OPERATION
AND USE OF
TELESCOPIC SIGHT

WAR DEPARTMENT • *28 SEPTEMBER 1943*

The front cover of War Department Technical Manual TM 9-270, 28 September 1943. The World War II ordnance pamphlet detailed the workings of the M1903-A4 and M73B1 telescopic sight. Photo Credit: Peter R. Senich.

Taking advantage of a lull in combat, an Army marksman tends to his '03-A4 sniping issue somewhere in Italy, 1944. Although U.S. snipers rarely made extensive use of personal camouflage, in this case the familiar helmet form has been effectively altered. Photo Credit: U.S. Army.

However, since the rifle had to be rezeroed each time the scope was removed, it was left in place more often than not.

Approximately thirty-two thousand mount assemblies were furnished by the Redfield Gun Sight Company for use with the A4. In an effort to facilitate rapid production, the Ordnance Department had deemed it inadvisable to redesign the receiver bridge or introduce additional machining operations necessary for mounting conventional sights. As a result, iron sights were not furnished with M1903-A4 rifles.

Although the 330 sight was officially designated M73B1, the first rifle/scope combinations finding their way to the combat zones utilized regular commercial Weaver sights originally manufactured for the civilian market. The commercial Lyman

Alaskan telescope was also authorized for use with the M1903-A4 rifle and was to phase out the Weaver on a "one-to-one" replacement basis beginning late in 1944. However, this sight could not be furnished in quantity since the Lyman firm was operating at capacity on small parts contracts for the government. While about two thousand receiver mounts (rings, etc.) were procured from Redfield to accommodate the Alaskan, according to Remington records, delivery of the Lyman sight never materialized and (excepting the few scopes used for evaluative purposes), only the Weaver sight was furnished with the A4.

Although variations in 330/M73B1 markings have been noted, the following legends are representative of those appearing on the adjustment plate:

U.S. troops advancing cautiously through a village in Italy, 1944. The soldier (left) is armed with an M1903-A4 rifle. Photo Credit: U.S. Army.

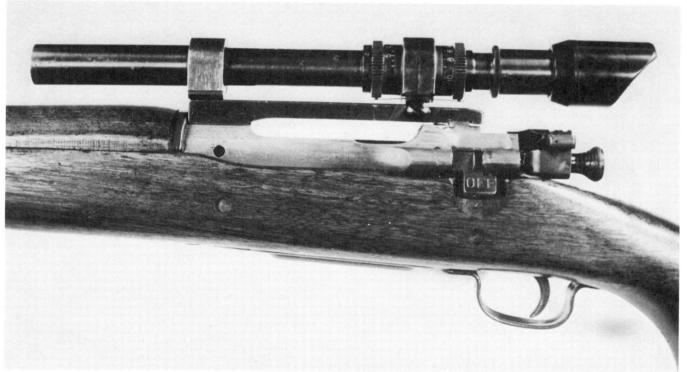

Unique and relatively rare, Telescope M73B2, the "French Weaver," was manufactured in Paris in 1945 under U.S. Ordnance auspices to improve on Weaver features and still fit the Redfield (base) mounting on the M1903-A4 rifle. Photo Credit: Peter R. Senich.

Army personnel "going at it" with the Japanese during isolated action for control of the Burma Road in 1945. Note the rifleman (center) sighting an A4 rifle. Photo Credit: U.S. Army.

Model 330
Pats. Pend.
W. R. Weaver Co.
El Paso, Tex. USA

330 Scope—M8
Patents Pending
W. R. Weaver Co.
El Paso, Texas

Telescope M73B1
Pat'd.—Pats. Pend.
W. R. Weaver Co.
El Paso, Tex. USA

While Weaver produced the bulk of the telescopic sights intended for use with M1903-A4 rifles (36,000), an unspecified, limited number of M73B1 sights were reportedly fabricated at Frankford Arsenal having "F. A." impressed on the adjustment plate.

Of further interest are variants bearing an "M8" designation, which the Weaver firm cites as having been manufactured for military use during World War II as well.

The M1903-A4 retains the distinction of being the only U.S. sniping arm manufactured in quantity or mass produced. Manufacture of the A4 was continuous and limited only by the availability of telescopes until June 1944, when the last orders were cancelled in favor of Army procurement of its successor, the U.S. Rifle, Caliber .30, M1C (Garand). As a result, the M1903-A4 was reclassified to "Limited Standard," out of production with its use temporary until replacement.

The brief interlude between V-J Day and the Korean conflict found the M1903-A4 unchanged. Despite official relegation to limited standard, the Weaver-A4 combination was brought forth and employed in large numbers during the Korean

Even though Lyman sights (Telescopes M81 and M82) did not see official issue, a limited number of these scopes were mounted on the A4 at the field level in Korea using rings procured from the Lyman Gun Sight Corporation. Photo Credit: Peter R. Senich.

An A4-equipped Army marksman in Korea. Exposure such as this was an open invitation to a Chi-Com sniper, among which many proved extremely deadly. Photo Credit: U.S. Army.

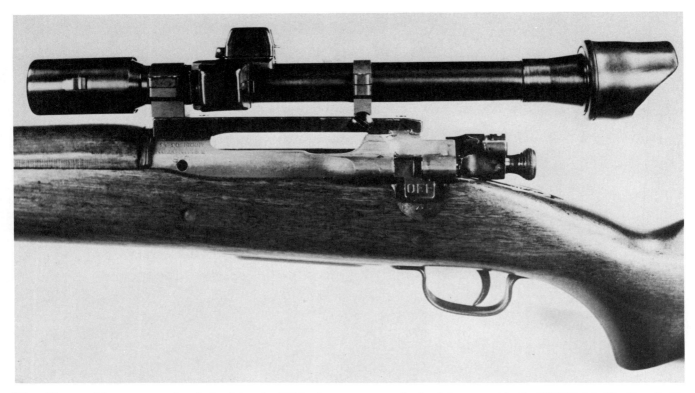

When Weaver sights were rendered obsolete, the M84 telescope was authorized for use with the M1903-A4 rifle. Despite its vintage, the A4 saw limited use by Army marksmen during early combat in Vietnam when sniping arms were in short supply. **Photo Credit: Peter R. Senich.**

War by both Army and Marine Corps snipers. At this juncture, however, it shared this application with the M1C and M1D for harassing North Korean and "Chi-Com" forces.

Even though Lyman sights (Telescopes M81 and M82) were not issue items, a limited number of these scopes were reportedly mounted on the A4 at the field level in Korea. An unspecified quantity of base mounts and 7/8-inch rings were procured from the Lyman Gun Sight Corporation during this period.

While capable of producing satisfactory results when carefully prepared by qualified unit armorers, the M1903-A4 was not favored by U.S. marksmen, particularly among those possessing the knowledge to recognize its deficiencies. A Report of Sniping Activities, dated 25 March 1952, dealing with the tactical employment of snipers in Korea, presented the following consensus among snipers serving with the 2nd U.S. Inf. Div., 9th Inf. Regt., and the 2nd ROK (Republic of Korea) Div., 31st Regt.:

A discussion of issue sniper rifles and telescopes indicated the following:

A. Present telescopes do not have sufficient magnification (2 1/2x).

B. Adjustments for elevation and windage cannot readily be made.

C. The Weaver 330 telescope is easily thrown out of adjustment.

D. Telescope cross hairs are too coarse and obscure the target.

E. Stocks should be better designed to facilitate taking good firing position.

F. Trigger pulls are neither adjustable nor crisp enough to permit a good squeeze.

G. Accuracy of the M1903-A4 is questionable due to the bedding of the barrel and the fact that wartime production runs of M1903-A3 rifles are believed to have been converted to the M1903-A4 rifle, without screening out those rifles not suitable for such a purpose.

H. Present sniper rifles do not maintain their "zero" from day to day, thus requiring frequent targeting.

In deference to the inadequacies of sniping issue in Korea, the report further pointed out that

Many failures with present equipment occur due to the lack of proper ordnance support and the individual handling it not being trained in its care and use. Present sniper equipment is not being utilized in all cases as intended, but is frequently issued to a man that would like to "carry it."

Despite the fact that vast numbers of the A4 were declared surplus and sold by the government to commercial arms dealers in the years following the Korean War, the M1903-A4 continued to be referenced by the Department of the Army in various Technical Manuals and Ordnance Bulletins through U.S. involvement in Southeast Asia. While such reappearance of the A4 might suggest its use by U.S. snipers in Vietnam, except for infrequent use by Army marksmen during early combat activity, the A4 was not employed to any great degree.

An Army sniper from the 45th Infantry Division adjusting his telescopic sight near "Ice Cream Cone Hill," Korea, November 1952. Note the burlap wrapped around the helmet to alter its form. Photo Credit: U.S. Army.

An Army rifleman equipped with an '03 Springfield and World War I-era Maxim Model 15 silencer, Italy 1944. Despite its vintage, the Maxim rifle silencer also saw limited action against "select" North Korean and Red Chinese targets during the Korean War. Photo Credit: John Minnery.

Chapter 9 ◆◆

Sight Development—
The Global Conflict

When development of an M1 sniping variant finally went into high gear in late 1943, procurement of a suitable telescopic sight and mount proved to be a difficult task. By this time, the Weaver 330 had clearly demonstrated its unsuitability for the rigors of combat, as evidenced by reports from the Pacific. Combat use of the Weaver sight with the M1903-A4 sniping rifle revealed two basic deficiencies: its susceptibility to moisture and damage to the cross hairs. In deference to the Weaver, problems with the reticle were believed to have occurred from careless handling by military personnel rather than haphazard manufacture as indicated by some field reports.

Attempts to rectify cross-hair difficulties resulted in the adoption of a tapered-post reticle, and while various 330/M73B1 sights have been noted with reticle patterns other than those cited, the vast majority of sights furnished for military use utilized the standard .001-inch cross hairs.

Additional field complaints centered on the sight recoiling against the sniper's helmet, thereby damaging the telescope and/or lens. Moving the sight forward on the receiver and the development of a rubber guard to protect the tube were under consideration when the M1903-A4 was reclassified

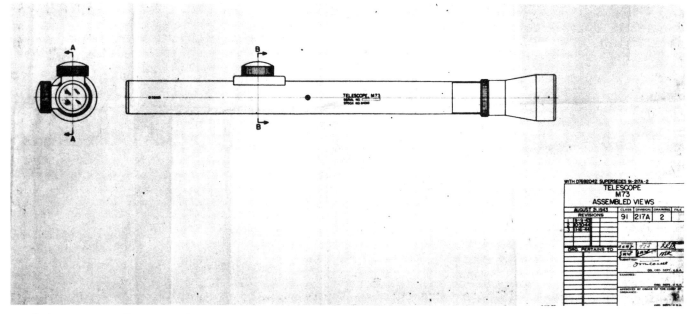

An Ordnance print illustrating the M73 Telescope Sight (Lyman Alaskan) as originally intended for military use without a sunshield or rubber eye guard. Photo Credit: Peter R. Senich.

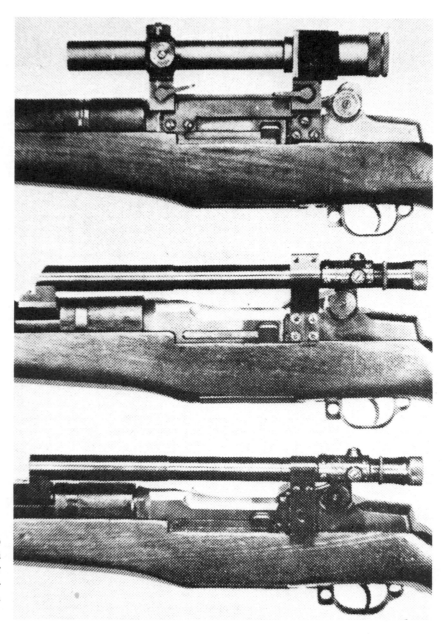

Initial efforts to adapt telescopic sights to the M1 Garand included evaluation of a 3 power prismatic sight (top) and Weaver 330 scopes in slightly modified Stith commercial side-mounts. Photo Credit: U.S. Army.

to "Limited Standard." Despite this status, efforts to improve existing sights included Ordnance Department experiments with a unique sight manufactured by the O.P.L. Company *(Optique et Precision de Levallois),* known as the "French Weaver." It was designed as an improvement on Weaver features that would still fit the Redfield (base) mounting on the M1903-A4 rifle.

The Army also considered adoption of an optical attachment manufactured by the Litschert Manufacturing Company. This device increased magnification of the 2 1/2 power 330/M73B1 sights to 6 power. Although orders for a number of these devices were reportedly placed, none were delivered before the war ended. Neither the French

M73B2 nor the 330/Litschert sights ever reached issue status.

Reviewing telescopic sight/mount development during this era, efforts were under way to adapt the Weaver 330 sight to the M1 Carbine as cited in records of the Ordnance Research and Development Service:

In June 1943, at the request of Headquarters, Army Ground Forces, a project was initiated to develop a suitable mount for the adaptation of a 2 1/2 power telescope to the carbine without interfering with ejection of empty cartridge cases. The M1E7 Carbine, so assembled, was submitted to test at Aberdeen. It was found that the mount would not stand up under sustained firing and the endurance

One of the countless camouflage patterns evaluated by the Army during World War II. To be effective, it was essential to make the clothing look less like a uniform and more like the terrain where it was worn. Photo Credit: U.S. Army.

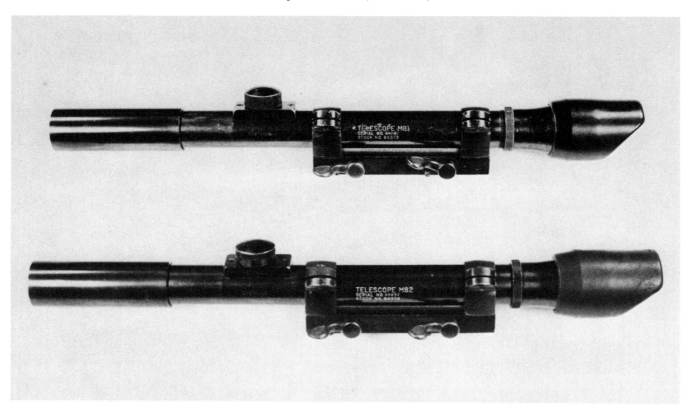

Comparative view of M81 and M82 telescopes with Griffin & Howe mounting as issued with the M1C sniper rifle late in World War II. Except for reticle patterns and minor details, both scopes were identical. Photo Credit: Peter R. Senich.

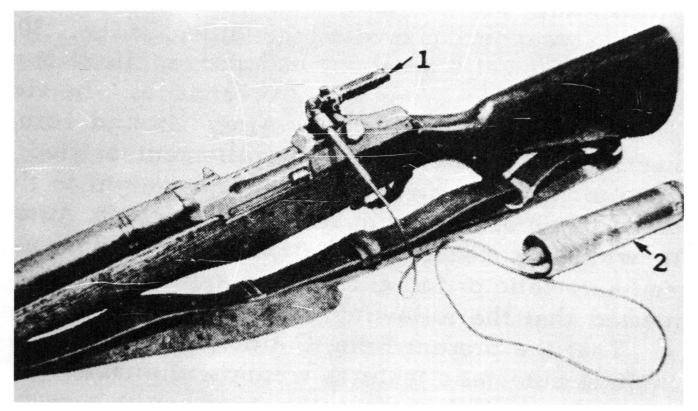

Collimator sight T53 (1) and instrument light T12 (2) as tested in 1944 with the M1 rifle for night use by Army snipers. Photo Credit: U.S. Army.

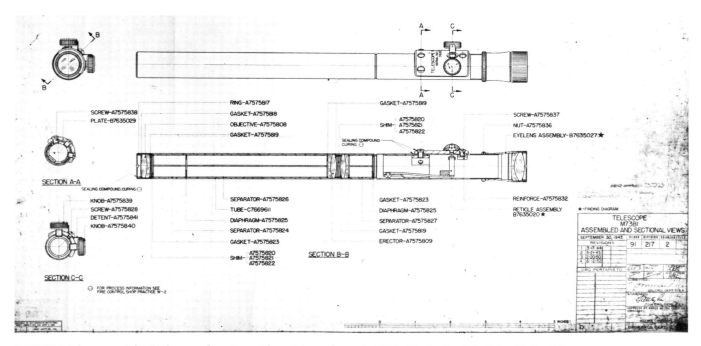

A M73B1 telescope-sight Ordnance drawing with revisions through 1952. Photo Credit: Peter R. Senich.

test was suspended. Inland Manufacturing Division of General Motors Corporation was directed to fabricate a carbine with a brazed-on telescope mount similar to the mount of the M1903-A4 Sniper's Rifle that would overcome the weakness of the first M1E7 Carbine.

Two carbines equipped with copper brazed sight mounts were tested at Aberdeen in January 1943. These tests indicated that the mounts were satisfactory from the standpoint of mechanical stability, but that there was interference with ejection. Malfunctions occurred more frequently after the ejector spring became weakened from use. Other models of the same basic design, but with the front portion of the mount cut away so as to be flush with the rear of the chamber, proved to be satisfactory, but in view of little interest shown by using services, the item, as a lightweight sniper's rifle, was not considered for service test.

Development work with the M1E7 Carbine was not in vain, because this system later served as the basis for development of the T3 Carbine used with infrared viewing devices.

Initial efforts to adapt telescopic sights to the M1 Garand included evaluation of a 3 power prismatic telescope, developed by International Industries, which was mounted offset to the left of the receiver with the eyepiece centered over the bore. In this form the test item was designated M1E2. Based upon the results of an Infantry Board test of the M1E2 and the M1, mounting commercial Weaver 330 scopes in slightly modified Stith side mounts, Headquarters, Army Ground Forces, made the following recommendations:

A. No further consideration be given to the two items.
B. That the mounting of the telescope be modified as follows:
1. So as to lower the telescope to bring the optical axis as nearly as practicable on a level with the standard iron sights when set for medium ranges.
2. So as to bring the axis of the telescope as nearly as practicable to the vertical plane through the axis of the bore and still permit clip loading.
3. So as to bring the rear end of the telescope forward to a position one-quarter inch in front of the forward edge of the elevation knob on the iron sight.
4. So as to permit fore and aft adjustment of the telescope tube of at least one-half inch to fit the conformation of the individual.
C. Consideration be given to the substitution of a rear sight similar to the ramp-type sight on the M1903-A3 Rifle for the present standard M1 sight on all M1 rifles modified for use as sniper's rifles.
D. That an adjustable cheek pad be supplied with the M1 type sniper rifles.

A drawing study was initiated to determine the advisability of developing a left side mount telescope and utilizing a ramp-type rear sight similar

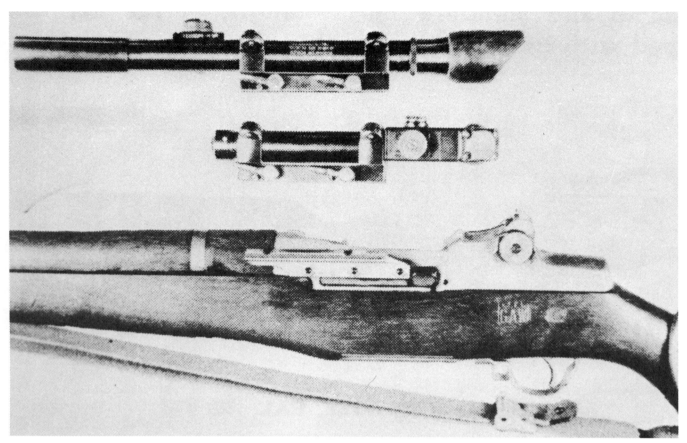

Rifle, U.S. Caliber .30, M1C with an experimental night sight, reflex-collimator T110, which could be mounted in a regular issue Griffin & Howe mount as illustrated. Photo Credit: U.S. Army.

to that of the M1903-A3 Rifle in order to permit usage of the iron sights with the telescope in position on the rifle. This study resulted in the decision that the M1E6 Rifle of this design would be undesirable from the standpoint of the extensive M1 rifle receiver modifications.

In line with the requirements of Headquarters, Army Ground Forces, the M1E7 (M1C) and M1E8 (M1D) were developed, evaluated, and subsequently adopted. In both cases, the M73 (2 1/2 power Lyman Alaskan) or the Weaver 330/M73B1 telescopes were authorized for use. Even though the 330 had been designated as an alternate sight, its application never progressed beyond the testing stage with the M1.

The Lyman firm had curtailed scope production due to pressing government contracts, and, excepting the few commercial Lyman Alaskan telescopes used for evaluative purposes, they were not available in quantity. When Lyman was able to resume telescope production, representatives from Frankford Arsenal visited the company on 29 and 30 September 1944 to finalize manufacture of Alaskan sights with a combination rain-sun shield for the objective end of the telescope and a protective rubber eyepiece for the ocular end. During this visit, pilot parts were carefully examined and retoleranced where necessary in order to facilitate rapid production.

On 2 October 1944, Headquarters, Army Ground Forces, approved the military version of the Alaskan and authorized manufacture of 2,000 sights with "cross-wire reticles." Efforts to supplement initial Lyman production included Springfield Armory's furnishing cross-wire reticle assemblies for the new telescopes.

In military configuration, the Lyman Alaskan was designated Telescope M81. However, in view of Frankford Arsenal studies which had indicated a definite preference for a tapered-post reticle with this type telescope, shortly after the M81 was approved, manufacturing drawings were revised to incorporate a tapered-post reticle (Lyman Catalog Number 6). This variant then became Telescope M82. Except for their reticle patterns, the telescopes were identical.

Experimental Carbine, Caliber .30, M1E7 with 2.5 power Weaver sight as evaluated for use as a "lightweight sniper's rifle" in 1943. The Weaver sight is a pure commercial 330S (Silent) variant having adjustment screws (windage and elevation) equipped with lock nuts, as opposed to the 330C scope with "click" adjustments. Photo Credit: U.S. Army.

A Litschert optical attachment of the type intended for use with 330/M73B1 sights during World War II. The 3 3/4-inch long, 1 1/4-inch objective attachment increased magnification to 6 power. Photo Credit: Donald G. Thomas.

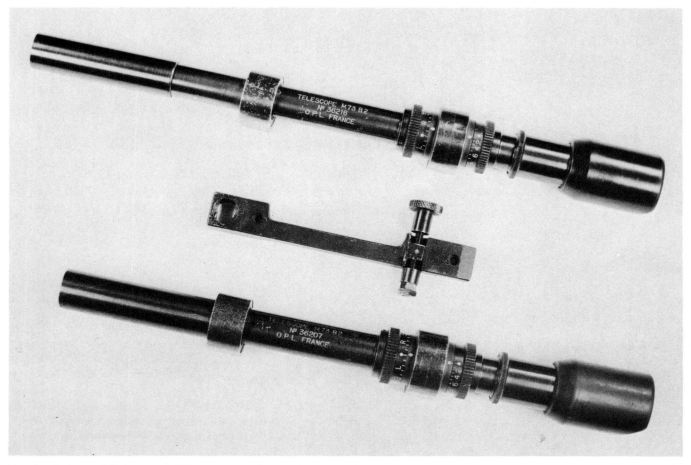

Two variations of Telescope M73B2 as manufactured in 1945 for ordnance evaluation with the M1903-A4 sniper rifle. The sight (top) with sunshade extended has an integral range-scale reticle pattern. The improved sight base (center) was specially made by Redfield for mounting the M73B2 to the A4. Photo Credit: Peter R. Senich.

The first M81 telescopes furnished to the Army were designated:

The Lyman Gun Sight Corp.
Alaskan
Made In U.S.A. Middlefield, Conn.
U.S. Patent No. 2078858
Telescope M81
Serial No. 31502
Stock No. 84373

Following a brief period of production when components (scope tubes) originally made for commercial use were expended, all reference to their Lyman origin was deleted, leaving only the model identification serial and federal stock numbers.

Telescopic sights having the tapered-post reticle were designated:

Telescope M82
Serial No. 35692
Stock No. 84374

Variations in federal stock numbers will be encountered with this sight, however.

In commercial form, two types of this sight had been produced by Lyman. The early type, with an aluminum alloy tube and exposed windage and elevation dials, was discontinued when alloy could no longer be obtained. The newer steel tube model, dubbed the "Alaskan All Weather" scope, was modified to include protection for the windage and elevation dials by means of screw-on dust and moisture covers.

All scopes furnished for Army use had a standard commercial blue-black finish. A web carrying case (M65), with "lift-the-dot" flap fastener and belt hooks, was designed to hold the telescope and mount when removed from the rifle. Leather lens

A part of extensive World War II efforts to develop satisfactory camouflage uniforms and techniques. A "camouflaged sniper in lightly covered terrain" during field evaluations held at the U.S. Army Desert Training Center, Mojave Desert, California (January 1943). Photo Credit: U.S. Army.

Comparative view of the standard Redfield M1903-A4 receiver base (right) and an M73B2 mount. Although virtually identical, the improved base made use of a threaded shaft on which a large, knurled knob with a screwdriver slot, and a threaded sleeve having an integral nut and jam nut, were tightened to lock the sight in place as opposed to the fragile windage screws used with the standard A4 base. Photo Credit: Peter R. Senich.

Developed at Frankford Arsenal late during World War II, an M84 telescope with the mounting used for M1D sniper rifles from the Korean War era to the present. Photo Credit: Peter R. Senich.

caps were not furnished with either M81 or M82 telescopes.

Early in 1945, the Wollensak Optical Company of Rochester, New York, commenced production of M82 scopes for use with the M1C. Initial production tests at Springfield Armory indicated that "the optics became loose and out of adjustment after sustained test firing (3,000 rounds)." This problem was rectified following a series of meetings between representatives of the Ordnance Department and Wollensak engineers. While the exact quantity of M82 scopes produced by Wollensak remains obscure, according to its records, "thousands of these instruments were supplied to the Army for sniper use." Although the government had acquired a second source in this case, Lyman remained the primary supplier of M82 telescopes through the end of the war in August 1945. On an overall basis, a substantial quantity of M82 telescopes were procured for military use.

Frankford Arsenal, a principal source of optical fire-control systems for the Army's artillery, in response to a pressing need for telescopic sights for small arms embarked on research and development in quest of "an optimum telescope for sniper use" shortly after the beginning of the war. Early sniper experience indicated that a telescope had to be fungus-proof, waterproof, and practically shock-proof. Development of such a telescope to replace the commercial types commenced in earnest after it became obvious that no commercial sight possessed the attributes necessary for sustained military use. The Weaver 330 was to be replaced by the Lyman scope on an overall basis, as noted by Frankford Arsenal records, and the Lyman sight in turn: "The Telescope M73 (Alaskan) is to be used until a superior telescope is developed and

standardized." Consideration was even given to the Lyman Alaskan type in a somewhat modified form with "new reticle patterns." But the M73E1 and M73E2 telescopes, as they were designated, did not progress beyond the testing stage.

Following the adoption of the M1C, telescope development advanced rapidly with a number of designs brought to fruition. The most unusual perhaps were the collimator sights intended for target sighting during day or night. By early 1945, however, a conventional 2.2 power sight, designated T134, had emerged as the most practical among those considered for adoption. Although the development of 3 power and 4.5 power variants, having characteristics similar to the T134 device, had been initiated and were to be available for field testing in June 1945, they were ultimately rejected for reasons that remain obscure. Telescope T134 was chosen, designated M84, and standardized on 12 April 1945.

The M84, a 2.2 power straight tube telescope with vertical post and horizontal cross-hair reticle, was designed to incorporate an optical system sealed with synthetic rubber gaskets in an effort to make the scope impervious to moisture. The M84 was intended primarily for the M1C, but it was also authorized for use with M1903-A4 sniping rifles.

Designed to replace M81 and M82 telescopes as they became unserviceable, M84 standardization at the end of the war found only a handful produced for testing and evaluation. The M84 was not available in quantity until the Korean War when Libby-Owens-Ford (L.O.F.) became the prime contractor. In final production form, the scope was finished in black-oxide and issued with a web carrying case. An identification plate, attached to the right side of the sight, bore the designation:

Standing in full view, the soldier displays the "field experience sniper's suit" developed at the Desert Training Center (January 1943). Photo Credit: U.S. Army.

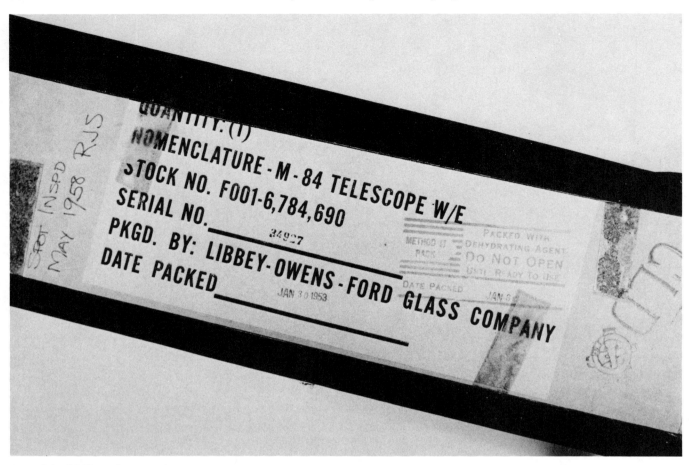

An original M84 telescope shipping carton for sight No. 34927 as packed by L.O.F. on 30 January 1953. The heavy cardboard cartons were 17 inches long, 6 inches wide, and 3 inches high, with a sealed foil pouch containing a dehydrating agent. Photo Credit: Peter R. Senich.

Pachmayr commercial "Lo-Swing" telescope mount as tested and approved for Army sniper use with the M1 rifle in 1953. Photo Credit: U.S. Army.

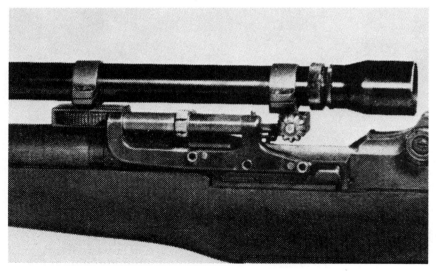

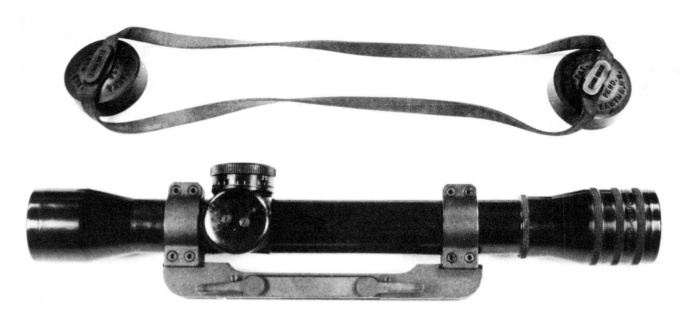

USMC Stith-Kollmorgen Model 4XD telescope, Griffin & Howe mounting, and issue Storm Queen molded rubber lens covers. Photo Credit: Peter R. Senich.

Comparative view of Griffin & Howe telescope mounts used with the Army M1C (left) and the USMC Kollmorgen 4XD scope. The levers on both mounts are in the unlocked position. Photo Credit: Peter R. Senich.

Telescope
M84
Serial No. 18410

As a result of inadequacies and field reports from Korea expressing dissatisfaction with the low magnification power of the M84 telescope, in 1951 the U.S. Army Infantry Board (USAIB) commenced testing commercial telescopes for the purpose of selecting "a more suitable sniper rifle scope." During these tests, twelve different commercial scopes and various mountings were evaluated with the M84 serving as the control and comparison item. The commercial telescopes, some fixed and some variable-power, ranged from 2.5 power to about 6 power magnification.

The conclusion of the USAIB following the last test in 1953 was that the Stith "Bear Cub" 4 power Telescope (Kollmorgen), with .001 crosshair reticle pattern, and the Pachmayr "Lo-Swing" Telescope Mount were the most suitable items for use with the M1C. The Pachmayr "Lo-Swing" mount positioned the telescope over the bore, but

could be swung aside to permit clip loading of the M1 magazine. It was the Board's opinion "that a fixed 4 power magnification telescope, in consideration of field of view, obscure target definition, and resolution capability, was the most satisfactory for military use."

The USAIB therefore recommended that the Stith Telescope and the Pachmayr Mount be standardized for Army use. On 15 September 1953 the Chief of Army Field Forces Office approved the recommendation of the USAIB and recommended that both telescope and mount be issued to replace the M84 telescope and the Griffin & Howe mount. But with the Korean War almost over at this juncture, no procurement action took place.

Even though commercial telescopic sight development would attain a highly sophisticated level in the years following the Korean War, the M84 sight was to remain as the principal sniper telescope for both the Army and Marine Corps until the early 1960s, when United States military involvement in Southeast Asia emphasized the upgrading of existing sniper equipment.

Griffin & Howe mounting developed for Marine Corps use with the M1C (MC-1) and Kollmorgen 4XD telescopic sight. Mount locking-levers were furnished with both round and flat ends, as illustrated. Photo Credit: Peter R. Senich.

USMC Griffin & Howe mounting for the Stith-Kollmorgen Model 4XD telescope (top view). The Federal Stock Number (FSN 1240-647-1107) appears above the item identification (Mount Telescope). Note the locking-levers with round ends. Photo Credit: J. B. Anderhub.

A 24th Infantry Division sniper with an M1C in Korea, August 1950. Photo Credit: U.S. Army.

Chapter 10 ◆ ◆

Semiautomatic Sniping System

In the years following the adoption of John Garand's semiautomatic rifle design, continuing refinement of the new service arm precluded any consideration of its suitability for sniping. However, when combat requirements brought about a reassessment of priorities during the initial stages of World War II, the demand for telescopic-sighted rifles resulted in the hasty adoption of the bolt-action 03-A4 variant and authorization to develop a sniping arm based on the M1 rifle as well: "At the time that Headquarters, Army Ground Forces recommended the standardization of the M1903-A4 Sniper's Rifle, it was also recommended that the M1 be equipped with a telescope in such a manner as to permit clip loading and normal functioning of the weapon," Headquarters noted in a report.

Further development included the evaluation of a prismatic type telescope, offset to the left with the eyepiece centered over the bore, and two versions of slightly modified Stith commercial side mounts with Weaver 330 telescopes. By 1944 attempts to adapt a satisfactory telescope mount to the M1 according to guidelines established by Headquarters, Army Ground Forces, proved fruitless. In the face of mounting pressure, a concerted effort saw the emergence of two designs: the M1E7 Rifle and the M1E8 variation, both of which were reportedly developed at Springfield Armory.

The M1E7 incorporated a dovetail, cam-operated pressure-plate type of scope mount, requiring the drilling and tapping of three holes and the drilling of two tapered holes in the left side of the receiver

World War II vintage Springfield Armory M1C sniper rifle with M2 flash hider, T4 cheek pad, and serial No. 67 M82 telescopic sight believed to represent a late-war Wollensak Optical Company contract sight. Photo Credit: Canfield Collection.

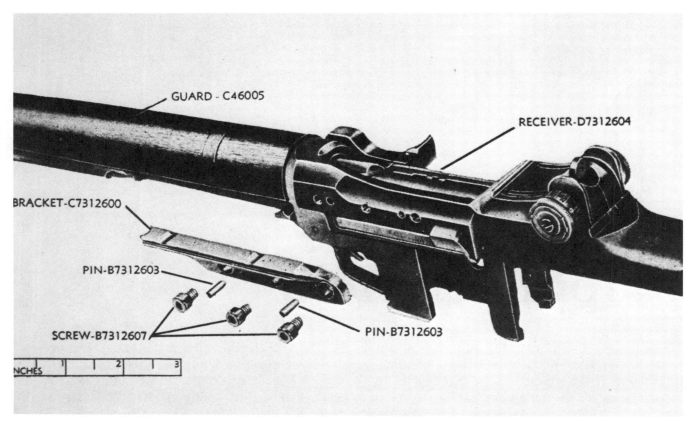

An excerpt from an Army Technical Manual illustrates the base, screws, pins, and receiver mounting area of the M1C sniping rifle. Photo Credit: Peter R. Senich.

A close view of the M1C with M82 telescope. Although extremely few matching rifles have been noted, in addition to the receiver bases, Griffin & Howe telescope mounts were also stamped with the rifle serial number as originally assembled at Springfield Armory. Photo Credit: Canfield Collection.

Korea presented a formidable battleground for American combat forces and even the most proficient snipers, since the rugged terrain, in most cases, necessitated long-range shooting that rested beyond the resolving power of the issue telescopes. A Marine marksman prepares to fire on enemy positions from "Siberia Hill" in Korea. Photo Credit: U.S. Marine Corps.

An M1C-equipped Marine Corps marksman during action in Korea. Although M1 sniping variants proved to be more than satisfactory, combat sniping reports indicated the maximum effective range as 600 yards. Photo Credit: U.S. Marine Corps.

With a capability for engaging multiple targets in rapid succession, the M1C was favored by many USMC snipers during the Korean War. Photo Credit: U.S. Marine Corps.

to adapt the base. The M1E8 design, on the other hand, called for use of a machined block-type mount pinned to the chamber end of the barrel, which required a shortened rear hand guard to provide necessary clearance.

Even though both systems proved satisfactory and conformed to the Ground Forces requirements, the M1E7 design fitted with the Griffin & Howe telescope mounting was chosen, as ordnance records recount, "because of its rugged characteristics."

On the basis of Infantry Board Tests of the M1E7 and M1E8 Rifles, the M1E7 Rifle equipped with a two and one-half power telescope was standardized in June of 1944 as U.S. Rifle, Caliber .30, M1C (Sniper's), thus making the M1903-A4 Sniper's Rifle Limited Standard. In order to assure production

meeting requirements, the M1E8 Rifle was adopted in September 1944 as a Substitute Standard and designated as U.S. Rifle, Caliber .30, M1D (Sniper's).

In both instances the M73 (Lyman Alaskan) or Weaver 330/M73B1 telescopes were authorized for use. Even though the 330 had been tested and designated as an alternate sight, its application never progressed beyond the testing stage. As a matter of interest, the Griffin & Howe telescope mount group was not designed specifically for the M1C, but rather was an adaptation of a mounting popular with sportsmen on bolt-action rifles prior to the war.

The initial government contract placed with Griffin & Howe in mid-1944 called for 8,300 telescope mounts for use with the M1C rifle. Four-

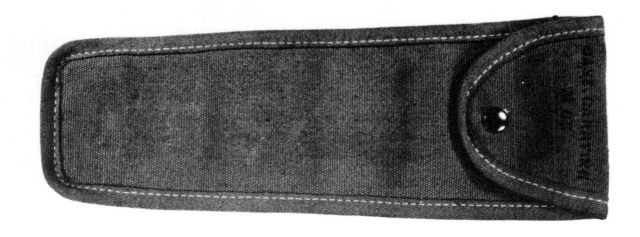

Web cases were issued for carrying the telescope when removed from the rifle. The top case (M65) was intended for M81 and M82 scopes; the other is for the M84. Photo Credit: Peter R. Senich.

teen thousand were completed by VE Day (8 May 1945), and on VJ Day (12 August 1945) only 2,000 remained in work. Upon completion of its final contract, Griffin & Howe had furnished a total of 37,000 mount assemblies (rings, mount, and receiver base).

In order to compensate for the offset position of the telescope, it was necessary either to make special stocks for the sniping variants, to modify regular issue stocks, or to develop an adapter that would permit the sniper to see through the telescope and still keep his face supported by the stock. The final solution: the T4 cheek pad consisting of a leather cover with a pocket containing three removable felt inserts. This enabled the sniper to adjust the thickness of the cheek pad to suit himself. The pad was laced to the left side of the stock to bring the right eye in line with the telescope.

Since some sniping was expected during periods of semidarkness (dawn-dusk), a funnel-shaped flash hider was provided. The flash hider (M2) was fastened to the muzzle of the rifle by means of a bracket similar to that used with the M7 Grenade Launcher, utilizing the bayonet stud as a point of anchorage. Ordnance studies indicated that this device would eliminate approximately ninety percent of muzzle flash at one hundred yards, but it did not reduce the smoke emitted from the barrel and, in fact, could reduce accuracy due to its relatively loose fit and method of attachment. Further experiments conducted some years later found the M2 design to be definitely inferior and resulted in the adoption of the "prong-type" T-37 flash hider. The T-37 device replaced the M1 gas cylinder lock and became an integral part of the gas cylinder assembly. If the rifle was zeroed with the flash hider, its removal and replacement with a conventional gas cylinder could cause a change in zero. It was recommended that

An Army patrol with Chi-Com prisoner, Korea 1952. The rifleman (left) is holding a partially obscured M1 sniping rifle. Photo Credit: U.S. Army.

Outfitted in winter camouflage, Army marksman Bill Krilling is pictured with his M1C in Korea. Photo Credit: Courtesy of Donald G. Thomas.

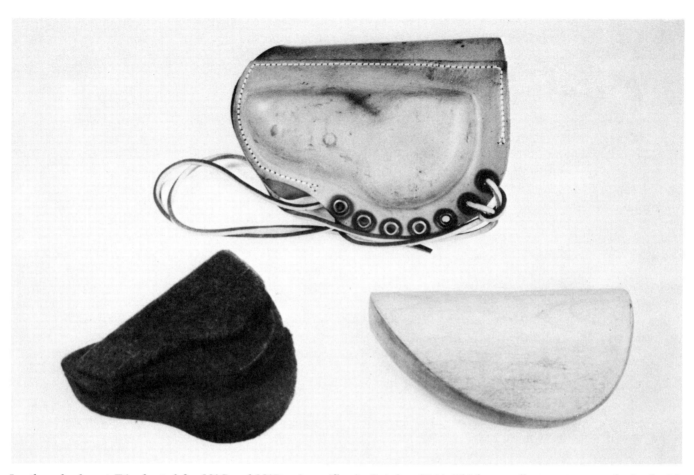

Leather cheek rest T4 adopted for M1C and M1D sniper rifles in October 1944. Thickness adjustments were obtained with three felt pads that were removed or inserted as desired. Cheek rests fashioned from wood (lower right) received brief consideration for use with M1 sniping rifles during the Korean War. Photo Credit: Peter R. Senich.

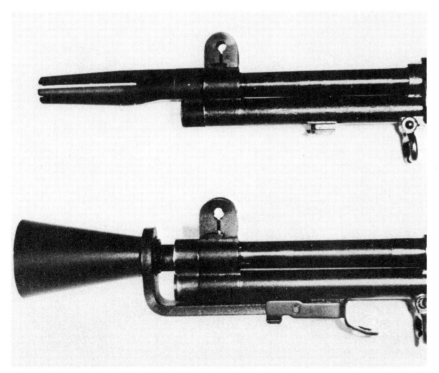

Flash hiders designed for use with M1 sniping rifles. The funnel-shaped M2 variant was adopted as an accessory in early 1945; the prong-type T37 in 1958. According to various Army and USMC snipers, both devices were more impressive in design than beneficial in actual use. Photo Credit: Peter R. Senich.

the flash hider be left on the sniper rifle and kept tight at all times. The T-37 device was not manufactured and issued in quantity.

According to government production figures, 6,896 M1 sniping rifles were manufactured at Springfield Armory from late 1944 through August 1945. This total is believed to represent the M1C variant in entirety, inasmuch as available records indicate only a few M1Ds were produced for testing purposes during this period. An unspecified number of M1Cs were also manufactured at Springfield in the years immediately following the war.

As originally fabricated, both the receiver base and the Griffin & Howe mount were stamped with the corresponding rifle number. Telescopes, however, were not numbered to the rifle (stamped or etched), but were instead hand numbered with white paint on the underside of the tube using the last four digits of the rifle serial number when issued.

Precious few M1C rifles reached the front lines by war's end, particularly in the European Theater where "the M1C was heard of, but never encountered." Even though the war lasted an additional three months in the Pacific, the scarcity of the M1C prevailed there as well. Consequently, little opportunity existed to judge the combat effectiveness of the M1 sniping system until it was reissued for the Korean War.

Although the M1C was to remain as the Army's principal sniping arm during this era, efforts to field additional sniper equipment included Springfield Armory's manufacture of "D" barrels to be used for producing the M1D variant. Unfortunately, inconclusive records have relegated the circumstances surrounding the manufacture and issuance of the M1D to obscurity. However, Springfield reportedly produced "D" barrels continuously for a period of about one year, from January 1952 through February 1953. The point of contention in this matter rests with whether the M1D was actually manufactured as such during the Korean War, or simply based on "rebuilt" M1s as some experts contend. Regardless, the M1D was to serve only as a supplement and did not see extensive issue during the Korean conflict.

M1 sniping variants proved to be more than satisfactory. Combat sniping reports from Korea indicated the maximum effective range as 600 yards, with rather consistent results between 400 and 600 yards. In deference to the M1, limitations

of the telescopic sights and ammunition used with the system did not help to increase the chances of long-range hits. While adequate at short to medium ranges, the resolving power of the M81, M82, and M84 telescopes made long-range target definition extremely difficult. Special or match grade ammunition was not available or even considered for sniping purposes. Army snipers drew regular .30 caliber ball ammunition that showed up fairly well at shorter ranges but was not reliable at 500 to 600 yards. When obtainable, .30 caliber armor-piercing ammunition was employed since its heavier bullet provided increased stability over longer ranges.

Marine Corps snipers had made extensive use of armor-piercing ammo during World War II, and they continued to do so in Korea. Marine Corps snipers, equipped primarily with the Springfield 03-A1/Unertl combination, also employed a number of M1Cs originally intended for Army use. The M1C was not officially recommended for Marine Corps adoption until 1951.

During early Korean involvement, Marine Corps stocks of sniper rifles were quickly depleted. Before additional procurement was undertaken, it was considered desirable to examine existing sniper materiel to ascertain whether a more suitable sniper rifle was available or whether one should be developed. On 9 February 1951 the Commandant of the Marine Corps directed the Marine Corps Equipment Board to establish a project to evaluate both military and commercial sniper materiel to determine which would meet Marine Corps requirements. Efforts to arrive at a satisfactory conclusion involved a series of exhaustive studies conducted through the balance of 1951.

Based on its *Study of Sniper's Rifles, Telescopes and Mounts,* it was the opinion of the board that:

(1) The U.S. Rifle, Caliber .30, M1C with the Griffin & Howe mount (fixed receiver base), is suitable for interim and long-term Marine Corps use as a sniper's rifle.

(2) The Stith (Bear Cub) 2 3/4x Telescope is suitable for interim Marine Corps use after modification of the range and windage adjustment to include click adjustments.

(3) The Griffin & Howe removable mount as issued with the U.S. Rifle, Caliber .30 M1C is suitable for interim Marine Corps use after modification of the telescope holding bracket to accept the Stith (Bear Cub) Telescope.

A Marine sharpshooter sights an M1D from a rooftop in Santo Domingo during the Dominican Crisis in 1965. Photo Credit: U.S. Marine Corps.

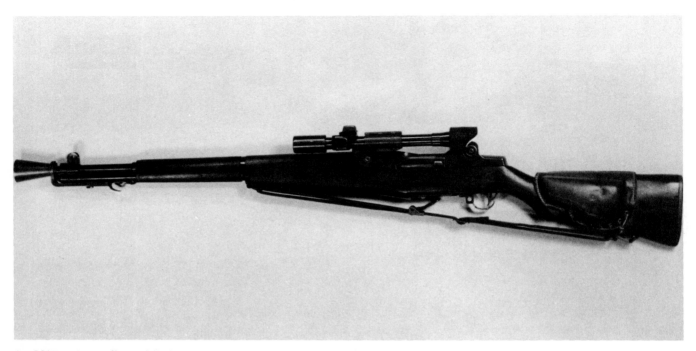

An M1D sniper rifle with M84 telescopic sight. Although developed late in World War II, this variant did not see general service use until the Korean War. Photo Credit: Canfield Collection.

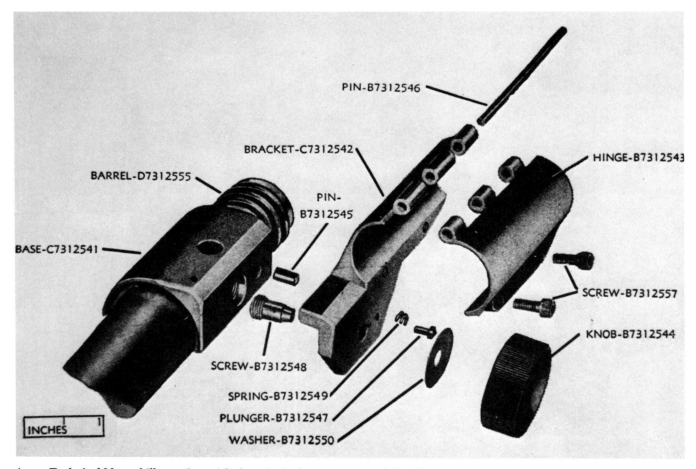

Army Technical Manual illustration with the principal components of the M1D sniper system. Photo Credit: Peter R. Senich.

A close view of the M1D rifle. Made in considerable numbers, M84 telescopes saw extensive issue with Army and USMC sniping arms throughout U.S. involvement in Southeast Asia. Photo Credit: Canfield Collection.

A 3rd Marine Division sniper in Vietnam, January 1966. M1Ds were pressed into service during early combat in RVN and in some cases were accurized and glass-bedded by USMC armorers to improve performance. Photo Credit: U.S. Marine Corps.

(4) There is no requirement for the development of a sniper's rifle to meet long-term Marine Corps requirements.

(5) There is a requirement for development of a telescope to meet long-term Marine Corps requirements.

(6) It is recommended that the U.S. Rifle, Caliber .30, M1C as outlined, be standardized in the Marine Corps for interim use.

Of all the military and commercial telescopes evaluated, the board considered the Stith "Bear Cub" as the most suitable. However, as cited in point five of the evaluation, the sight was to be modified to conform to Marine Corps require-

ments. Therefore, in 1952 the Stith Company, in conjunction with the Kollmorgen Optical Corporation (the actual manufacturer of this sight), submitted a fixed focus, 4 power telescope having audible click, range, and windage adjustments.

When accepted by the USMC on an experimental basis, the Stith-Kollmorgen Model 4XD was considered by most scope-wise men to be the "best" telescopic sight then available. This sight was not developed strictly for military use, however, as commercial variants were available for sport-shooting as well.

Overall telescope length of the Model 4XD ran about eleven inches, tube diameter 1.023 inch,

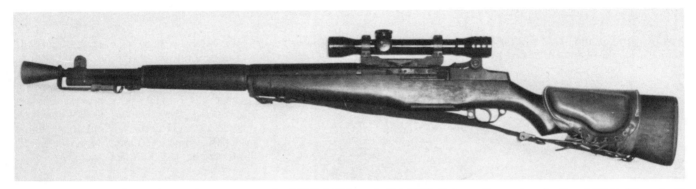

Variously cited in Marine Corps documents as the M1C, MC-1, and MC-1952 Sniper, the vast majority of M1C rifles rebuilt for the USMC during the Korean War have Springfield Armory barrels dated 1951, 1952, or 1953. Sniping arms based on various manufacture M1 Garands were assembled at USMC Ordnance Depots well into the 1960s. Photo Credit: Peter R. Senich.

A close view of the USMC M1C with Kollmorgen 4XD telescope and Griffin & Howe mounting. Photo Credit: Peter R. Senich.

KOLLMORGEN

RIFLE TELESCOPE

4XD, MC-I

MADE FOR

THE U. S. MARINE CORPS

BY

KOLLMORGEN
optical corporation
NORTHAMPTON, MASSACHUSETTS

The cover of a six-page pamphlet furnished to the Marine Corps detailed the workings of the Kollmorgen 4XD telescope sight. Photo Credit: Peter R. Senich.

and objective and ocular ends approximately 1.250 inch in diameter. Cross-hair reticles were furnished to the Marine Corps and eye-relief was cited as being three to four inches. Commercial "Storm-Queen" lens covers consisting of molded rubber cups connected by narrow stretch bands were issued for protective purposes. In addition to the manufacturer's legend, located on the ocular end of the telescope, there was the inscription:

STITH MOUNTS S.A., TEX.
4X DOUBLE
KOLLMORGEN OPTICAL CORP.
BROOKLYN, N.Y.
PAT. PEND.

A Marine Corps serial number appeared on the top or side of the tube: MC 1288-P. Variations stamped U.S. with a Federal Stock Number (FSN) have also been noted. Since the telescope tube

was fashioned from aluminum alloy, conventional metal-finishing methods could not be employed. Therefore, a black "enamel type" coating, compatible with this material, was used instead.

Griffin & Howe ultimately furnished the telescope mounting used with the Marine Corps M1C. The "double-lever" side mount made for the Stith-Kollmorgen sight was, in effect, a scaled-up version of that originally adopted for the Army's "C." Although it was designed to fit the standard M1C receiver base, the USMC mounting was substantially stronger and 5.125 inches in length as compared with the 3.875-inch mount utilized with Army telescopes. Unlike the Army, USMC mounts were not numbered to the rifle on which they were issued. Mounts were carefully fitted to the receiver base and serial numbers were either taped to the telescope or simply noted in stock (supply) records.

According to Marine Corps records, a portion of

the M1Cs used in Korea by its Scout-Snipers were originally manufactured as such by Springfield Armory in 1944–45. These were rebuilt at Springfield through 1952–53 and reallocated to the Corps following their standardization. In addition to this, "select M1 rifles were modified to M1C specifications at various ordnance depots on an as-needed basis."

Despite its eventual acceptance by the Marine Corps, the Stith-Kollmorgen 4XD telescope reportedly did not see combat use in Korea, since it was in service use from about 1954 through 1962 when the M1C-USMC rifle was obsoleted by the Corps. Even though the M84 telescope was manufactured during the Korean War, Model 81 and 82 scopes saw extensive use with the M1C by both the Army and the Marine Corps.

Contrary to the definition of obsolete, the M1C and M1D remained as quasiofficial sniping arms of the Army and Marine Corps through the mid-1960s, when combat requirements in Southeast Asia necessitated the upgrading of sniper equipment. Even though the M1 sniping rifle has been long removed from "Standard Type" classification, a substantial number of these rifles still repose in National Guard Armories across the United States.

Chapter 11 ◆◆

2000 Yard Kills— .50 Caliber Sniping

During the early stages of the First World War, the Germans were the first to employ cleverly concealed steel plates in and about their trench works for sniper protection.

The heavy plates, having small loopholes cut into them, afforded adequate protection from return fire since a bullet had to pass directly through the opening to render any harm. From behind these innovative plates, German snipers exacted an awesome toll on the Allied Armies during the first winter of combat in 1914–15.

At that point, riflemen of the British, French, and Belgian forces, with precious few telescopic sights or the benefit of armor-piercing ammunition, were hard-pressed to either penetrate or accurately place their shots through the German loopholes, even at comparatively short ranges. While there were a number of Allied marksmen capable of hitting the small apertures, they were so few in number that such efforts were to prove of little value.

Sizing up the situation, a few imaginative British officers decided that the next best measure would be to simply "bash-in" the German plates. To accomplish this, high-velocity, large-bore rifles once used on the African continent for elephant hunting were brought up. As anticipated, they worked exceedingly well.

The Germans, ever mindful of these events, in addition to effective use of armor-piercing small-arms ammunition against Allied plates, were to employ their heavy 13mm bolt-action Mauser antitank rifles. These were originally intended to neutralize British tanks and for counter-sniping as

well. Interestingly, a number of German sharp-shooters, active during World War II, indicate that they had also employed antitank rifles to some extent.

The later weapons, developed for early Wehrmacht use against lightly armored vehicles, utilized a 13mm case necked down to 7.92mm which gave extremely high velocity and penetration. It must be emphasized, however, that use of such rifles for sniping in both wars was not based on weapon accuracy, but rather, to drive opposing snipers and machine-gun crews from protective cover. While effective under certain circumstances, antitank rifles were awkward and comparatively heavy. Owing to considerable dispersion, Wehrmacht snipers generally limited such use to 300 to 400 meters.

Continuing development of a satisfactory .50 caliber machine gun by the United States Army following World War I entailed the use of captured 13mm German antitank guns for test purposes. In order to enable Frankford Arsenal to develop ammunition for the new weapon, the Department of Experiment at Springfield Armory made up several Mauser antitank rifles modified to chamber .50 caliber test rounds.

Subsequent development resulted in a succession of Browning machine guns in both water and air-cooled variations. Design efforts culminated with the two most common types employed by United States Forces during World War II, the air-cooled .50 caliber M2 aircraft and M2 heavy-barreled machine guns.

The infantry or ground .50 "M2 Heavy Barrel Flexible" variant made use of a forty-five-inch barrel with no jacket of any kind beyond the short one incorporating a bearing surface which was firmly screwed into the receiver. Unlike most heavy machine guns, the M2 possessed both automatic and semiautomatic fire option.

Although original design had intended the use of semiautomatic action for sighting in or targeting, unlocking the bolt latch release and alternately pressing the trigger and bolt latch release permitted semiautomatic or, simply, single-round firing. Fitted with conventional leaf and blade type sights, the rear sight base incorporated a dovetailed groove in which a telescopic sight could be mounted.

Under favorable circumstances and the right combination of gunner, telescopic sight, barrel quality, and ammunition, the "big fifties" accounted for some phenomenal shooting at ranges of 2,000 plus yards during World War II. Against enemy positions, personnel, and unarmored vehicles the air-cooled Brownings were considered indispensable. Following the invasion of Fortress Europe when long-range shooting requirements became greater than they had been in the Pacific, German forces developed a healthy respect for the .50s.

Based on its single-shot capability in conjunction with telescopic sight, utilization of the air-cooled .50 Browning in a sniping capacity (to supplement long-range limitations of existing .30 caliber sniping rifles) was officially considered late in World War II and again when United States Forces became involved in Korea a few years later.

Unsuited as they were, ground .50s were employed in Korea with marginal success for sniping purposes. This depended, of course, on what constituted effective sniping, which in itself was a subject of considerable opinion difference within the military establishment through the years.

Nevertheless, frequent use entailed placing two .50s at separate points, firing single shots simultaneously at the same target. This doubled the probability of a hit while confusing the enemy as to the weapon's position. As a long-range weapon, the .50 was found to be invaluable for enfilading enemy trenches.

The First Marine Division included instruction in the use of the .50 in its sniper training program in Korea. Major Norman W. Hicks, USMC, citing this activity, related:

Each student trained not only with the .30 caliber M1 rifle (or the 03 Springfield, depending upon his preference) [Ed. Note: M1C or 03A1 with Unertl scope] but also with the .50 caliber machine gun, fired single shot. Scopes were mounted on the machine guns and they proved to be effective for ranges up to and beyond 1200 yards.

Unquestionably, the most innovative application of .50 caliber sniping weapons in Korea involved adaptation of World War II vintage British and Russian antitank rifles by imaginative Ordnance personnel.

An Army Ordnance officer serving in Korea in 1951, Captain William S. Brophy, observed that issue sniping rifles were in a poor state of first and higher echelon maintenance. Investigation disclosed that no special use was being made of the sniper's rifles, that the individuals who had been issued the rifles were not properly trained in their use, and that the rifles presented maintenance problems which Ordnance personnel were unable to handle because of a lack of spare parts.

Capt. Brophy, who had served in the Pacific Theater as an Infantry Officer during World War II, was aware of the inadequacy of the arms issued for sniping purposes. Therefore, in order to demonstrate the effectiveness of sniping when a trained rifleman and good equipment were employed, Brophy procured, at his personal expense, a commercial Winchester Model 70, .30 caliber target rifle fitted with a 10x telescopic sight. Following numerous demonstrations by Brophy and others instructed in its use, the effectiveness of the Winchester was clearly evident.

However, targets were frequently observed beyond the range considered maximum for .30 caliber accuracy. Therefore, Brophy, drawing on his extensive shooting experience, had a .50 caliber aircraft machine-gun barrel assembled to a Soviet PTRD 14.5mm anti-tank rifle. A butt rest and bipod were fitted and a 20x Unertl telescopic sight was mounted on the receiver.

Using issue .50 caliber ammunition, Capt. Brophy and individuals instructed by him in the use of the weapon demonstrated its effectiveness at ranges between 1,000 and 2,000 yards, rendering more than a few Red soldiers *hors de combat.*

Field conditions in Korea did not permit extensive testing of the weapons so employed. Consequently, it was considered desirable to conduct accuracy tests of these weapons using the M1D rifle, .50 caliber M2 Heavy Barrel machine gun, and .30 caliber commercial rifles as controls in order to obtain a comparison of the effectiveness of each.

The results, conclusions, and recommendations of these tests, conducted under the auspices of the Development and Proof Services, Aberdeen Proving Ground, Maryland, from 2 December 1953 to 20 June 1954, are herewith presented in their original form.

DESCRIPTION OF MATERIEL

A. Weapons
1. Rifle, Caliber .50 Sniper. This weapon is a rotating-bolt action, single-shot shoulder weapon equipped with bipod and stock rest. Two barrels were used in this test. One was from a Browning caliber .50 M3 aircraft machine gun. The rifle consists of the receiver group, trigger assembly, and stock from the Soviet 14.5 mm PTRD-1941 anti-tank rifle. The receiver group was altered to accommodate the caliber .50 M2 ball cartridge. An adjustable rest from a 57 mm recoilless rifle was added for butt-stock support and elevation adjustment.
2. Rifle, Caliber .30 M1D. This is the standard, gas operated, semi-automatic, clip-feed shoulder weapon equipped with the M84 telescope and used for sniping.
3. Gun, Machine, Caliber .50, Browning, M2, Heavy Barrel, Flexible. This weapon is an automatic, recoil operated, belt-fed, air cooled machine gun.
4. Rifle, Winchester, Caliber .30, M70 Sniper, Serial

An Army Firing demonstration conducted with the prismatic machine-gun telescope shortly before WW II. Photo Credit: Donald G. Thomas.

Sight, Telescope, M1, manufactured by the Prefix Corp. in Milwaukee, Wisconsin, in 1942, was intended for precise long-range shooting with the Browning Machine Gun, Caliber .50, HB, M2. Photo Credit: Steve Fleischman.

The .50 Browning rear sight was provided with a dovetail groove in which the M1 telescopic sight was attached. Photo Credit: Steve Fleischman.

No. 254544. This weapon is equipped with a modified Mauser-type rotating-bolt action, heavy barrel, trigger mechanism providing an adjustable trigger pull, an integral box-type magazine, and sporter stock.

5. Rifle, Winchester, Caliber .30, M70 National Match. This is a commercial match rifle and is equipped with the same trigger assembly, magazine, and rotating-bolt action used in the M70 Winchester Sniper rifle described above. It differs from the M70 Sniper rifle in weight of barrel and

in being equipped with the heavier, target-type stock.

6. Rifle, Winchester, Caliber .30, M70 Bull Gun. This rifle differs from the M70 National Match Rifle only in that it is equipped with a longer, heavier barrel.

B. Ammunition

1. Cartridge, Armor Piercing, Caliber .30 M2, Lot FA895. This ammunition was used with the caliber .30 M1D rifle.

While effective for single-shot firing, M1 sights saw limited issue during WW II. The range dial was graduated in yards and mils; the deflection dial in mils. Photo Credit: Steve Fleischman.

2. Cartridge, Ball, Caliber .50 M2, Lot WRA 22405. This ammunition was used in tests involving the Caliber .50 Sniper Rifle and the .50 M2 heavy-barrel machine gun.

3. Cartridge, Remington, Caliber .30 Palma Match, Lot C238157. This cartridge, using a 180 grain, metal-cased, boat-tailed bullet, was used in tests involving all three Winchester rifles mentioned in this report.

4. Cartridge, Peters, Caliber .30 Match, Lot A23D2. This cartridge, using a 180 grain, metal-cased, boat-tailed bullet, was used in a 1400 yard accuracy test of the Winchester M70 Bull Gun.

5. Cartridge, Caliber .30, hand-loaded. This cartridge was specially loaded with 53 grains of 1MR 4350 smokeless powder and a Sierra 150 grain boat-tailed bullet. It was used in a 1400 yard accuracy test of the Winchester M70 Bull Gun.

C. Telescopic Sights

Name	Serial No.	Weapon
Telescope, Lyman, Super Targetspot	48	Rifle, Win., M70 Bull Gun Rifle, Win., M70 Sniper
Telescope, Unertl, Ultra-Varmint	29494	Rifle, Caliber .50 Sniper (heavy and light barrels)
Telescope, Unertl, Target, 2 inch	28022	Gun, Machine, Cal. .50 M2 Heavy Barrel
Telescope, M84	31348	Rifle, Cal. .30, M1D

D. Weights and Measurements

Weights are given in pounds and measurements in inches, unless otherwise noted.

1. Winchester Rifles

	National Match	Sniper	Bull Gun
Overall length	44.6	44.3	48.5
*Weight	9.15	9.80	12.48
Trigger pull	2.2	2.9	3.3
Height of sight above bore	1.1	1.0	1.0

	National Match	Sniper	Bull Gun
**Drop of stock:			
Line of sight to forward part of comb.	1.6	1.8	1.4
Line of sight to heel of butt	1.8	3.0	1.5
**Pitch	2.4	2.4	3.7
Distance, trigger to butt	13.3	13.0	15.2

	National Match	Sniper	Bull Gun
Barrel dimensions:			
Length	24.0	24.0	28.0
Diameter	0.600	0.790	0.842
Sight radius	28.2	28.2	32.4
Width of front sight	.050	.050	.039
Diameter, rear aperture	.039	.039	.039
***Differences in height, line of sight of telescope to line of sight of metallic sights.	.07	.07	.08

*With metallic sights and without sling.

**Sight set for 300 yards—metallic sights.

***Measured at rear sight.

2. **Rifle, Caliber .50 Sniper**

Length:	Overall with heavy barrel	69.0
	Overall with light barrel	60.0

*Weight:	With heavy barrel	42.80
	With light barrel	27.65

Height of bipod:	With heavy barrel	9.4 to 14.5 adjustable
	With light barrel	11.0

Adjustment in butt rest	0 to 5.25
Distance, trigger to butt	15.0
Trigger pull	11.0

*Not including telescope or mount.

3. **Telescopic Sights**

	Unertl Ultra-Varmint	Unertl Target	Lyman Super Targetspot	M84
Magnification	23.3	10	12	2
*Field	6 ft.	10 ft.	9.25 ft.	33 ft.
Diameter, exit pupil	2.6 mm	5 mm	2.9 mm	8.8 mm
Luminosity factor	6.8	25.0	8.4	77.4
Eye relief	3.5-4.5	3.0	2.0	4.0
Overall length	24.0	24.0	24.3	**11.5
Diameter, objective cell	57 mm	57 mm	35 mm	17.0 mm
Diameter of tube	1.0	1.0	.75	.875
Diameter of eyepiece	1.3	1.125	.75	1.0
Weight with detachable mount	1.95	2.52	1.51	1.56

*Measured at 100 yards

**With sunshade 12.4

DETAILS OF TEST

A. Procedure

1. To obtain data allowing comparison of their inherent accuracies, the M1D rifle and three Model 70 Winchester rifles, differing in stock dimensions and weight of barrel, were fired at a range of 100 yards using metallic sights with post front sights. The ten-inch bull's-eye of the "A" target provided a distant point of aim. After sighting in, the ten-shot groups were fired from each weapon using a bench rest followed by two ten-shot groups fired from each weapon from the prone position using a sling. During the record firing, sight settings remained unchanged in order that any change in the center of impact could be determined.

2. To determine the magnitude of any error which might exist because of the use of metallic sights, the Winchester M70 Sniper Rifle and M1D rifle were fired according to the procedure set forth above, using telescopic sights.

3. To compare the performance of the M1D rifle, the Winchester M70 Sniper Rifle, and the Caliber .50 Sniper Rifle with respect to accuracy when fired at clearly distinguished targets at gradually increased ranges, the following procedure was used.

    A. Four ten-shot groups were fired from each weapon at a range of 300 yards using the bull's-eye of the "A" target on the aiming point. The caliber .30 rifles were fired from the bench rest. The caliber .50 Sniper Rifle was fired from the prone position employing bipod and butt rest for support. Both heavy and light barrel versions of the weapon were tested for comparison of accuracy. Telescopic sights were used on all weapons tested.

    B. The M1D rifle, Winchester M70 Sniper Rifle, and the light-barrel version of the caliber .50 Sniper Rifle were fired to obtain one ten-shot group per day per weapon on a "B" target at 600 yards range. In testing each weapon, one target was superimposed on another, the first being removed, recorded, and replaced by another every ten rounds. The second target remained in place to record the full fifty-shot group. Before firing each day, the bore was wiped out with a clean patch. No fouling or sighting shots were used once the

initial targets were fired. Each hole on the target was numbered, and the vertical and horizontal distance from the center of the target were recorded. Sights and aiming point remained undisturbed during the test. Telescopic sights were used on all weapons.

    C. The procedure followed in paragraph 3A was repeated with the exception that the range was increased to 1000 yards, a "C" target replaced the "B" target, and only the light barrel was employed with the Caliber .50 Sniper Rifle.

4. To determine the dispersion characteristics of the Browning caliber .50 M2 heavy-barrel machine gun when fired single shot on a clearly defined aiming point, two series of four ten-shot groups were fired—the first using telescopic sights and the second using metallic sights. The "A" target was used at a range of 300 yards.

5. To determine its effectiveness under conditions of sighting similar to those met in combat, the Browning caliber .50 M2 heavy-barrel machine gun was fired single shot at man-sized silhouette targets mounted on a large background, colored to provide contrast simulating that of a soldier uniformed to blend with the terrain.

    A. The first of two tests of this type was conducted with the type of "E" silhouette target mounted on a background 8 x 8 ft. stationed at 1000 yards. Ten rounds were fired for sighting; fifty rounds were fired for record using the standard metallic sights. The procedure was then duplicated employing telescopic sights.

    B. In the second test, the range was increased to 1400 yards and the background size was increased proportionally to 12 x 12 ft. Ten rounds were used for sighting and fifty rounds were fired for record. Telescopic sights were employed in this test.

6. In order to establish the extreme range at which a satisfactory number of hits might be expected on a man-size target from the accurate caliber .30 rifle, sixty rounds of match-quality ammunition were fired from the Winchester Model 70 Bull Gun at an "E" type silhouette mounted as in paragraph 5B, and stationed at 1400 yards. The weapon was fired from a bench rest employing telescopic sights.

RESULTS

1. Test at 100 yards with .30 caliber rifles. Four targets were fired with each rifle. Two targets were fired from a bench rest and the remaining two by using a sling. Measurements are in inches.

Target Measurements

Rifle	MR	MVD	MHD	EVD	EHD	ES
Winchester M70 Bull Gun	0.6	0.4	0.4	1.6	1.4	1.5
Winchester M70 Nat Match	0.9	0.5	0.6	2.2	2.5	2.5
Winchester M70 Sniper	0.8	0.4	0.6	1.6	2.4	2.5
Caliber .30 M1D	1.6	1.2	0.8	5.2	3.1	5.7
Fired using telescopic sight						
Winchester M70 Sniper	0.7	0.4	0.5	1.6	1.6	2.0
Caliber .30 M1D	1.3	1.0	0.7	4.0	2.9	4.0

KEY:
MR — Mean Radius   EVD — Extreme Vertical
MVD — Mean Vertical   EHD — Extreme Horizontal
MHD — Mean Horizontal   ES — Extreme Speed

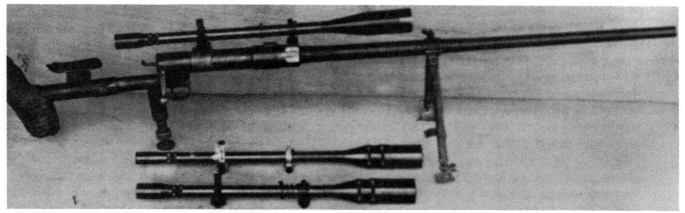

The .50 caliber sniper rifle used by Capt. William S. Brophy to reach targets beyond the limits of .30 caliber accuracy. Photo Credit: U.S. Army.

2. Test at 300 yards with .30 and .50 caliber rifles. Four ten-shot groups were fired from each rifle using telescopic sights. The caliber .30 rifles were fired from a bench rest and the caliber .50 from the prone position using a bipod and butt rest.

Target Measurements

Rifle	MR	MVD	MHD	EVD	EHD	ES
Winchester M70 Sniper	2.2	1.4	1.5	4.6	5.4	6.5
Caliber .30 M1D	4.0	2.2	2.6	9.0	9.9	12.1
Caliber .50 Sniper, light barrel	4.9	2.8	3.3	11.6	13.7	16.2
Caliber .50 Sniper, heavy barrel	3.0	1.7	2.2	6.6	7.6	8.3

Four ten-shot groups were fired from the caliber .50 M2 machine gun using metallic sights, and an additional four were fired using telescopic sights.

Metallic	5.8	3.4	3.9	13.7	15.6	18.2
Telescopic	4.8	3.2	3.0	12.6	12.4	15.8

3. Test at 600 yards. One ten-shot group was fired by each rifle on each of five days. A target containing composite of five groups was produced simultaneously for each rifle. The caliber .30 rifles were fired from a bench rest and the caliber .50 rifle from the prone position using bipod and butt rest. Telescopic sights were used with each weapon. Target measurements are given in inches.

Target Measurements

Rifle, U.S. Caliber .30 M1D

Trial No.	MR	MVD	MHD	EVD	EHD	ES
1	10.1	5.8	7.1	27.3	25.4	30.0
2	14.1	6.5	11.8	25.2	45.3	47.0
3	9.2	5.3	5.7	30.1	26.2	30.5
4	12.4	6.8	9.0	31.0	39.9	41.3
5	11.3	7.6	6.7	29.0	25.0	35.4

Rifle, Winchester M70 Sniper

Trial No.	MR	MVD	MHD	EVD	EHD	ES
1	5.4	3.0	4.0	11.7	13.6	17.4
2	6.7	3.9	5.0	15.1	13.4	18.0
3	4.5	2.2	3.5	9.5	12.8	12.8
4	5.7	2.8	4.0	10.9	23.2	23.4
5	4.0	2.9	2.3	8.3	9.5	11.7

Rifle, Caliber .50 Sniper, Light Barrel

Trial No.	MR	MVD	MHD	EVD	EHD	ES
1	7.1	4.7	4.5	15.1	19.2	19.7
2	8.2	7.3	5.0	31.7	10.1	31.7
3	7.3	3.9	5.5	12.8	29.0	29.0
4	8.3	4.4	6.7	20.8	23.2	31.2
5	12.2	6.1	9.5	21.9	33.5	33.9

The measurements in inches of the composite targets are shown below. A type "E" silhouette was superimposed on each target, and the hits within the area so defined were recorded.

Rifle	Hits on Silhouette	EVD	MHD	ES
M70 Winchester Sniper	38	17.4	29.7	30.4
Caliber .50 Sniper	41	33.9	38.0	39.2
Caliber .30 M1D	23	47.4	56.3	61.1

4. Test at 1,000 yards. One ten-shot group was fired from each rifle on each of the five days. A composite target of five day's firing of each weapon was made by superimposing the targets to contain the daily ten-shot groups over the target recording the fifty round group produced by the total of five trials. Telescopic sights were used on all rifles. The caliber .30 rifles were fired from a bench rest, and the caliber .50 rifle from the prone position using bipod and butt rest. Target measurements are given in inches.

Trial Measurements

Rifle, Caliber .30 M1D

Trial No.	MR	MVD	MHD	EVD	EHD	ES
1	11.5	7.6	7.1	39.4	36.5	40.4
2	21.6	13.4	13.9	62.0	63.3	77.4
3	One shot missed the 12 X 12 ft. panel					
4	19.6	16.0	8.1	71.0	40.4	71.8
5	20.4	12.6	15.3	46.2	58.2	69.4

Rifle, Winchester M70 Sniper

1	10.4	5.1	7.6	23.9	27.6	27.6
2	8.5	5.3	4.8	26.4	19.5	25.3
3	12.8	11.4	5.2	36.2	29.1	36.7
4	11.4	7.1	7.9	31.7	29.9	39.2
5	13.1	10.1	5.5	39.8	24.6	40.1

Rifle, Caliber .50 Sniper, Light Barrel

1	13.7	8.7	8.6	30.3	37.6	37.8
2	22.2	13.6	15.6	39.3	55.1	61.6
3	20.6	14.1	13.0	74.4	48.4	64.8
4	21.4	16.4	8.7	66.2	38.0	60.0
5	14.8	10.5	7.8	43.3	58.8	45.9

An "E" silhouette was superimposed on the bull's-eye of each composite target and the hits falling within the area covered were recorded.

	Hits	MVD	EHD	ES
M70 Winchester Sniper Rifle	23	58.3	44.3	65.2
Caliber .50 Sniper Rifle	12	84.1	74.5	92.2
Caliber .30 M1D Rifle	6	—	—	—

Fifty-shot groups were fired from the caliber .50 M2HB machine gun using first, metallic sights and second, telescopic sights. The M3 tripod mount was used for support of the weapon. An 8 x 8 ft. panel was used as a background for a type "E" silhouette target centrally located. Measurements are in inches.

Sight	Hits on 8' x 8' Panel	Hits on Silhouette	MVD	EHD	ES
Metallic	49	11	84.3	86.5	86.7
Telescopic	49	16	79.0	75.0	80.5

5. Test at 1,400 yards. One fifty-shot group was fired from the caliber .50 M2 HB machine gun with telescopic sights, using the M3 tripoc mount for support of the weapon. The type "E" silhouette target was mounted centrally on a 12 x 12 ft. background. Target measurements are given in inches.

Hits on 12' x 12' Panel	Hits on Silhouette	MVD	EHD	ES
49	8	128.0	88.5	135.5

Three twenty-shot groups were fired from the Winchester M70 Bull Gun equipped with telescopic sight and supported by a bench rest. The type "E" silhouette was mounted centrally on a 12 x 12 ft. panel as in the preceding test. Measurements are given in inches.

Ammunition	Silhouette Hits	MR	MVD	MHD	EVD	EHD	ES
Remington	—	—	—	—	—	—	—
Palma Match	6	20.7	16.8	9.2	82.2	44.1	85.8
Peters Match	1	30.5	27.4	9.0	99.3	48.4	102.0
Sierra Hand Load	2	25.8	22.7	8.6	87.6	59.6	88.0

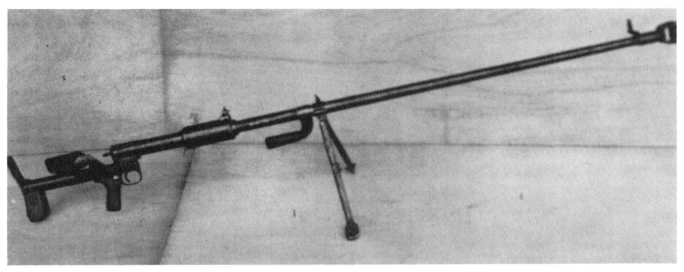

Soviet PTRD1941 14.5mm antitank rifle, employed by Communist forces during the Korean conflict, served as the basis for Capt. Brophy's special .50 caliber sniping weapon. Photo Credit: U.S. Army.

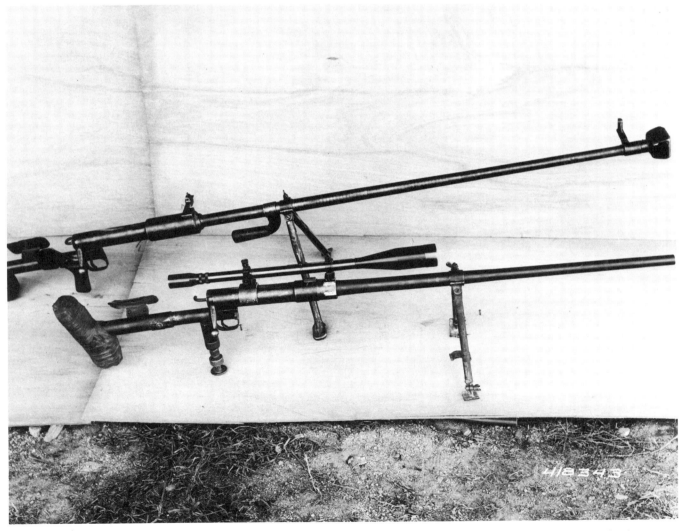

A direct comparison, the Soviet 14.5mm PTRD-1941 antitank rifle in original form (top), and as modified for long-range sniping in Korea. Photo Credit: U.S. Army.

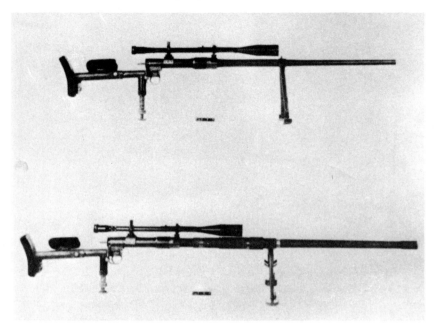

An Aberdeen Proving Ground photo (9 June 1954) of the "Rifle, Caliber .50 Sniper" based on the Soviet PTRD anti-tank rifle. The unique weapon was tested with a light barrel (top) and a heavy barrel as well. The telescope is a Unertl Ultra-Varmint commercial model. Photo Credit: U.S. Army.

OBSERVATIONS

1. The caliber .50 Sniper Rifle was first tested for accuracy at 300 yards using the barrel from the caliber .50 M3 aircraft machine gun (hereafter called the light barrel).
   A. The comparison of results after this barrel was replaced by a barrel from the caliber .50 M2 heavy barrel machine gun shows the heavy barrel version capable of producing a group having approximately one half the extreme spread of that from the light barrel. The loss of accuracy caused by use of the light barrel might be attributed to its chrome-plated stellite-lined bore.
   B. The groups fired from the heavy-barrel weapon have an extreme spread approximately two-thirds the size of those using the caliber .30 M1D rifle, a control weapon in this test. They are comparable at this range to those fired from the Winchester M70 Sniper Rifle.
   C. There was no noticeable change in center of impact in the groups fired by the Winchester rifles. The M1D rifle, however, produced groups showing marked changes in the center of impact.
2. The light-barrel version of the Caliber .50 Sniper Rifle was tested again at 600 yards range with the M1D rifle and Winchester M70 Sniper Rifle as control weapons.
   A. This test differed from the other accuracy tests in that:
      (1) Firing on the target was limited to ten rounds per weapon per day, being completed when a fifty-round group had been produced by each after five days.

(2) A type "E" silhouette was super-imposed on the bull's-eye used as the aiming point, and the number of hits within the area outlined were recorded.
   B. The accuracies of these weapons were compared in terms of hits described above. The best, therefore, shows the effectiveness of the weapons under varying conditions against a clearly defined target the size of a man.
   C. The results of the test show the accuracy of the light-barrel version of the Caliber .50 weapon to be comparable to the Winchester M70 Sniper Rifle and superior to the M1D rifle.
3. The above test was repeated at 1000 yards employing the caliber .30 M1D rifle and Winchester M70 Sniper Rifle as control weapons.
   A. The number of hits scored by the caliber .50 Sniper Rifle fall to approximately half the number scored by the Winchester M70 Sniper Rifle, a result consistent with the findings at 300 yards. The number of hits scored by the caliber .30 M1D rifle was reduced on approximately twenty-five percent of its 600 yard figure, only six having been scored of the fifty rounds fired.
   B. Since the accuracy of the caliber .50 Sniper Rifle with the heavy barrel compared favorably with that of the Winchester M70 Sniper Rifle at 300 yards, it is likely that this weapon would equal the performance of the Winchester at longer ranges. In addition to its accuracy, this weapon, because of its heavier projectile, has the advantage of longer range, flat trajectory, and less affectation by wind variation than a caliber .30 weapon.

4. The accuracy characteristics of the caliber .30 M1D rifle compared more with those of three commercial caliber .30 rifles manufactured by the Winchester Repeating Arms Company.

    A. Testing these weapons at 100 yards with metallic sights showed the most inaccurate of the three Winchester M70 rifles to be capable of producing an extreme spread only one-half that of the group fired by the M1D rifle.

    B. A subsequent firing of the M1D rifle and the Winchester M70 Sniper Rifle employing telescopic sights produced results substantiating the results of the above test.

5. The caliber .50 M2 heavy-barrel machine gun was tested at 300, 1000, and 1400 yards.

    A. The first test at 300 yards with metallic sights produced groups with extreme spreads larger than those fired by the M1D rifle at the same range. The use of telescopic sights in the following test offered little improvement indicating that the weapon's accuracy is inherent in its construction and in the construction of the mount.

    B. The test at 1000 yards was fired using a type "E" silhouette mounted on an 8 x 8 ft. background. The tests were run first with metallic sights and second with telescopic sights. It was the observation of the gunner that the silhouette was as indistinguishable through the metallic sights as would be a man camouflaged to blend with the terrain. Aim was accomplished by aligning the front sight post with the 8 x 8 ft. background. For this reason, metallic sights were not used in the test of the caliber .50 machine gun at 1400 yards.

6. The Winchester M70 Bull Gun was fired at 1400 yards from bench rest at a type "E" silhouette mounted on a 12 x 12 ft. background. Three twenty-shot groups were fired, each with a different brand of ammunition. Telescopic sights were used, and care was taken to fire only during a calm. No large difference in accuracy was observed between groups although the ammunition brands differed.

7. Miscellaneous observations of the rifleman on the performance of the caliber .50 Sniper Rifle are as follows:

    A. It was observed by the rifleman that firing in groups of ten to fifteen rounds during a short period of time resulted in fatigue caused by the violent recoil of the weapon. Fatigue results in a tendency to flinch, reducing the effectiveness of fire.

    B. The bipod from the M1919A6 machine gun used on the heavy-barrel version of the caliber .50 Sniper Rifle was found superior to the modified Soviet bipod used with the light-barrel. The short, widely separated legs of the former tend to increase the weapon's stability during firing.

    C. With the ground frozen during the cold weather, the ability of the bipod to grip was diminished, and recoil caused a large displacement of the weapon. The continual realignment of the weapon may have had some effect on group size at the target.

    D. During the test of the caliber .50 Sniper Rifle, the weapon was accidentally dropped, denting slightly the tube of the telescope, but causing no additional damage.

    E. Play developed between the receiver and trigger housing after firing approximately 50 rounds.

8. The following observations were made on the caliber .30 M1D rifle used as control weapon in this test.

    A. The elevation adjustment on the M84 telescope did not allow enough travel to obtain a zero at 1000 yards. The center of impact appeared approximately six feet below the

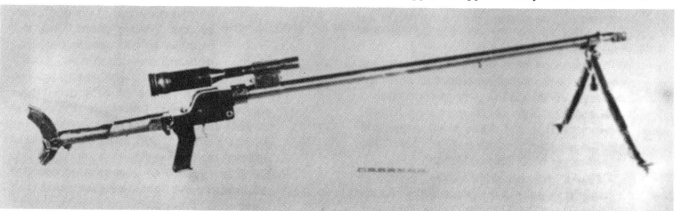

World War II PzB 39 antitank rifle modified for .50 caliber sniping by Colonel Frank Conway in 1946. Colonel Conway is recognized as the originator of the .50 caliber AT-rifle sniping concept. Photo Credit: Lieutenant Colonel F. B. Conway (Retired).

Colonel Conway sighting the .50 caliber PzB 39 from a prone position. Photo Credit: Lieutenant Colonel F. B. Conway (Retired).

line of sight once the telescope reached the end of its adjustment.

B. The telescope had insufficient magnification for identifying and accurately aiming at a man-sized target more than 600 yards distant.

C. The side mounting of the telescope and the instability of the leather cheek rest detract from the comfort of the rifleman. The stock of a rifle designed for use with telescopic sights should have sufficient height at the comb to permit the rifleman to rest the cheek comfortably during sighting. Examples of such a stock are those used on the Winchester M70 National Match Rifle, M70 Bull Gun, and M70 Target Rifle.

D. Upon removal and replacement, the M84 telescope failed to return to its original position. This defect, in addition to backlash found in the adjustment knobs, detracts from the weapon's ability to hold zero. The covers for the windage and elevation knobs were found to loosen during firing.

E. The post-type reticle used with the M84 telescopes was observed to obscure small targets at long ranges because of the excessive width.

9. The following observations pertain to telescopic sights:

A. It was the observation of the rifleman that telescopes of 12 diameters magnification, similar to those used in this test, are not adequate for recognition and aiming up to 1500 yards range. Telescopes of this magnification still retain sufficient field width.

B. Large objective lenses should be employed with telescopes of high magnification in order to obtain the high luminosity necessary for easy definition of the target by the rifleman under conditions of pool illumination.

C. The telescopes used in these tests are too long for use with the caliber .50 M2 heavy-barrel machine gun. Excessive length inhibits loading of a new belt of ammunition and makes transportation of the receiver more difficult. A prismatic telescope, more rigid and compact, has been designed for this use and designated Sight, Telescopic, M1. To accommodate this sight, a mounting assembly is incorporated on the receiver. The use of the prismatic telescope has been discontinued for reasons unknown.

10. Since the data for the report were taken, a new caliber .30 rifle and telescopic sight have become available commercially. Based on the results of this report, it is believed that these items contain the qualities of a good sniper weapon more than those tested.

A. The rifle is the Winchester M70 Target model and is basically the Winchester M70 Sniper Rifle with a target-type stock replacing the sporter stock. The high comb of the target

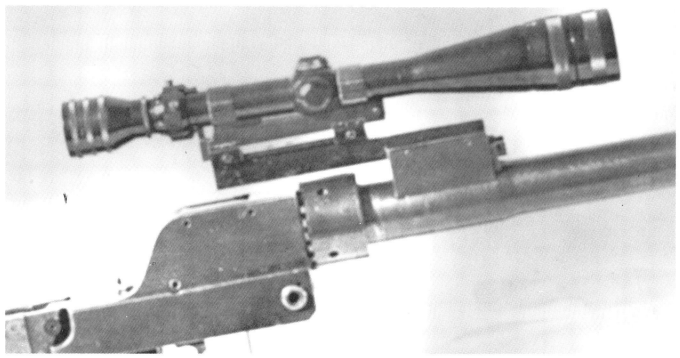

Although an improved Redfield 6x18 variable-power Adjustable Ranging Telescope (ART) was mounted on the .50 caliber PzB for use in Vietnam, the de-escalation prevented subsequent combat evaluation of this system. Photo Credit: Lieutenant Colonel F. B. Conway (Retired).

Double-baffle muzzle brake fabricated by Colonel Conway for the .50 caliber PzB rifle. Photo Credit: Lieutenant Colonel F. B. Conway (Retired).

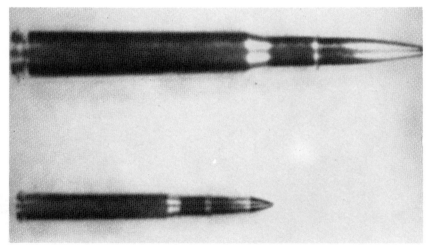

A comparison of .50 (5.45 in.) and .30 (3.34 in.) caliber ammunition. The .30-06 M2 Armor-Piercing round was favored by Army and USMC snipers during WW II and again in Korea. There was no questioning the authority of a .50 caliber bullet at any range. Photo Credit: Peter R. Senich.

stock provides firm cheek support when a telescopic sight is used. This rifle is lighter than the Winchester Bull Gun and, due to its shorter length, can be more easily handled. Based on the tests of the M70 Sniper model, the M70 Target rifle should be more accurate than the Winchester National Match Rifle.

B. The telescope mentioned above is the Unertl "Vulture" telescope. It features light weight, relatively high magnification and luminosity. Equipped with target type mounts, it has ease and permanence of adjustment. Basically it is shorter than the 20x target telescope and is less objectional from this standpoint.

C. Differences in ammunition fired in these tests may affect the results, particularly at long range. The ammunition used with the M1D rifle was the caliber .30 A.P. cartridge, while the Winchester rifles used a cartridge containing heavier, boat-tailed bullets. The latter has a flatter trajectory and longer range and is less affected by wind.

CONCLUSIONS

A. The following specific conclusions refer to characteristics of the particular items involved in this test.

A Boys antitank rifle manufactured in Canada in 1943 by the John Inglis Co., as fitted with a .50 caliber Browning machine gun barrel. Similar conversions have become popular among long-range shooting buffs in recent years. Photo Credit: Lieutenant Colonel F. B. Conway (Retired).

An alternate view of the .50 caliber PzB 39 with Redfield Adjustable Ranging Telescope (ART). When subjected to official testing, the special weapon consistently fired ten-inch groups at 1,300 meters. Photo Credit: Lieutenant Colonel F. B. Conway (Retired).

1. Over the ranges included in this test and among the weapons tested, the caliber .30 Winchester Sniper Rifle equipped with high power telescopic sights gave superior results, and is best suited against individual targets. It fired groups consistently smaller for a given range and number of rounds than did the light-barrel version of the caliber .50 Sniper Rifle. The caliber of .30 M1D rifle proved itself the least accurate of the three types of weapons tested.

2. Based on the accuracy tests made at 300 yards, it is apparent that the utilization of the heavy-barrel with the caliber .50 Sniper Rifle improves its inherent accuracy, giving it dispersion characteristics comparable to those of the Winchester M70 rifles. In addition, the flat trajectory, long range, and small wind deflection of the caliber .50 M2 ball bullet make the comparison between .30 caliber and caliber .50 weapons more favorable to the latter as the range increases.

3. The caliber .50 M2 heavy-barrel machine gun was found inherently less accurate as a single-shot weapon than the M1D rifle. The metallic sights, standard equipment on this weapon, are not adequate for aiming at ranges past 1000 yards. From test results, the maximum range at which a reasonable number of hits could be obtained using a suitable optical sight would increase to 1500-2000 yards.

B. The following general conclusions pertain to the general problem of sniper equipment, of which some aspects have been elucidated by the results of the present test.

1. Neither the caliber .30 nor the caliber .50 cartridge possesses characteristics satisfactory for employment in a long range sniping weapon. The exterior ballistic properties of the caliber .30 are capable of considerable improvement in a practical shoulder-weapon cartridge, but the heavy recoil of the caliber .50 cartridge is objectionable.

2. Neither the M1D nor the various commercial and special rifles tested possess the most desirable characteristics for employment as sniping equipment, although the accuracy of the commercial weapons was superior to that of the M1D.

3. Neither the M84 telescope nor the various commercial telescopes tested are completely suitable for employment as sniper rifle sighting equipment, the M84 being greatly inferior with respect to magnification and resolving power, and the commercial telescopes being of inconvenient size and too fragile for sustained military use.

RECOMMENDATIONS

A. It is recommended that none of the specific experimental weapon-sighting combinations tested be regarded as suitable for adoption, but that cognizance be taken of certain advantageous features of each.

B. It is recommended that consideration be given to the development of a rifle having more suitable characteristics than M1D for employment as a sniper's weapon, and that such development take the following course:

1. Development of a cartridge having exterior ballistic properties such as to minimize the effect of errors in range estimation and variation in atmospheric conditions, but characteristics suitable for employment in a shoulder weapon of practical dimensions.

2. An investigation be conducted to establish with reasonable certainty all of the important factors contributing to rifle accuracy in order that design of a sniper's weapon can proceed in accordance with well founded principles.

3. Consideration be given to development of telescopic sighting equipment having higher resolving power than does the M84, and more suitable military characteristics than have the various commercial telescopic sights currently available.

William S. Brophy
Major, Ordnance Corps
Proof Director

Interestingly, despite these qualified recommendations, as generally transpired with Ordnance reports intended to spur development of satisfactory sniping systems through the years, they were reviewed, filed, and forgotten by all, except by those cognizant of such a need.

Another significant application of .50 caliber sniping during the Korean fracas involved the use of Boys anti-tank rifles by the noted gunsmith, Ralph T. Walker of Selma, Alabama. The circumstances surrounding this use, though unofficial, are indeed noteworthy. Recollecting his .50 caliber sniping exploits, Walker relates:

I was assigned as small arms officer to the Nationalist Chinese Ordnance Corps in 1952 as part of the original M.A.A.G. (Military Advisor Assistance Group) charged with rebuilding the old Japanese arsenal at Taipei, Formosa.

As a matter of course, I had made several trips to the Nationalist held offshore islands. This was during the period when we had our own little war going on while Korea was in full swing. Things got a

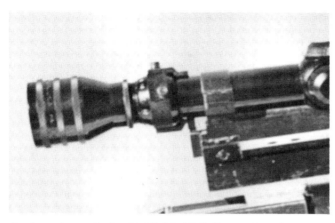

A close-view of the Redfield ART illustrating the spring loaded base, the ballistic cam as it rests on the base, and the power adjustor ring. Application of the Adjustable Ranging Telescope to .50 caliber machine guns was part of the original concept as fostered by the Limited Warfare Laboratory (LWL). Photo Credit: Lieutenant Colonel F. B. Conway (Retired).

bit hot during this time, resulting from Nationalist raids on the Communist mainland. We were looking for a full scale invasion at anytime. With only 250 Americans on Formosa, our concern was running high.

Just off Quemoy are two islands, one Nationalist, the other Communist. These were the outposts with the Commies' artillery holding the largest of the two. The Nationalist island, hardly more than a pile of sand, offered little room for artillery or its concealment. Heavy six-foot thick bunkers gave adequate protection, but it was rather noisy with incoming rounds falling on and about.

The Communists could not take the small island as Nationalist artillery on Quemoy protected it. With a shallow stretch of water separating the two, it was too deep to walk, and too shallow for boats . . . a stand-off, and it's still there.

The 1100 yards between islands made firing with a .30 caliber rifle a joke, due primarily to the incessant wind blowing across the water.

With American guns pouring into the arsenal on Formosa, we were pressed for storage space. While inspecting the warehouses, we came across some .55 caliber British Boys, antitank rifles, undoubtedly used against the Japanese, but not one round of ammunition. Remembering the two islands, the idea to build a supreme sniping rifle using the big .50 caliber machine gun round to buck the wind struck my fancy. With a small machine shop and the help of Chinese Ordnance personnel, we built the rifle.

The barrel shank of the .55 Boys, larger than an M2 .50 barrel, necessitated cutting the existing barrel forward of the receiver ring, followed by boring and threading the inside of the remaining section—sleeve affair. The .50 barrel was then turned down and threaded to match.

After severe proof firing with loads made by pulling the .50 bullets and packing the cases with powder, we concentrated on smoothing out the action somewhat. Finding it necessary to load rounds singly, we installed a block of steel in the magazine well which served to strengthen the action and function as a loading block.

Although the Boys was equipped with decent open sights, for the shooting planned, a scope would be necessary. The first, a Weaver 330 from an 03-A4, soon shattered from the recoil force.

Among the leftovers from the Japanese were some 20x spotting scopes intended for tank use. These had fixed reticle, with external mounts, but could not be satisfactorily adapted to the Boys in their original forms. Consequently, we made up external mounts

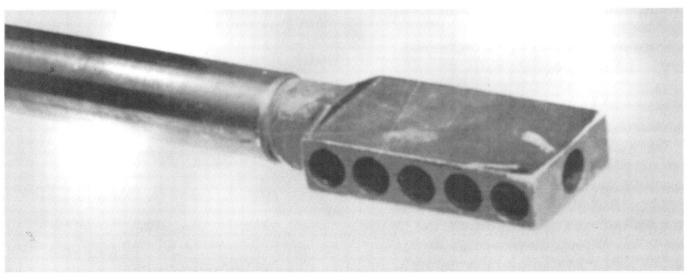

A close view of the Canadian Boys AT-rifle muzzle-brake as refitted to the Browning MG barrel. The muzzle-brake served to dampen recoil. Photo Credit: Lieutenant Colonel F. B. Conway (Retired).

for the two inch diameter scope closely resembling those used with Lyman or Unertl target scopes, only double in size.

On a 500 yard test range the rifle performed reasonably well. We moved back to 1000 yards and went through at least six barrels looking to increase accuracy. These were machine gun barrels, however, and were not intended for pin-point accuracy.

A .50 caliber round straight out of the box hardly qualifies as accurate ammunition. We found an amazing variance in both loading and bullets. In an effort to overcome this deficiency, we built a king-sized Pacific loading press, made dies, unloaded, and carefully remeasured the powder charges. Reloading improved accuracy somewhat, but not enough to compensate for the effort.

Although the Boys had a bipod in front and a monopod on the rear with a small built-in recoil system, it really rattled you to fire it. Three to five shots was about all a man could stand at one time even from a prone position.

The Nationalist Chinese became interested in the rifles and we wound up building twelve of the Boys anti-tank guns into .50 caliber snipers. Picking the biggest and best shots, they put them through a training program with the .50's. While they couldn't equal the accuracy of the original test rifle, groups ran about two feet long—still adequate for what we had in mind.

About half of the rifles and their unwilling new owners were sent over to the small off-shore island. Although the front office would not let me accompany them, I read the results in a subsequent report.

On a usual basis the Chinese Reds would go down to the beach and bathe. At the first sound of any artillery firing at them from Quemoy, the Reds would scurry for cover and beat the first rounds coming in. With initial use of the .50 caliber rifles, their report barely audible, a dozen or so Chi-Com soldiers had their beach privileges permanently rescinded.

It is general consensus, however, that the initial adaption of an antitank gun for .50 caliber sniping must be credited to the incomparable Lt. Col. Frank B. Conway (Retired). Assigned to a detachment supporting the Ordnance Board at Aberdeen Proving Ground, Maryland, in 1946, Conway was fully cognizant of the limitations of .30 caliber rifles based on first-hand sniping experiences in Europe. He considered the practicality of modifying an antitank rifle to provide an effective means for long-range firing.

Possessing a PzB39 rifle, the type converted to grenade launching by the Germans after tank armor had proven too thick for their 7.92mm

antitank rifles in Russia and North Africa, Conway, late in 1946, set about fitting a heavy .50 caliber machine gun barrel to his PzB39 action.

Following a full three days' work adapting the barrel, modifications included repositioning the bipod forward to the barrel end for increased stability, and the addition of a double-baffle muzzle brake much the same in principle as those used with artillery. In place of the original iron sights, a 3x8 degree telescopic sighting device from a Wehrmacht tow gun was mounted over the receiver. With bipod and sighting system the rifle weighed in at forty-six pounds. In its first use, Conway mentions, "Recoil was never a problem, but with that muzzle brake, ear protection was highly recommended."

Despite demonstrated effectiveness, little official interest could be generated at Aberdeen. At this point, immediately following the war, consideration of new innovative weapons, especially with regards to sniping, were of limited concern. In what appears to have been a chronic common problem with .50 caliber sniping rifles, Conway comments further:

> Ammunition was always a problem, not because of a lack, but rather, its quality. Some bullets were misaligned with the case to the extent that when rolled on a flat surface, the nose of the bullet would rotate through a quarter to three-eighths circle. The fact that they could be fired at all speaks well for the big Brownings. I was fortunate enough to secure small amounts of satisfactory ammo packed in ten round cartons for the .50 PzB.

Subsequent testing of the modified PzB at Ft. Bliss, Texas, in the early 1950s indicated positive results at ranges of 1,400 yards. When fired at an adobe shack some 2,800 yards distant, "we could usually place the second or third round through a small window."

While engaged in test and development of the Adjustable Ranging Telescope (ART) with the M14 rifle at the Marksmanship Training Unit (MTU) in Ft. Benning, Georgia, during the late 1960s, Frank Conway actively involved himself with the Limited Warfare Laboratory's concept of applying the ART to .50 Browning machine guns, in addition to the M14. Feasibility testing of this system was conducted, with Conway's .50 caliber PzB serving as one of the test weapons.

In adapting the ART, an early four by twelve Redfield variable, with an ART reticle and cam-

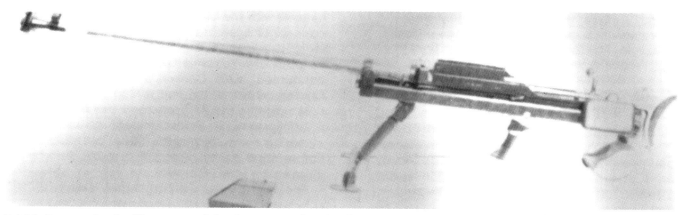

British Boys antitank rifle converted for long-range shooting by Browning specialist Steve Fleischman. A 36-inch aircraft barrel has been installed along with the original Boys muzzle-brake and sights. Photo Credit: Steve Fleischman.

A .50 caliber Flechette Rifle developed in 1969 for use against enemy personnel in Southeast Asia. A Boys AT-rifle action, smooth-bore barrel, and Weatherby telescope formed the nucleus of this unique weapon. Photo Credit: Donald Stoehr.

ming computed for the .50 caliber round at 600 to 1,800 meters, was fitted to the PzB by means of a special mount.

Testing involved firing at an Army "E" silhouette target (nineteen and one-half inches wide by forty inches high) at distances unknown to the shooter. One individual, who had not fired the rifle previously, was instructed to fire three rounds returning the ART to 6x between each shot as if searching the area for a target. Following this firing, examination of the target disclosed a triangular formed group (ten inches wide and four and one-half inches high) well centered on the target.

Upon informing the shooter that the target was 1,300 meters distant, his remarks were typical of those who had also fired the .50/ART: "Where in the hell can I get one of these?"

Without exception, those who had participated in the test firing were extremely impressed with the first round hit capability and ten-inch groupings at 1,300 meters.

As followed, the .50 caliber PzB was slated for field testing in Southeast Asia (Vietnam), mounting an improved 6 x 18 Redfield variable. As the reticle for the 3 x 9 scope was used, the horizontal stadia ranging lines were spaced at sixty inches, or double that used in the regular 3 x 9 ART. However, the de-escalation came about and, as Frank Conway put it, "So once again, the big .50 went into retirement."

Actual employment of converted .50 caliber antitank rifles for long-range sniping in Vietnam remains obscure and, at best, highly unlikely. In general, specifics dealing with weapon use and deployment in Southeast Asia, owing to the proximity of final U.S. involvement with the present, for the most part remain officially shielded in lieu of the fact that virtually all weapons used there are still current issue.

Nonetheless, a variety of "special use" .50 caliber weapons, including the venerable Browning HB M2 machine gun, were experimented with and

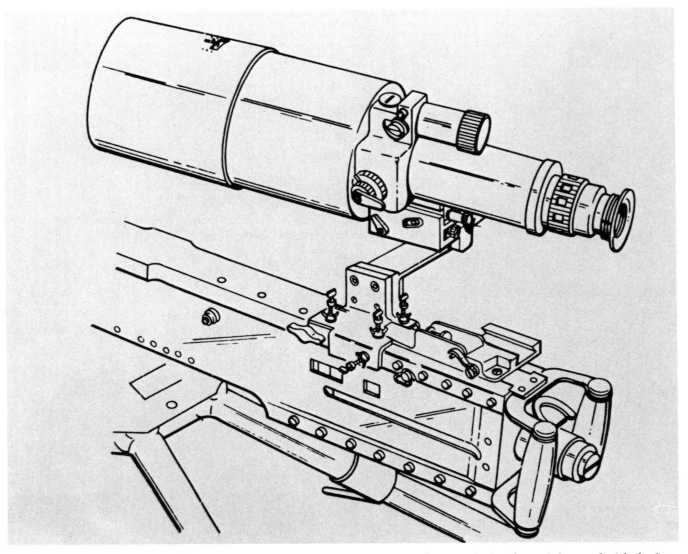

Although principal use of an optical sighting system with the .50 caliber machine gun in Southeast Asia rested with the Starlight Scope, the Marine Corps made frequent use of target telescopes with the "Big Browning" in Vietnam, as they had in Korea. The scope is an early AN/TVS-2 crew-served night-vision sight. Photo Credit: U.S. Army.

utilized by the Army, Navy, and Marine Corps with varying degrees of success.

In 1969, under the auspices of the Department of Defense, Advanced Research Projects Agency, a commercial firm undertook development of .50 caliber Flechette Rifles based on modified Boys anti-tank guns. A total of sixteen rifles were made up, including two prototypes. Weighing approximately thirty-five pounds, the Boys actions were fitted with unrifled smooth-bore barrels. The cartridge, a .50 caliber case with flechette projectile, gave a recorded muzzle velocity of 4,500 fps (feet per second).

While the original design was intended for use against individual personnel in a quasi-sniping role, its only salient feature was an extremely flat trajec-

tory since accuracy proved to be extremely poor. At 600 yards, a typical ten-shot group would be six to eight feet in diameter. On the other hand, at close range, the flechette round would defeat two inches of steel or two feet of concrete, but against personnel it was hopeless.

Unquestionably, the most effective, basic deployment of .50 caliber weapons in Vietnam rested with the Browning M2, Heavy Barrel machine gun, much the same as it had in Korea. The "Big Browning" saw most frequent service with conventional open sights, but various units of the Marine Corps were known to employ high-power telescopic target scopes with special receiver mountings. Perhaps its most sophisticated use came in conjunction with the crew-served night-vision sight, the Starlight Scope.

Deployment of .50 caliber machine guns as a marginal sniping weapon by the First Battalion (Mech.), 5th Infantry, proved particularly effective when its sniper teams were trained to engage targets out to a realistic range of 1,000 meters using the AN/TVS 2, Starlight Scope and firing single-shot. Intended to bolster their sniping capabilities rather than to supplant the use of conventional snipers, in initial use, a Starlight-Browning combination eliminated its target at a range of 800 meters with a single round.

In turn, sniper teams so trained were charged with instructing Battalion gunners for the purpose of enhancing their defensive posture by increasing the volume of accurate fire during periods of limited visibility. The Brownings were fired from regular M3 ground mounts and, when warranted, at secured areas such as Fire Control Bases, from fortified towers twenty to thirty-five feet high using special mounts designed to permit rapid changes in fire direction.

After many years and three major conflicts, the "Big Browning" continues to serve.

A prime example of ultralong-range firing with machine-gun-mounted telescopic sights. The .50 caliber Browning is equipped with an 8x Unertl telescope (Korea, December 1951). Photo Credit: U.S. Army.

A current issue, second generation AN/TVS-5 crew-served weapon sight (Starlight Scope) mounted on the .50 caliber machine gun. Photo Credit: Excalibur Enterprises.

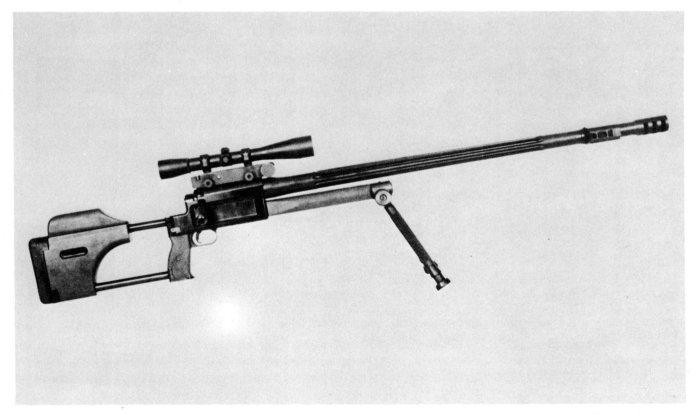

A state-of-the-art .50 caliber sniping rifle reportedly furnished to the U.S. Government in quantity. According to the manufacturer, the Research Armament Industries (RAI) Model 500 long-range rifle system "is capable of extreme accuracy at ranges in excess of 2,000 yards." Photo Credit: Jim Shults, Gung-Ho magazine.

The 30-lb., bolt-action sniping rifle is fitted with a 33-inch full fluted, free-floating barrel. Barrel vibration is dampened by an adjustable tuning rod. The rifle also features an adjustable trigger pull and can be broken down into compact components without the use of tools. Jim Shults (<u>Gung-Ho</u> magazine) is shown test firing a .50 caliber RAI rifle mounting a Leupold & Stevens scope. The weapon is in full recoil. Photo Credit: Jim Shults, <u>Gung-Ho</u> magazine.

A special purpose "extended long range" sniping system developed by the Gale McMillan Company of Phoenix, Arizona. The lightweight .50 caliber (12.7 x 99mm NATO) Model M87 ELR Sniper Rifle has been tested by the government. Photo Credit: John Mason.

Chapter 12 ◆◆

The Target Rifle in Combat

Never officially adopted for combat use, the Winchester Model 70 bolt-action rifle was utilized to some extent by both Army and Marine Corps marksmen during World War II, Korea, and again in Southeast Asia for sniping purposes. From the time of its introduction, some five years prior to World War II, the Model 70 in its various forms was considered to be one of, if not the finest, commercial rifle then available for hunting and competitive match-shooting. As such, the Model 70 was highly regarded by many of the military who considered this rifle both extremely efficient and readily adaptable for specialized use, in this case sniping.

Even though the Marine Corps had seriously considered the Model 70, it ultimately decided against its adoption in 1941. According to first-hand accounts, though, a fair number of unauthorized, "personal" telescope-sighted Model 70s brought the reality of war to Japanese combat personnel during the early stages of World War II in the Pacific.

In the years following the war, Winchester continued development of its Model 70 with extremely heavy barrels to meet the requirements of long-range target shooting. The Model 70 came in three target weights of about nine and one-half, ten and one-half, and thirteen pounds, and after having first been designated the National Match and Target Grade, was later redesignated Standard and Heavy Weight with the twenty-eight-inch barrel Bull Gun rounding out the trio. The target variants, for the most part, were similar to the early sporting version introduced in 1936. All three rifles were correctly stocked for target scopes or high receiver peep and target front sights, which by design could be easily mounted.

There is little to be said about the quality and desirability of these rifles, which were just about

Winchester Model 70, Serial No. 47262, manufactured in 1941 with commercial Unertl target telescope and heavy barrel (24 inches by .790-inch muzzle diameter), a part of the Marine Corps Museum Collection at Quantico, Virginia, is one of the rifles evaluated by a USMC Equipment Board in 1941 for possible sniper use. Photo Credit: Peter R. Senich.

the only over-the-counter factory arms made for target shooting following the war. There just were not enough "big-bore" shooters to induce other manufacturers to get into the picture. As a result, Model 70 target rifles gained considerable favor among Army and Marine Corps rifle teams for match-shooting purposes.

Early in 1952, in what some considered "a one-man campaign" to focus attention on the inadequacies of Army sniping equipment in Korea, Captain William S. Brophy, while attached to IX Corps Ordnance, visited several field units for the purpose of discussing sniping activities, tactical employment of sniping, and required characteristics of sniping equipment.

Using a commercial Winchester Model 70 target rifle to demonstrate what the right combination of weapon and trained marksman could achieve in a combat environment, Captain Brophy related, "The first reaction was not encouraging due to the feeling that the equipment I was demonstrating would be easily damaged and could not be handled properly by the average soldier." However, in view of the limits of existing Army sniper issue at ranges greater than 600 yards, interest was shown in trying the target Winchester to determine its potential in certain tactical situations. As a result of

1,000-plus yard shooting, during which several "Chi-Com" casualties were registered, the .30-06 Winchester Model 70 Bull Gun (28-inch barrel, .842-inch diameter muzzle), mounting a Unertl 10 power, two-inch objective telescope, was considered nothing short of phenomenal.

Nevertheless, the military viewpoint regarding sniper weapons of special configuration (other than standard issue) remained one of particular disdain, due to the difficulty in field supply and replacement of nonstandard parts. Consequently, bolt-action target grade rifles saw limited combat sniping use in Korea despite Captain Brophy's efforts.

In a segment of the extensive *Study of Sniper's Rifles, Telescopes and Mounts,* conducted by the Marine Corps Equipment Board at Quantico, Virginia, in 1951, the Winchester Model 70 was reconsidered, but rejected for basically the same reasons that were cited just prior to World War II. According to the 1951 study:

> There is no Marine Corps requirement for a special rifle for use by snipers in the Marine Corps. It is undesirable to inject another rifle into the supply system, and if another rifle is injected into the supply system, it is necessary to inject non-standard ammunition for this rifle into the supply system in order to

Rear mounting typical of those furnished with prewar Unertl target telescopes. (Winchester M70, USMC Trial, 1941.) Photo Credit: Peter R. Senich.

Front mount and recoil spring assembly that brought the scope back into position after firing. (Winchester M70, USMC Trial, 1941.) Photo Credit: Peter R. Senich.

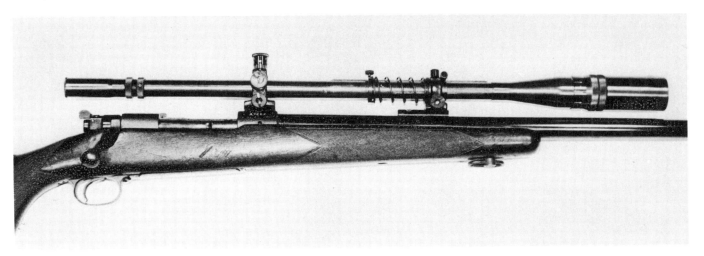

A close view of the 8 power Unertl target telescope with M70 Winchester used for USMC evaluations in 1941. Photo Credit: Peter R. Senich.

Captain William S. Brophy with Winchester target rifle, Korea, 1952. Photo Credit: U.S. Army.

exploit fully any gain in accuracy. The U.S. Rifle, Caliber .30, M1C is sufficiently accurate for use by snipers in the Marine Corps.

Aside from its rejection, the review board held the Winchester in high regard: "Investigation of the better grades of commercial rifles indicate that the Model 70 Winchester is the most accurate American made, Caliber .30 on the market."

When the Vietnam conflict heated to the point at which full-scale United States intervention became a reality, the Model 70 Winchester wound up as the quasi-official sniping arm of the Marine Corps. This was in 1965, when, according to a Marine Corps spokesman, "M14 rifles with conventional sights were found inadequate for precise long-range shooting."

Starting out as its sole specialized sniper armament, the first Model 70s pressed into service in Vietnam, from the Third Marine Division Rifle Team, were originally used in rifle matches, including the National Matches at Camp Perry. Events leading to their combat use were cited by Frank McGuire in the *American Rifleman,* in 1967:

> Efforts were made to get a suitable match rifle for Marine Corps rifle teams that would meet the NRA's weight limitations for such equipment in competition. The late Brig. Gen. George O. Van Orden, USMC (Ret.), head of Evaluators, Ltd., went to Winchester and had some Model 70s made up with a heavy barrel on a sporter stock. This rifle met the weight requirements (since changed by NRA) and also happened to be the same configuration which Brig. Gen. Van Orden had recommended for sniper use in the early 1940s. It was this configuration of the Model 70 which S/SGT Don L. Smith, USMC used in 1953 to win the National Match rifle championships at Camp Perry. The rifle team of the 3rd Marine Division had been using the Model 70 with the heavy barrel and the heavy Marksman stock, in view of the changed weight limitations. When the need

arose for more Model 70s, the rifles procured by Brig. Gen. Van Orden, including Smith's championship-winning rifle, were shipped out as supplemental equipment in Vietnam.

When these turned out to be too few, additional Model 70s, all equipped with target barrels, were shipped to the Republic of Vietnam (RVN) and fitted with either sporter or target stocks. The sporter stocks were favored most by Marine snipers because they were lighter and easier to carry.

Glass-bedded and accurized by Marine Corps Rifle Team Equipment Armorers (RTE), the Model 70s fired .30-06 M72 match ammunition having a 173-grain, boat-tailed bullet. In some cases, Douglas barrels were fitted to the Winchester actions to attain optimum accuracy. A limited number of 3x to 9x variable power "Marine Scopes" of Japanese manufacture saw early use, but target mount, 8 power Unertl telescopes, unchanged basically from those first adopted in 1941, were fitted to the Model 70s as were many of the original World War II Unertl contract scopes, which had survived official obsolescence and the post–Korean War surplus sell-off. Despite their effective use, the official Marine Corps point of view regarding target scopes remained unfavorable for basically the same reasons that were cited by the Marine Corps Equipment Board in 1951: "A small exit pupil, small field of view, and high magnification require that targets be designated for the sniper by an observer. The lack of durability of the target telescope is another undesirable feature of this equipment."

Hits were recorded at 1,000-plus yards (approximately 900 meters), but the most effective range for the average Marine sniper equipped with the Model 70 Winchester lay between 500 and 700 yards, this being the range at which most targets were detected and engaged. While the USMC used

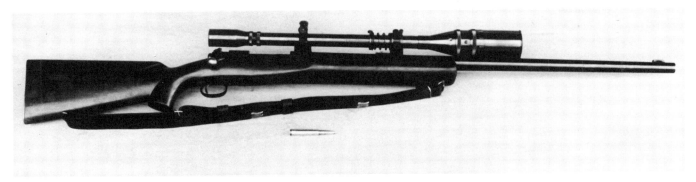

Winchester Model 70 "Bull Gun" used for 1,000-yard sniping in Korea. Photo Credit: U.S. Army.

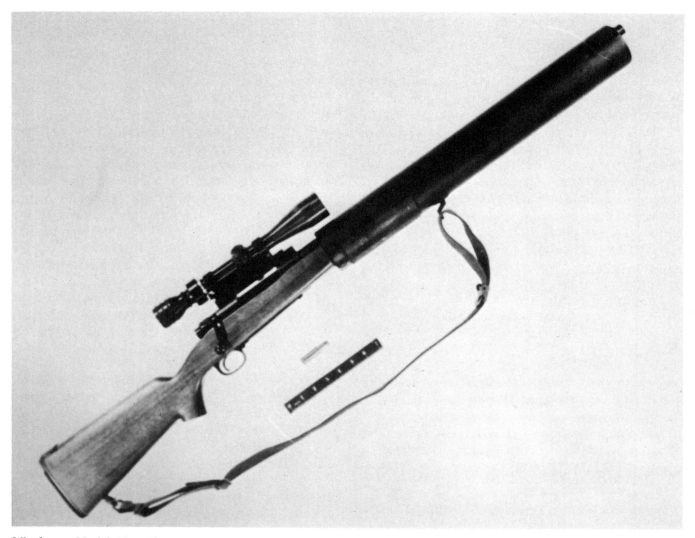

Winchester Model 70 .458 Magnum Cartridge silent sniper system as used for Army evaluations in Vietnam. Photo Credit: Donald G. Thomas.

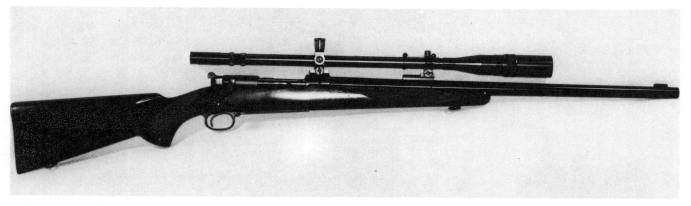

A heavy barrel Model 70 Winchester, with Unertl USMC contract sight and sporter stock, represents one of the lot made up under the auspices of the late Brigadier General George O. Van Orden, USMC Retired, head of Evaluators Ltd., for Marine Corps use in the early 1950s. Photo Credit: Peter R. Senich.

Third Marine Division sniper candidates on the firing line at Da Nang, January 1966. Note the use of both sporter and target stocks with the Model 70 rifles. Photo Credit: U.S. Marine Corps.

The Model 70 Winchester extended the Marine Corps kill radius to 1,000 yards during early action in South Vietnam. Photo Credit: U.S. Marine Corps.

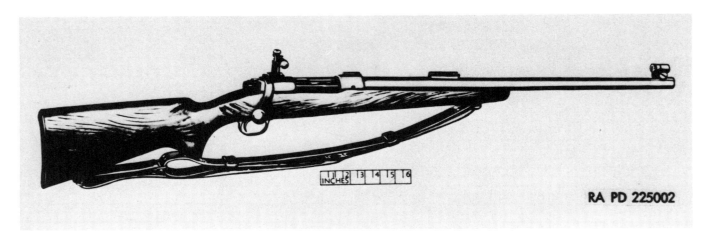

A Model 70 target rifle of the type utilized by Army Rifle Teams. Photo Credit: U.S. Army.

Marine Corps armorer preparing a Model 70 rifle for a Unertl telescope, Vietnam, 1966. Photo Credit: U.S. Marine Corps.

USMC marksman sighting his Unertl-equipped M70 on the rifle range. The Marines were the first branch of the U.S. forces in Vietnam to establish a sniper unit. Photo Credit: U.S. Marine Corps.

Limited numbers of 3x-9x variable power "Marine Scopes" manufactured in Japan were used with the Model 70 for early USMC sniping activity in Vietnam. Photo Credit: U.S. Marine Corps.

The principal Marine Corps sniping weapon during early involvement in South Vietnam. The Winchester Model 70 rifle with an 8x Unertl telescopic sight. Photo Credit: U.S. Marine Corps.

A Marine Corps sniper team selecting "their mark" during early action against the Viet Cong. Photo Credit: U.S. Marine Corps.

Marine snipers proved their worth in Vietnam by denying free movement to "Old Charley" in his own backyard. Photo Credit: U.S. Marine Corps.

the Model 70 to greatest advantage during this period, a limited number were also employed by Army personnel for sniping, and Model 70s with silencers mounted on them were utilized for covert operations in Southeast Asia.

The most intriguing Army application of the Model 70 evolved as a result of the U.S. Army Limited War Laboratory (USALWL) efforts to develop a Silent Sniper System for use by sniper teams in Vietnam. A description of this unique weapon was set forth in *Technical Report No. 71-73,* by Elmer K. Landis, Chief, Munitions Branch, USALWL.

The Silent Sniper System was comprised of three elements, including: the weapon, the sighting system, and a specially loaded subsonic ammunition.

The weapon is a heavy, bolt-action rifle with an integral noise suppressor. The sighting system is based on a 3x to 9x variable power range-finding telescope which is retained in a flexible mount. A ballistic cam, physically attached to the telescope power adjusting ring, automatically provides the proper super-elevation for a given range. This is the same sighting system as the LWL-developed Adjustable Ranging

Telescope used as an element of the XM21 Sniper System.

The ammunition is specially loaded for subsonic velocity and is a modification of the commercial .458 Magnum Cartridge. The case has been purposely shortened to prevent inadvertent loading and firing of the standard cartridge for safety reasons. Capability for night operations is supplied by the use of a Starlight Scope mount base adaptor which will accept the AN/PVS-1 and the AN/PVS-2A Starlight Scopes.

In February 1971 Franklin Owens of the USALWL accompanied five .458 magnum silent sniper rifle systems to the Twenty-third Infantry Division (American) Sniper School in Vietnam for evaluation purposes. The systems were tested by the sniper school cadre and division snipers during March, April, and May on the sniper range near Chu Lai. Two rifles were sent to the field with snipers who volunteered to evaluate them during missions under combat conditions.

The result of thorough test and evaluation indicated that the XM21 was far superior to the .458 magnum silent sniper system in all respects except

Although never officially adopted, the Model 70 Winchester saw considerable Marine Corps sniper use. A rifleman is shown checking his Unertl telescope on the range. Photo Credit: U.S. Marine Corps.

A 3rd Marine Division sniper with heavy barrel Model 70 Winchester mounting the 8 power Unertl telescope. Photo Credit: U.S. Marine Corps.

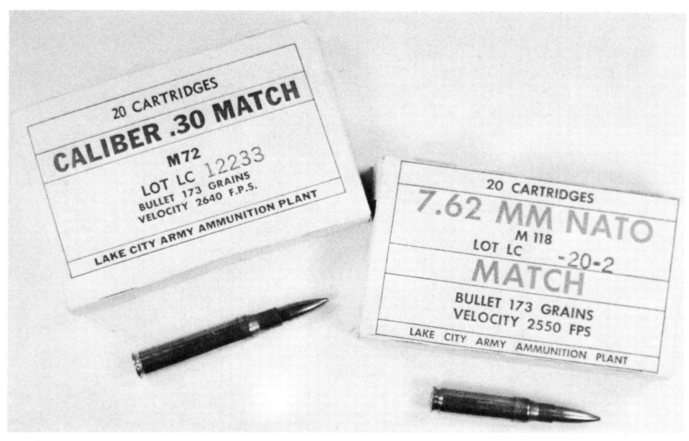

Match Grade ammunition as utilized by Army and USMC snipers in Vietnam. Photo Credit: Peter R. Senich.

A USMC Lance Corporal holds a Unertl scope hit by a bullet during an encounter with the Viet Cong. Photo Credit: U.S. Marine Corps.

Winchester Model 70 Center Fire Target Rifle circa 1972. Photo Credit: U.S. Marine Corps.

noise suppression, and as a result the special rifles were deemed unsuitable for further field use. Curiously, the utilization of noise suppressors with bolt-action sniping rifles never reached practical proportions in Vietnam. Although the Marine Corps conducted tests with a Sionics variant on the Remington M40 and employed suppressors of unknown design with its telescope-sighted M70 Winchesters in the mid-1960s, the circumstances surrounding their field use remain obscure.

Chapter 13 ◆ ◆

Night Vision Sights – The Eyes of Darkness

Throughout the history of armed conflict, the cover of darkness has provided a tactical advantage for one side or the other. The earliest efforts to remove this cover were effected by the use of torches, flares, and rockets. During World War I, formal research work was initiated in the realm of night vision, but such efforts were confined to searchlight illumination.

Television research by RCA in the 1930s led to development of an image tube which could be used to convert infrared images to visible displays. The military significance of this was quickly seized upon by the Army with the development culminating in 1944 with the introduction of an operational small-arms-mounted infrared unit—the "Sniperscope."

The Sniperscope, first conceived in 1943 by a group of Army officers at the laboratories of the U.S. Army Engineer Board at Fort Belvoir, Virginia, utilized a recently invented infrared image converter tube telescope which was being explored for use in night convoy driving applications.

These officers fashioned a crude arrangement consisting of an electronic telescope and an infrared-filtered, sealed-beam headlight fastened to an M1 .30 caliber carbine. A lead-acid aircraft battery carried in a knapsack was used to power the device.

Although the prototype Sniperscope had an approximate range of only one hundred feet, it served to show that such a device could provide aimed fire in total darkness. Although Frankford Arsenal had fabricated "tool room prototypes," the first Sniperscopes to see combat were fabri-

cated at Electronic Laboratories, Inc., Indianapolis, Indiana, in 1944, incorporating the RCA IP25A infrared-image converter tube.

At the request of the Chief of Engineers, U.S. Army, a study to determine the most practical method of modifying the carbine receiver to accept the electronic viewing telescope was necessitated by the less than satisfactory manner in which the prototype units had been mounted.

Based on the results of feasibility tests conducted with conventional 2 1/2x telescopic sights on the carbine (M1E7) in 1943, the following models were submitted for inspection and test:

A. Carbine with brazed-on telescope mount, base centrally located with respect to the center line of the bore, and special scope rings.
B. Carbine with brazed-on telescope mount, base 5/8-inch to the left of the center line of the bore.
C. Carbine with brazed-on telescope mount having the front portion of the mount cut away so as to be flush with the rear of the chamber.

Resulting from these tests, the M1E7 type of carbine, having a modified stock for attaching the infrared light-source bracket to the fore-end, was approved February 1944 and designated Carbine, Caliber .30, T3 "Sniperscope."

In addition to the Sniperscope, a companion device, the Snooperscope, was developed to supplement night observation and signaling. While similar in configuration to the Sniperscope, it was hand-held and not weapon-mounted. These instruments were later named "Molly" and "Milly" by

177

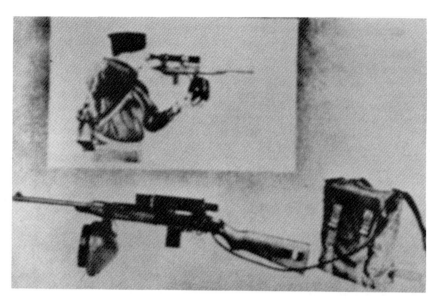

Prototype infrared device as originally tested by the Army in 1943. Photo Credit: U.S. Army.

members of the Armed Forces.

Original operation and maintenance instructions for the early infrared units were set forth in War Department Technical Manual TM 5-9340, dated September 1, 1944. Classified "SECRET" at that time, it was downgraded to unclassified some time after 1946. Unique and comparatively rare, surviving copies are eagerly sought after by U.S. military buffs and collectors.

When the infrared units were entrusted to civilian manufacture, Electronic Laboratories and Bell & Howell became prime contractors, utilizing components from various sources. Bell & Howell manufactured all optics while the image tubes were government-furnished. The instruments were assembled on a preliminary basis at the subcontractors. Upon receipt of these units, the assemblies were disassembled and subjected to thorough inspection and testing prior to final shipment to the Army.

Inspection tests included thorough shock and function testing of the highly sensitive image tubes. Bell & Howell records indicate such tests eliminated approximately 90 percent of the tubes furnished. Operational infrared devices, designated Sniperscope M1, utilized the service-designed T120 telescope. Subsequent development by Bell & Howell necessitated "complete redesign and engineering" resulting in the introduction of Sniperscope M2 having a vastly improved T230 electronic telescope.

Sniperscope M2, similar to its predecessor, differed in mechanical detail to the extent that most parts were not interchangeable. The Snooperscope was eliminated as a separate assembly with

the addition of a hand-held mount, included with the M2 equipment. The light source and telescope could now be removed from the weapon and readily affixed to the hand mount as circumstances dictated. The power-pack and six-volt storage battery furnished with the new instruments, although modified somewhat, could still be utilized with existing M1 devices.

Following acceptance of Sniperscope M2, as Ordnance records indicate, Headquarters, Army Ground Forces, recommended that the Carbine T3 be standardized for use with this unit. The basic weapon was to be either an M1 Carbine or an M2 Carbine modified to allow only semiautomatic action. However, tests conducted by the Engineer Board indicated there was no appreciable difference between the effects of automatic and semiautomatic fire from the Carbine, Caliber .30, M2 on the electrical and optical components of the Sniperscope.

There were to evolve two variations of T3 Carbine to permit mounting the electronic telescope on the receiver. The first, or original pattern, had a bridge-type mount extending from the forward portion of the receiver rearward to the rear section. Subsequent models dispensed with the bridge mount altogether.

Approximately 2,000 to 3,000 T3 Carbines were manufactured by General Motors Corp., Inland Division, Dayton, Ohio, and Winchester Repeating Arms Co., New Haven, Connecticut. The T3 was to be the only weapon manufactured specifically for use with night-vision instruments.

Use of the Sniperscope involved pointing the device toward some sound heard in the darkness,

An early production Sniperscope, the carbine mounted M1 infrared system with the lamp (light source) positioned beneath the weapon. The original M1 model and the first issue of sniperscope M2 were produced with the lamp below the carbine on the stock using a mount with a grip and trigger switch for the lamp. Photo Credit: U.S. Army.

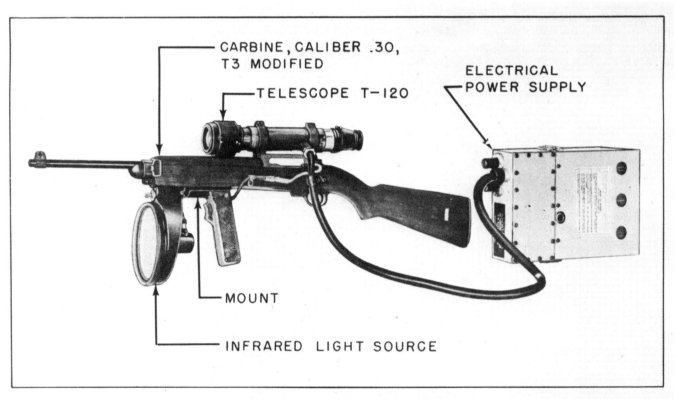

Figure 3. Sniperscope. Complete assembly

The first operational infrared system (M1) issued for combat use late in WW II. Night-vision equipment proved invaluable against Japanese infiltration tactics at Okinawa and final action in the Philippines. Photo Credit: U.S. Army.

switching on the power supply, and scanning the forward area until the cause of the sound was located or determined. Infrared rays, visible only to the operator, were projected over the sighting area. The reflected rays, picked up by the electronic telescope, were converted to a visible image and magnified according to the power of the telescope. Sighted objects appeared in varying shades of green, regardless of their daylight color.

A night-vision capability was to prove particularly effective in combating Japanese infiltration tactics conducted during periods of darkness in the Pacific. It was reported during the first seven days of action of the Okinawa Campaign that the Sniperscope accounted for approximately 30 percent of the total Japanese casualties inflicted by small-arms fire.

Combat reports cite approaching groups of Japanese being thoroughly decimated while attempting to pick their way through American lines. From that point forward, night activity of the Imperial Japanese soldier was to be infinitely more hazardous. Although several thousand infrared units were manufactured during World War II, only about 200 were actually employed in the South Pacific. The Japanese military, cognizant of infrared principles and techniques, was in fact developing units for small-arms use late in the war. However, operational devices were not known to be employed in actual combat.

The Germans, on the other hand, had successfully developed a myriad of infrared instruments which were used in aircraft, vehicle, and fire control applications.

In 1943, an energetic program was started to develop a portable infrared night sight for the Maschinenpistole 43 (MP 43) Assault Rifle series to protect armored units from tank-destruction troops and infantry attacks during periods of darkness. The sight, designated Zielgerat 1229 (ZG 1229), bore the code name "Vampir."

Successful tests of German infrared were conducted by the Panzergrenadiere (armed cavalry) during the months of February and March 1945. Against single persons, a range of approximately seventy meters was established. Interestingly, the German concept of such use called for the Panzergrenadiere equipped with infrared devices to be transported in an armored vehicle fitted with infrared driving equipment.

In anticipation of Allied use of infrared, the Germans produced a simple device to detect its

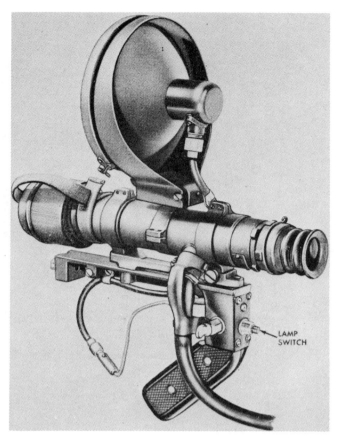

The original M1 infrared was designated sniperscope when mounted on a carbine and snooperscope when used with the hand-held for signaling or searching operations. Photo Credit: U.S. Army.

use. The device consisted of a small paper tube having an infrared window and lens on one end and a sensitive screen on the other. The screen possessed a remarkable property that, after exposure to strong sunlight, became so sensitized that for a long time afterward it would respond by emission of red visible light when illuminated by invisible infrared light. While in a sensitized state, the detector permitted German troops to pinpoint the source of any infrared device directed against them. Approximately 10,000 detectors were produced for use by the Wehrmacht.

Infrared light, invisible to the naked eye, irradiates objects which then can be seen with the viewer. The main objection to infrared use was that the user could be readily spotted by a foe similarly equipped with infrared instruments or detection equipment. Although British and American forces did employ infrared searchlights in Europe during World War II, owing to priorities that had been established for weapon-mounted instruments in the South Pacific, use of such devices following Allied

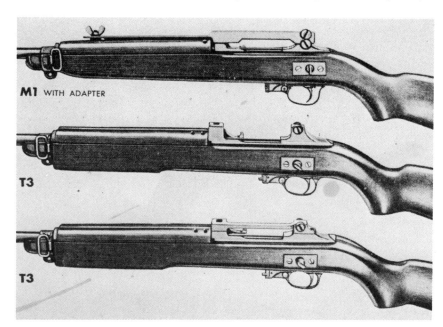

T3 Carbines developed for use with the Sniperscope during WW II. An adapter was eventually designed to mount the infra-red assembly on conventional carbines. Photo Credit: U.S. Army.

invasion of the Continent was nonexistent or at best extremely limited.

On the original Sniperscope M1 and the first issue of Sniperscope M2, the light source lamp was mounted below the carbine on the stock using a mounting bracket with grip and switch for operating the light source. Field reports indicated that such mounting was not entirely satisfactory. Modification Work Order ENG 9340-1 provided for relocation of the lamp above the telescope to provide increased use of cover and decreased reflection from brush and grass particularly when sighting and firing from a prone position. The switch for actuating the infrared unit was then incorporated directly into the light source mechanism.

Existing M1 and early M2 models thus modified were fitted with a lamp mounting clamp on top of the telescope housing. On later M2 models, this clamp was to serve as a holder for the power cable as well.

With the light source so mounted, the requirement for a special stock was eliminated. Consequently, following the end of the war, Carbine, Caliber .30, M3 was adopted and standardized. The M3 carbine, while still utilizing a special receiver for mounting the electronic telescope, was now fitted with a conventional stock typical of those employed with the selective-fire M2 carbines.

Concurrent with standardization of the Carbine, M3, a flash hider (T23), adjudged to be 95 percent effective in hiding muzzle flash, was adopted for use with Sniperscope units and selective-fire M2

carbines. The flash hider, supplied as an accessory with M2 Sniperscopes, was not supplied with the M1 variant as originally issued.

Sniperscope M1 bore serial numbers on each major component. The M1 telescope serial number, which had commenced with number 1, was considered the instrument serial number. Sniperscope M2 had only one serial number, located on the telescope. Early variants were numbered beginning with 5001.

Following sustained test and field trials, it was found that elimination of the forearm grip made handling extremely difficult for the operator during periods of prolonged scanning. Later models of Sniperscope M2 have a hand grip mounted under the carbine fore-end. The hand grip, acting as a handle, permitted greater weapon stability when sighting, especially during periods of full-automatic fire. The switch for operating the light source was removed from the lamp and incorporated into the revised grip.

In conjunction with reestablishment of a hand grip, an adapter mounting which permitted affixing a Sniperscope to any standard carbine was formulated. Henceforth, Sniperscope mounting could be effected by an operator or a unit armorer using basic hand tools. With production of special carbine receivers terminated, Sniperscopes could be readily employed on all .30 caliber carbines. The later, or last-issue M2 Sniperscopes, bear serial numbers from M2-1-50 through M2-1700-50.

In the years immediately following World War II, experiment and development of small-arms

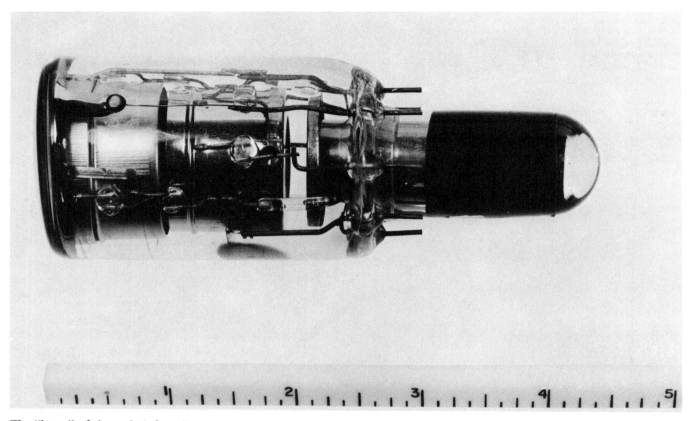

The "heart" of the early infrared system; RCA IP25A image converter tube. Photo Credit: U.S. Army.

T3 carbine with bridge-mount and first issue M2 Sniperscope mounting the light-source lamp below the stock. Photo Credit: U.S. Army.

A 25th Infantry Division rifleman equipped with the M2 infrared unit and modified-mount T3 carbine, Korea, August 1950. Photo Credit: U.S. Army.

infrared units was to continue at a vigorous pace. In some quarters of the Army, applying the Sniperscope to the Rifle Cal. .30 M1, Garand was being pushed. While infrared mounting was thoroughly tested with the M1 Garand, the use of the available night-vision instruments was to remain with the carbine.

The principal reason for this decision rested with the considerable weight of existing devices. The electronic telescope and light source weighed about five pounds, with the power supply adding another fifteen pounds. A carbine with a fully loaded 30-round magazine closely approximated 5.53 pounds, with an overall length of 35.58 inches. In comparison, the M1 Garand at 9.5 pounds and a length of 43.60 inches was deemed excessively heavy and unwieldy with the addition of infrared equipment. Although comparative accuracy between the carbine and M1 was heavily in favor of the latter, the carbine, having a full-automatic fire option and reasonable weight, was to see its retention as companion to the Sniperscope through the Korean War as well.

When the Peoples Army of North Korea assumed a totally aggressive posture, pouring across the 38th Parallel in mid-1950, the Armed Forces of the U.S. were to find themselves involved shortly thereafter in the initial concept of Limited Warfare, or as it was then considered in some quarters, a "Police Action."

By whatever guise or name, men were called from their short-lived peacetime routines, while vast quantities of equipment and weapons stockpiled in Ordnance storage depots were brought into a state of combat readiness. With few exceptions, the tools of war employed by the U.S. during World War II were brought to bear against the North Korean invaders with the Republic of South Korea as the battleground.

Included, of course, were existing M1 and M2 infrared Sniperscopes and what was to become the last in the series of carbine-mounted units, the "Set No. 1/M3 20,000 volt" Sniperscope that had been developed and introduced as operational, concurrent with initial United States Korean involvement. Although identical in principle to its predecessors, the new device provided increased image clarity, resolution, and brightness. Of particular significance was extension of the effective range to almost double that of the M2 variant under optimum conditions.

The primary difference of M3 operation consisted of the addition of a reticle rheostat and improved electrostatic focus which, in effect, gave the operator greater fine adjustment latitude. The rheostat, located on the right side of the light source, permitted the operator to make adjustments commensurate with the brightness necessary for sighting.

The electrostatic focus (potentiometer) located opposite of the rheostat made effective focusing of the telescope possible during day or night. As the operator looked through the telescope, the electrostatic focus knob was rotated until the viewing image was sharpest.

Unlike the earlier M1 and M2 units which incorporated a desiccant inside the electronic telescope, the M3 possessed an external desiccant assembly which could be removed. The desiccant, a silica gel, was blue when completely effective. When it turned pink, it had absorbed moisture from the telescope and was changed or restored. Desiccant effectiveness could be restored by baking at 250 degrees Fahrenheit until the blue color returned.

Incorporation of an improved desiccant assembly was fostered by the experience gained from severe moisture conditions during initial infrared use in the Pacific. Prolonged jungle use had wrought havoc on the early electronic mechanism.

As a further protective measure, the power pack and battery assembly were now carried in a special neoprene-coated, water- and fungus-proofed knapsack-type carrying case. By comparison, earlier units were toted about in regulation knapsacks made of ordinary web material. A special bracket included with M3 equipment permitted mounting the instrument on a 3.5 rocket launcher for night sighting.

Specific operation and deployment techniques for the M3 units appeared in Department of the Army Technical Manual TM 5-9342, *Operation and Maintenance Instructions for Sniperscope Infrared Set No. 1, 20,000 Volts,* dated August 1951.

GENERAL

(1) **Uses.** The sniperscope is useful in both offensive and defensive night operations. It is most effective on dark nights, but may be used in moonlight. The uses of the sniperscope are dependent on the originality, initiative, and resourcefulness of local commanders responsible for specific operations.

(2) **Operator's vision.** An operator using the sniperscope should have normal vision. He should adapt his eyes before leaving on a night mission by subjecting his eyes to complete darkness for about 30 minutes beforehand. If this is impossible, he should avoid looking at lights around him. Wearing red goggles helps adapt eyes to darkness. Covering one eye to keep out the light will dark-adapt that eye.

Defensive Uses

The sniperscope is used most effectively in perimeter defense and in establishing general outpost lines at night. The use of sniperscopes in pairs is desirable to obtain cross illumination and additional range.

(1) It can direct the fire of machine guns and other weapons. One sniperscope between a pair of machine guns can effectively direct fire along protective lines and save ammunition. Tracer ammunition is often used from sniperscopes to point out targets to other weapons.

(2) When trip flares and trip grenades are used in setting up a perimeter defense at night, the sniperscope is used to scan the area where the flare or grenade was fired.

(3) Antitank-gun squads often use it for covering roads and possible tank approaches.

Marine Corps riflemen receiving instruction in use of the M1 Sniperscope during the Korean Conflict. Photo Credit: U.S. Army.

(4) Forward observers can warn of approaching enemy patrols and direct mortar fire on such groups. Within signaling range of sniperscopes, rearward sniperscope operators must be able to receive and transmit signals received from such observation posts.

(5) The sniperscope may be used to detect enemy use of similar devices.

Offensive Uses

In offensive night operations, it may be used for infiltration; attack and advance through woods, jungle, or rough terrain; attack of fortified positions; or combat in cities and towns.

(1) Night combat and reconnaissance patrols use the sniperscope for detecting and bypassing or destroying enemy patrols.

(2) Sniperscope "looking and listening" posts at critical points behind enemy lines provide accurate means of observing and counting enemy traffic and movement.

(3) Effectiveness of ambushes can be increased by using the sniperscope to observe the ambushed party. The enemy party and its weapons can be reconnoitered and the most favorable moment to open fire can be chosen. Exploitation of the ambush can be increased by observing the defensive measures taken by the enemy after the action has begun.

Concealment

Concealment afforded by trees, bushes, and underbrush effectively screens personnel because infrared light is reflected from vegetation with such intensity that objects or persons behind it are not readily discovered by the use of a single device. Movements of foliage and of brush by concealed troops is, however, easily detected.

Cross Illumination

Cross illumination is effective in reducing glare from vegetation and the discovering of concealed objects or personnel. For example, when an infrared light is shone at about right angles to the line of sight of a telescopic viewer, objects or persons hidden in brush appear as brighter objects against a darker background. For this reason, sniperscopes should be employed in pairs, whenever possible.

Signaling

Sniperscopes are useful for secret communication at night. The Morse code can be transmitted between two sniperscopes by turning the lamp ON and OFF. Signaling is possible at ranges of 1,000 yards or more.

Effect Of Ammunition

The firing of ball ammunition from the carbine of the sniperscope has little effect on the operator's vision. The firing of tracer ammunition causes streaks to appear on the viewing screen, because the bright

The improved M2 infrared unit shown during a field demonstration in Korea. As redesigned, the infrared light source (lamp) was positioned above the telescope to provide increased use of cover and decreased reflection from brush and grass when sighting from the prone position. Photo Credit: U.S. Army.

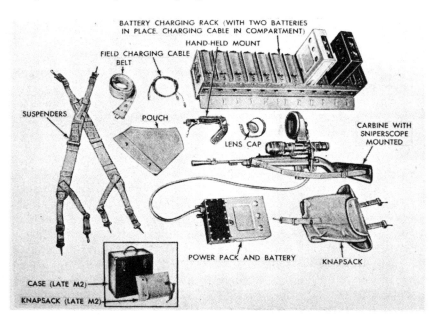

Sniperscope M2 with carrying cases and various accessories. This variant has the rotary light-source switch which was designed for use with M1 and M2 units. No hand grip was used with this model. Photo Credit: U.S. Army.

Army marksman firing from a defensive position in Korea. The M2 infrared device has the top-mount lamp assembly. Photo Credit: U.S. Army.

flash of light directly in front of the telescope causes the screen to give off a bright glow.

Warning:

Always look through the telescope for enemy infrared before turning on the light source. Remember that your lamp is visible to enemy using infrared equipment.

A somewhat optimistic performance chart relating to M3 Sniperscope use in Korea was established by The Department of the Army in 1951. Interestingly, there remains considerable difference of opinion among those having actual combat experience with such devices.

PERFORMANCE CHART

Instrument Range. A crouching man wearing fatigue clothing and moving at a 45 degree angle to the line of sight can be detected at 125 yards against an open background on a moonless night.

Visual Security. The light source cannot be detected from distances greater than seventeen yards by a dark adapted observer who is unaware of the location of the light source.

Accuracy of Fire. The accuracy of fire depends on the accuracy of the carbine, the skill of the operator, and the telescope adjustment.

Battery. The life of a charge on the battery depends on the use to which the sniperscope is put. However, unless the use is extremely heavy, one charge should last throughout the night.

Temperature Range. The components of the sniperscope, less batteries, are made to operate at temperatures from –65°F to +140°F. However, because of the limitations of the battery at subzero temperatures, the minimum operable temperature at which the instrument is effective is 0°F.

Filter. The filter should last indefinitely with proper care.

Angle of View. 14° or 250 mils.

Compared to the receptive attitude of American combat forces in the Pacific during World War II, when infrared could have weighed one hundred pounds and still been most welcome, such devices were not popular in Korea. Objections to their use were manifold, and as reports indicate, they were centered on their bulk and susceptibility to damage during combat.

Although carbine-mounted infrared was utilized with varying results, its most practical application came late in the conflict when activity was relegated to trench lines and bunkers with more frequent use of the night-vision equipment in a defensive posture. The use of similar devices by North Korean and Chinese forces has not been substantiated even at this late date. The U.S.S.R., principal arms supplier to the Communist armies in Korea, was known to have operational infrared devices for small arms, however.

Model M2 and M3 Sniperscopes were issued to all branches of the Armed Forces in Korea. Major uses, other than by the Air Force for guarding aircraft installations, was by Army and Marine Corps combat troops. The designation "Sniperscope," actually a misnomer, did not require a specially trained marksman or sniper for satisfactory operation. In reality, the use of snipers in Korea, other than the highly respected Marine Corps Scout-Snipers, was an infrequent occurrence. Despite rather extensive use of infrared, few men participating in the Korean Conflict were aware that American Forces possessed a night-vision capability.

The last of the carbine-mounted infrared units (i.e., the M3) were pressed into service during the mid-1960s when they were furnished to indigenous troops in Vietnam for use against the Vietcong et al.

Following the Korean War, development work continued on weapon-mounted infrared units with primary efforts directed at improving their effective range as well as elimination of the cumbersome power pack. By the late 1950s, satisfactory devices meeting both criteria were developed for use with the M1 Garand.

Improved variants, designated T-1, Infrared Weapon Sight, were issued in limited quantities for the M1 Garand (Special), and later with its successor, the 7.62mm, M14 rifle in the early 1960s. Such units consisted of an infrared light source, the image-forming telescope, and, unquestionably the most significant aspect of the new devices, an integral, miniaturized high-voltage power unit which obviated the need for an awkward knapsack-carried power source. Power, supplied by a rechargeable 6 VDC Nicad battery, could now be easily carried by the operator by affixing it to his cartridge belt.

Unlike the M1 Garand which necessitated a special receiver mounting, ordnance design had provided for ready attachment of accessory devices such as infrared and telescopic weapon sights by incorporating a bracket-mounting groove and screw recess on the left side of the M14 receiver. As compared to the twenty-eight- to thirty-pound Korean War variants, the new Infrared Weapon Sight was vastly improved from this standpoint alone.

A 12-battery charging rack (M2) supplied as part of the Sniperscope maintenance equipment. A portable engine generator was used to supply the current for field charging the batteries. In forward areas, when necessary, the battery could be charged from a 6-volt vehicle generator by using a cable furnished with the Sniperscope. The Army Ordnance technician is shown separating a power pack from the 6-volt battery (Korea). Photo Credit: U.S. Army.

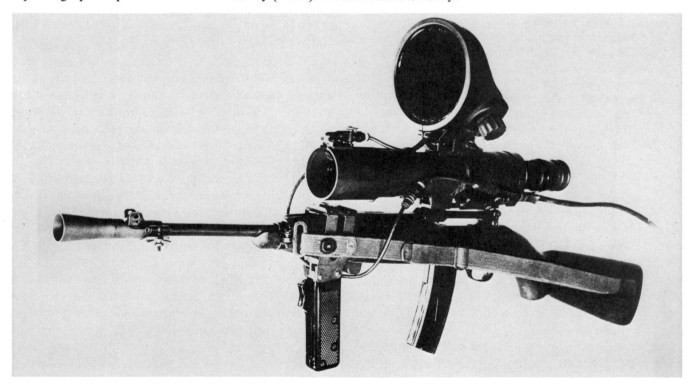

The last of the carbine-mounted infrared units, the M3 Sniperscope. Officially designated, Sniperscope Infrared Set No. 1, 20,000 volts, the M3 was manufactured by the American Optical Co., and Capehart-Farnsworth beginning about 1951. Photo Credit: Sam Bases.

Designed to replace the M2 infrared unit, the range of the M3 was approximately 400 feet with a fresh battery and eyes fully adapted to the dark. Photo Credit: U.S. Army.

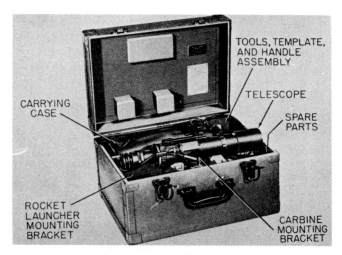

CARRYING CASE

TOOLS, TEMPLATE, AND HANDLE ASSEMBLY

TELESCOPE

SPARE PARTS

ROCKET LAUNCHER MOUNTING BRACKET

CARBINE MOUNTING BRACKET

A chest issued for the M3 Sniperscope and supporting equipment was intended primarily for storage and shipping. Photo Credit: U.S. Army.

Designed for use in temperatures ranging from minus twenty-five degrees to plus 115 degrees Fahrenheit, pertinent dimensions for the primary unit were thirteen by four and one-half by eleven inches. Effective at ranges approximating 200 meters under optimum conditions, the electronic telescope possessed 4.5X magnification.

Beginning in 1961, the improved Infrared Weapon Sights were furnished to the U.S. Army by its prime contractors, Varo Inc., of Garland, Texas, and Polan Industries, Inc., of Huntington, West Virginia. The sights were known as Models 9903 and P-155, respectively.

Subsequent and first combat use of the Infrared Weapon Sights by U.S. Special Forces units in Southeast Asia during the early 1960s revealed that reflections from foliage, grass, and branches restricted ranges significantly. Effective coverage up to 250 meters was achieved over river surfaces, and up to 150 meters over rice paddies. However, in grassy areas, where the view was partly obstructed by blades of grass and weeds, range was limited to only one hundred meters. Interestingly, the basis for original complaints registered during initial infrared use occurred in the Pacific in World War II.

Combat reports indicate that infrared use was most effective on clear, dark nights. Soft natural light, such as twilight, dawn, bright moonlight, or starlight, caused a hazy glow in the electronic telescope, thereby reducing image clarity.

By this time, Russian development, use, and supply of night-vision equipment to Communist-Bloc allies was well known to the U.S. military.

As with all infrared, an enemy soldier also equipped with an infrared weapons sight or detection viewer could pick up the beam projected by the light source and accurately pinpoint its location. General knowledge of this fact among U.S. ground forces engaged in Southeast Asia was to cause considerable concern during field operations employing Infrared Weapon Sights. Such devices were to be both the principal and the last in the long series of small-arms-mounted infrared devices utilized by U.S. forces.

With full cognizance of infrared limitations, in 1955 Army Warfare Vision personnel began development of light-amplifying tubes which would enable combat troops to fight more effectively at night with a passive system which could not be detected by the enemy.

Night-vision scientists produced and successfully demonstrated a two-stage cascade image-intensifier tube in 1957 whereby funds were allocated to enable them to continue their efforts. The need for passive night-observation devices was further emphasized in 1961 by U.S. Special Forces, anti-guerrilla warfare advisors, and Department of Defense studies. A special presidential advisory committee identified the lack of night-fighting capability as a serious drawback in the Army's preparedness for limited warfare.

Following acceleration of the night-vision program, based on tests of a feasibility model built in-house at the Night Vision Laboratory, a contract for Engineer Design models was awarded to the Bell & Howell Company in June 1962.

Production contracts for an Individual Weapons Night Vision Sight (Small Starlight Scope) were awarded to Electro-Optical Systems Inc. (a subsidiary of Xerox), in September 1964. In November 1965, the program was transferred from the Army Engineer Research and Development Laboratories and became a major element of the Army Electronics Command's Combat Surveillance, Night Vision and Target Acquisition Laboratories complex (ECOM).

At the same time, the Army Materiel Command, parent organization of ECOM, created a night-vision project-manager's office at Fort Belvoir, Virginia, to speed production of night-vision equipment as warranted. As a result of increased military activity in Southeast Asia (Vietnam), additional production contracts for Starlight Scopes manufacture were given to Varo, Inc., in June 1967.

Though reasonably effective in a combat environment, the cumbersome nature of the early carbine-mounted infrared units limited their value as an attack weapon. The most practical application came with the use of night-vision equipment in a defensive posture. Photo Credit: U.S. Army.

An Army ordnance sergeant with the M3 infrared weapon sight, Korea, June 1953. Photo Credit: U.S. Army.

The "Set No. 1/M3 20,000 Volt" infrared Sniperscope—an alternate view. The battery and power pack were strapped together and carried in a knapsack-type case. Held on the operator's back by shoulder straps, the neoprene-coated case was water and fungus-proofed. Photo Credit: U.S. Army.

Despite its vintage, a limited number of M3 infrared units were employed by South Vietnamese troops during early action against the Viet Cong. Photo Credit: U.S. Army.

Efforts directed at eliminating the cumbersome power pack and increasing the effective range of small arms infrared units resulted in the development of a satisfactory device for use with the M1 Garand during the late 1950s. Photo Credit: U.S. Army.

The heart of the new night-vision systems, the image-intensifier tube, consisted of three modular sections which are mechanically and optically coupled together to form a three-stage intensifier. The three modules with the multiplier sections of the high-voltage power supply are completely encapsulated; a recessed connector is provided for plug-in of the power-supply oscillator assembly.

The original 25mm image-intensifier tube used in the Small Starlight Scope and the Crew Served Weapon Sight was approximately seven inches in length and two and three-fourths inches in diameter. Contractors engaged in production of the first-generation image-intensification tubes were Machlett, RCA, ITT, and Varo.

Basically, such equipment permitted viewing at night without the aid of any light source other than the dim glow of the moon, stars, or even faint sky glow. Light from the night sky strikes the end of the objective tube. A "fiber optic"—a bundle of individual glass fibers—traps the light, bringing it into the tube where it strikes a photoemissive surface. The tube then discharges electrons into a vacuum. These electrons, energized by 15,000 volts of electricity, strike a screen similar to a television picture tube, giving off light. This process is repeated twice so that the electrons are energized to the point that when they strike the final screen near the eyepiece, the image is 40,000 times brighter than when it entered the tube.

The Small Starlight Scope could be hand-held for visual observation or, in conjunction with appropriate weapons adapter brackets, could be mounted on the M14 and M16 rifles. The larger sized scope was used on crew-served weapons, such as machine guns and recoilless rifles.

Although operational and dimensional characteristics were to vary somewhat through successive development, description of the original Starlight Scope, small hand-held or individual weapons-mounted units were set forth as follows:

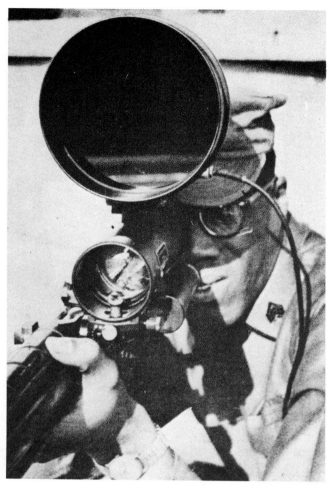

Marine Corps rifleman with an Infrared Weapon sight and M14 rifle. Photo Credit: U.S. Marine Corps.

Starlight Scope

Magnification .... 4 power
Field of view .... 171 mils (average)
Eyepiece focus .... +4 to -4 diopters
Objective lens focus .... 4 meters to infinity
Weight .... 5 pounds, 14 3/4 ounces
Length .... 18.50 inches
Width .... 3.35 inches
Height .... 5.52 inches
Range .... Dependent on ambient light level

Operating temperature ...... -65° to +125°F at humidity ranging from 0 to 100 percent

Battery

Type .... BA 1100 – u Mercury
Voltage 6.75
Use life .... Approximately 100 hours
Shelf life .... 2 years at optimum storage temperature at 70°F.

The function of the Starlight Scope was to provide an efficient viewing capability during night-combat operations. While the sight would not afford the clarity of daylight vision, a trained operator could see well enough to detect and fire on enemy targets while remaining free from detection by visual or electronic means. The Starlight Scope, however, was not without limitations.

An Army technician at Ft. Ord, California in June 1961 is shown with a pilot model of the Infrared Weapons Sight eventually employed by U.S. combat forces in Southeast Asia. Infrared binoculars are attached to his helmet. Photo Credit: U.S. Army.

The AN/PAS-4 Infrared Weapon Sight produced by Varo, Inc., and Polan Industries as used by Army and Marine Corps troops in Vietnam. Though utilized primarily with the M14 rifle, the sight could be adapted to the M16 with a special mount. Photo Credit: Sam Bases.

Using ambient light from the night sky, it would not function under absolute darkness. Optimum performance could only be expected on bright, moonlit nights. When the sky was overcast or the ambient light level low, the viewing capabilities of the Starlight Scope were greatly increased by the use of flares or illuminating shells on the flank or to the rear as circumstances warranted.

Fog, smoke, dust, and rain had an adverse effect on the instrument's viewing capability, decreasing both the range and resolution. Eye fatigue became a serious consideration when the scope was employed for extended periods. A point of instruction specified graduated periods of exposure beginning with ten minutes followed by a rest period of approximately fifteen minutes. After several periods of viewing, the time limit was extended. It was further recommended that the operator alternate viewing eyes frequently.

The greatest sensitivity of the Starlight Scope rested with its susceptibility to damage from exposure of the objective lens to bright light such as direct sunlight. It was mandatory to have the lens cover in position during daylight hours. When inadvertently exposed to bright light during night operations, the sight would automatically switch itself off to prevent damage to the operator's eye and to the image intensifier tube. When traversed to a darker area, the sight would automatically

turn on and normal operation could be resumed.

Despite careful and extensive instruction to destroy the Starlight Scope by small-arms fire, fragmentation, or thermite grenades when capture or loss was imminent, owing to combat circumstances and operator attrition, a number of these sights were captured and redirected against U.S. Forces by Vietcong and North Vietnamese combatants.

Although Starlight Scope variants were utilized in a myriad of applications by all branches of U.S. forces in Southeast Asia, mounting such devices on special sniping rifles provided an excellent means of achieving first round hits during periods of darkness.

The Infrared Weapons Sight, prior to its gradual replacement by the Starlight Scope, had been employed to some extent in early loosely organized sniping operations. However, not until an effective sniping program was finally instituted in Vietnam in the late 1960s did the significance of night-vision sighting reach practical realization in this capacity. Concurrent with organized sniper use and deployment, the improved AN/PVS-2 Starlight Scope became the principal night-vision instrument utilized by both Army and Marine Corps marksmen with telling effect.

The 9th Infantry Division, considered a trend-setter in Army sniper use and deployment in Vietnam, included night-firing instruction in its sniping

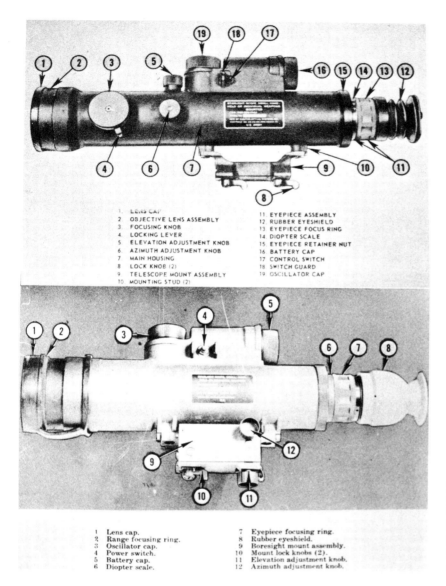

1. LENS CAP
2. OBJECTIVE LENS ASSEMBLY
3. FOCUSING KNOB
4. LOCKING LEVER
5. ELEVATION ADJUSTMENT KNOB
6. AZIMUTH ADJUSTMENT KNOB
7. MAIN HOUSING
8. LOCK KNOB (2)
9. TELESCOPE MOUNT ASSEMBLY
10. MOUNTING STUD (2)
11. EYEPIECE ASSEMBLY
12. RUBBER EYESHIELD
13. EYEPIECE FOCUS RING
14. DIOPTER SCALE
15. EYEPIECE RETAINER NUT
16. BATTERY CAP
17. CONTROL SWITCH
18. SWITCH GUARD
19. OSCILLATOR CAP

1 Lens cap.
2 Range focusing ring.
3 Oscillator cap.
4 Power switch.
5 Battery cap.
6 Diopter scale.
7 Eyepiece focusing ring.
8 Rubber eyeshield.
9 Boresight mount assembly.
10 Mount lock knobs (2).
11 Elevation adjustment knob.
12 Azimuth adjustment knob.

A comparative view of the original AN/PVS-1 Starlight Scope, fielded for use in Southeast Asia (top) and its eventual successor, the AN/PVS-2. The improved model provided better focusing characteristics and a clearer sight reticle. Photo Credit: U.S. Army.

syllabus. In addition to proficiency with the telescopic sight, each candidate learned to engage targets with the Starlight Scope at ranges of 150, 300, and 600 meters.

Students bring a Starlight Scope and mount to the sniper school when they report for training. The sight is mounted on the rifle and zeroed during training. The sniper retains that scope/rifle combination during subsequent operations. This procedure assures retention of zero even when the sight is dismounted during daylight operations and remounted for night operations.

Successful night-sniper deployment, although varied, included two particularly effective methods as recorded by Major Robert G. Hilchey in 9th Division records.

A xenon searchlight has been used to covertly illuminate an area with pink light. The Starlight Scope is sensitive to a portion of the infrared band that is pink and near the visible light portion of the spectrum. By using a pink filter on a xenon searchlight, an area can be illuminated with invisible light that registers in the Starlight Scope. This phenomena has been used successfully in two types of sniper activity: berm security and ambush operations.

Successful ambushes have been conducted by placing a searchlight-equipped one-fourth ton vehicle 1,200 to 1,500 meters from a road intersection. Snipers equipped with Starlight Scopes were placed 300 meters from the intersection. Maintaining radio contact with the searchlight operator, the snipers controlled the covert illumination of the intersection and surrounding areas. When Viet Cong appeared in the kill zone they were easily engaged by the sniper team. It has been found that by off-setting the sniper

Intensifier Tube

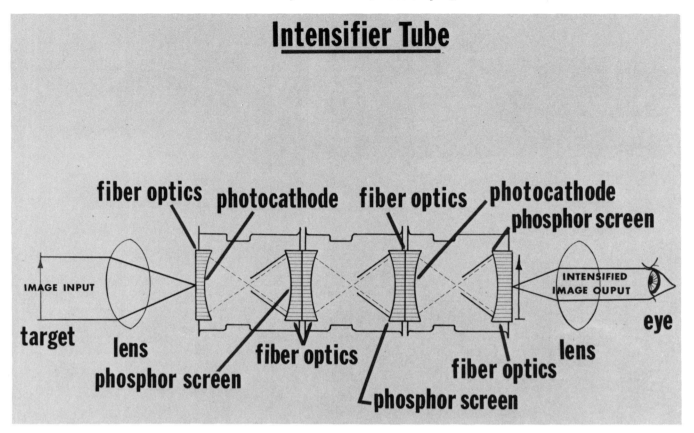

A schematic of the first generation Image Intensifier Tube, the prime component in the Starlight Scope night-vision system. Photo Credit: U.S. Army.

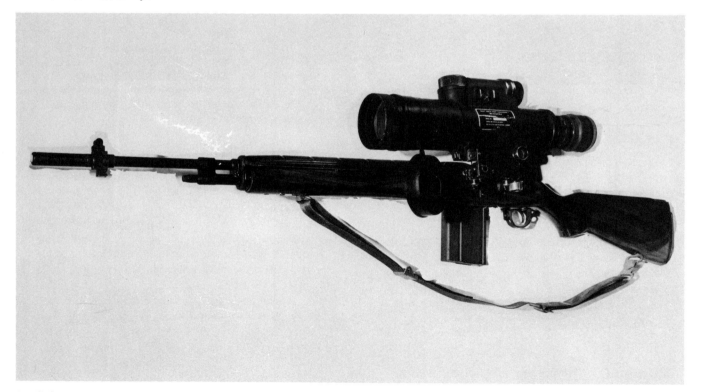

Starlight Scope variants were utilized by all branches of U.S. forces in Southeast Asia. Mounting such devices on special sniping rifles provided an excellent means of achieving first-round hits during periods of darkness. The M14 depicted mounts an AN/PVS-2 night-vision sight. Photo Credit: Sam Bases.

A 9th Infantry Division sniper attaches the AN/PVS-2 Starlight Scope to his XM21 rifle for night operations in the Mekong Delta. Photo Credit: U.S. Army.

Marine sniper with M16-mounted Starlight Scope taking aim at dusk during Operation Shelby south of Da Nang, September 1967. Photo Credit: U.S. Marine Corps.

A night scene as viewed through a Starlight Scope. Photo Credit: U.S. Army.

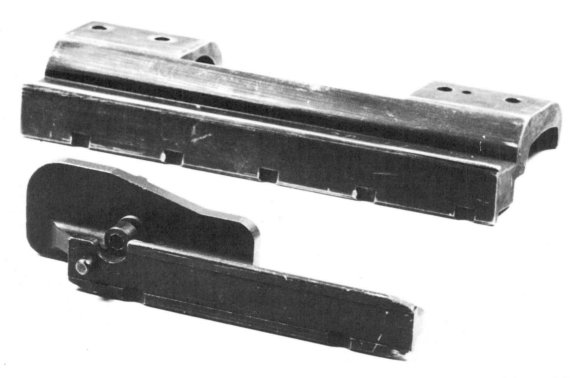

M14 night-vision sight adapter bracket (bottom) and a mount fabricated by the USAMTU to permit use of the Starlight Scope with the Winchester Model 70 rifle. The special mount was designed to fit on top of the receiver. Prior to 1970, bolt-action rifles used for sniping in Vietnam were without a night capability. Photo Credit: Lieutenant Colonel F. B. Conway (Retired).

Sections of one-inch-thick armor plate were used as targets for zeroing the night-vision system in darkness. The impact of the bullet against the plate when viewed at night through the Starlight Scope produced a very bright light or flash. Photo Credit: U.S. Army.

Silhouetted against the evening sky, a Starlight Scope–equipped Army marksman prepares for night operations in the delta. Before the buildup of American troops in Vietnam, it was said that "The night belonged to the Viet Cong." But as the use of efficient night-vision equipment mounted, the VC could no longer use darkness with impunity. Photo Credit: U.S. Army.

Chinese Communist 7.62 x 39mm Type-56 Carbine as fitted with an M3 infrared Sniperscope by the Viet Cong. Captured U.S. night-vision sights were highly prized by the Viet Cong and North Vietnamese combatants. Photo Credit: "Simonov SKS-45 Type Carbines" by Lamont & Fuller.

teams from the searchlight and placing the searchlight and one-fourth ton vehicle in a position remote from the ambush site, the enemy in the kill zone were not alerted by the noise of the running vehicle engine.

The pink light/sniper combination has been successfully employed in base camp security operations. The searchlight, mounted on a one-fourth ton vehicle, responds to radio equipped sniper teams in position either on the berm or on ambush positions outside the berm. The background noise of a fixed base camp effectively conceals the noise of engine and activity of the searchlight crew. In forward base camp, the searchlight remains in the center of the base camp and, by swinging its beam through 360 degrees, covertly illuminates avenues of approach into the position. With this method it is again essential that the sniper team maintain radio contact with the searchlight crew. The pink light is particularly useful during the dark of the moon period.

The following data reflects 9th Division sniper results during the period 1 January 1969 through 10 March 1969.

The crew-served weapon sight AN/TVS-5 (top), and the individual-served weapon sight AN/PVS-4. The second generation Starlight Scopes are currently issued to U.S. Armed Forces on a worldwide basis. Photo Credit: Excalibur Enterprises.

The AN/PVS-4 Starlight Scope mounted on the M16 rifle. Photo Credit: Excalibur Enterprises.

Kills in relation to time of day:

Kills	Time of Day
7	0600–1800
89	1800–2100
68	2100–2400
18	0001–0600

In 1970, based on Army results of extensive night sniping, development of a match grade Thermoluminescent 7.62mm round for use in conjunction with the Starlight Scope was requested. The special round, to be visible only when viewed through the Starlight Scope, would in concept permit observing the round in flight and adjustments to the point of impact should a second or third round be required. Subsequent

development and/or use remains obscure, however.

Use of the specially prepared M14 rifle (XM21) for sniping purposes was to provide the Army with a highly efficient night-sniping instrument as well. Marine Corps snipers, on the other hand, utilizing the 7.26mm M40 bolt-action rifle (Remington) as their primary sniping arm, were, by necessity, to employ regular-issue M14 and M16 rifles for mounting the Starlight Scope during sniper deployment. Active pursuance of a satisfactory mount bracket to permit Starlight Scope mounting to the M40 commenced late in 1969.

With the activity of the VC at high level during periods of darkness, the effectiveness of the Starlight Scope, particularly in the hands of a skilled sniper, was to prove invaluable by any standards.

Chapter 14 ◆◆

Almost A Sniping Arm—The M16

By the time the last combat forces had been withdrawn from Vietnam, the 5.56mm, M16A1 rifle manufactured by the Colt Firearms Division, Colt Industries, had emerged as the standard U.S. infantry weapon. From the standpoint of sniper use, contrary to most beliefs, the M16 did receive official consideration as a sniping arm, but could not match the consistent long-range accuracy of the M14, as proven conclusively when the M16 was subjected to innumerable tests over an extended period by various agencies. As a result, the specially prepared M14 rifle (M21) evolved as the principal sniping arm of the U.S. Army following military operations in Southeast Asia.

Unsuited as the M16 may have been for specialized long-range shooting, the right combination of marksman, rifle, ammunition, and telescope accounted for documented hits at ranges up to 700 meters. Nevertheless, results such as this were far from common.

For the sake of clarification, when the M16 came into Army use in Vietnam, it was considered a special item and therefore given an XM designation. As such it differed from the original Air Force M16 with the addition of a bolt-closing device and bore the designation XM16E1. On 23 February 1967, it was made Standard A and designated M16A1 as subsequently issued for Army use.

As compared to the M14, rather simple score mounts could be readily attached to the M16's integral carrying handle directly over the receiver

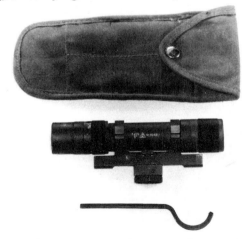

A Marine Corps 3 power telescopic sight manufactured by the A.I. firm (the Netherlands) and mounting made by Colt for the M16 as issued to USMC snipers for use in Vietnam during the mid-1960s. A scope-adjusting tool and web carrying case with cartridge belt hooks were a part of this issue. Photo Credit: Peter R. Senich.

Left view of a Colt rifle with the 3 power scope attached to the carrying handle. Photo Credit: U.S. Army.

A USAMTU gunsmith, Raymond Behnay (Master Sergeant, Retired), fabricated M16 telescope mounts, designed to accommodate the M84 telescope with Weaver rings, at his own expense for Army sniper use in RVN. Photo Credit: Lieutenant Colonel F. B. Conway (Retired).

The Colt Industries 3 power telescopic sight, originally made for the commercial market, was typical of those sights used extensively on M16 rifles with Army and Marine Corps snipers in Southeast Asia. Photo Credit: Peter R. Senich.

Cook mount with Weaver rings issued in 1967 for mounting the M84 telescope to the M16 rifle. The threaded knob secured the rib to the M16 carrying handle. Photo Credit: Lieutenant Colonel F. B. Conway (Retired).

The Behnay M16 telescope mount removed from the rifle. Photo Credit: Lieutenant Colonel F. B. Conway (Retired).

in-line with the bore. With this advantage, a considerable number of telescopic-sighted M16s were pressed into service in Vietnam well in advance of the match-grade M14s, the highly sophisticated XM21 system, and an organized sniping program.

As reports from this period indicate, 2.2 power M84 and 3 power Colt Realist scopes saw most frequent use. However, with telescopic sights in short supply on an overall basis, commercial sights were brought from the States or procured from the PX by enterprising units and individuals. Although military regulations prohibited bringing personal weapons to Southeast Asia, rifle scopes were not included. Consequently, a number of M16 sniping weapons were fielded under these circumstances.

Even though the Army's decision to "go with accurized M14s" for specialized sniper use had been implemented during the late 1960s, considerable efforts to increase the M16's long-range capabilities—based on the evaluations of heavy

The Cook M16 telescope mount removed from the rifle. Photo Credit: Lieutenant Colonel F. B. Conway (Retired).

An M16 scope mounting, developed and fielded for a combined Colt-Army sniper program, extended beyond the carrying handle to provide a balance point for the rifle and extra support to the scope. Photo Credit: Lieutenant Colonel F. B. Conway (Retired).

Marine Corps riflemen with Starlight Scope–equipped M16s prepare for night activity in Vietnam. The rifle (top) mounts an original night-vision variant with an improved AN/PVS-2 in use on the lower weapon. Photo Credit: U.S. Marine Corps.

Experimental Colt M16 sniper rifles mounting Realist autoranging telescope (ART) and Sionics (MAC) MAW-A1 noise suppressors. A number of special rifles, including heavy barrel variants, were developed by Colt to evaluate the M16's suitability for Army sniper use in Southeast Asia. Photo Credit: U.S. Army.

Starlight Scope AN/PVS-4 mounted to an M16A1 rifle for evaluation by the Army Infantry Board in 1974. Photo Credit: U.S. Army.

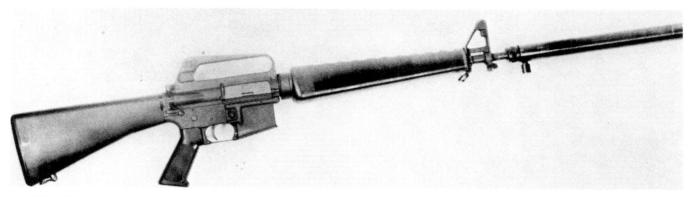

An M16 rifle fitted with the MAW-A1 Noise Suppressor. The Sionics attachment became the "standard suppressor" for use with the M16 system in Southeast Asia. Photo Credit: J. David Truby.

Patrolling in Vietnam. The M16 rifle is equipped with a noise suppressor, a part of the unconventional methods and hardware developed for use in Southeast Asia. Suppressed M16s were used to some extent by ground combat forces mainly for long-range recon patrols and ambush situations. At one point, there existed three suppressor variants for the M16: the M4, developed by the U.S. Army Human Engineering Lab (HEL); the Frankford Arsenal XM model; and the Sionics designed MAW series. From all accounts, however, the Sionics MAW-A1 suppressor emerged as both superior, and most frequently used with the M16A1 rifle. Photo Credit: U.S. Army.

A reconnaissance team member shown moving through the high grass. A suppressor is attached to his rifle. Should any period stand as the Golden Age of Silencers, it would certainly be the era of U.S. military involvement in Southeast Asia when a variety of silencer-equipped weapons were employed by "regular and covertly regular U.S. military personnel" for special operations in Laos, Vietnam, and Cambodia. Photo Credit: U.S. Army.

The AVN/PVS-4 is shown in use by an Army rifleman during suitability testing in early 1975. Photo Credit: U.S. Army.

Smith & Wesson Star-Tron passive night-vision riflescope with a Colt AR-15 semiautomatic rifle. Photo Credit: Smith & Wesson.

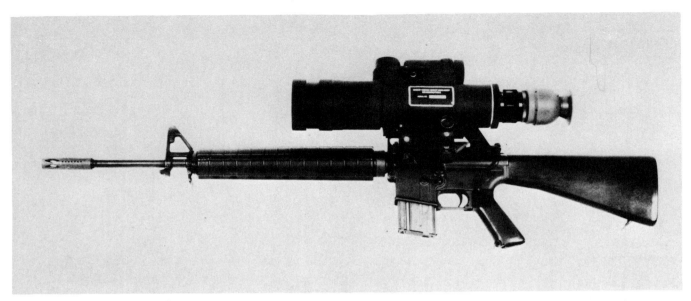

The AN/PVS-2 Starlight Scope, the principal night vision instrument utilized by both Army and Marine Corps combat personnel in Southeast Asia. Shown here with an M16, the AN/PVS-2 was employed for a myriad of applications. Photo Credit: Excalibur Enterprises.

A 5.56mm Armalite AR-18 in sniper trim with 3 power scope and and detachable mount. Considered by many as the "first cousin" of the M16, AR-18 rifles saw military use in "certain applications." Photo Credit: Armalite Inc.

The business end of an AN/PVS-2 Starlight Scope-equipped M16 rifle during field exercises held at Fort Hood, Texas, in 1970. Photo Credit: U.S. Army.

One of the variant first generation Starlight Scopes produced for the U.S. military services, an AN/PVS-3 weapon sight is mounted to the M16 rifle. A design progression, the 3-lb. instrument was smaller and lighter than the preceding models. Photo Credit: Excalibur Enterprises.

Considered to be one of the most efficient military sights now in use, the second-generation Leatherwood 3x-9x Adjustable Ranging Telescope (ART II) is shown with a Colt AR-15 rifle. Photo Credit: Charles Leatherwood.

A right view of the Leatherwood ART II system. Photo Credit: Charles Leatherwood.

barrels, different cartridge loadings, and bullet weights—were to continue through the course of hostilities in Vietnam. Despite such efforts and excepting limited field tests, the M16s utilized for sniping purposes in Vietnam were "as issued."

In the years following Vietnam to the present, both the individual and combined efforts of the Army, Navy, Air Force, and Marine Corps marksmanship training units, or their equivalent, have greatly enhanced the long-range accuracy stan-

dards of the M16A1 rifle. The M16A1 stands second to none in its own domain, with "carefully prepared, telescopic sighted models" reportedly available for "special applications" by various Army and USMC combat units. However, on the basis of the most important single characteristic required of a sniping arm, consistent long-range capability, at this juncture the USMC M40A1 and the Army M21 remain firmly entrenched.

A close view of the AN/PVS-4 Starlight Scope mounted to the M16 rifle. Photo Credit: Excalibur Enterprises.

Chapter 15 ◆━➤

Sniper Standard— The Marine Corps

When the Marine Corps deemed it necessary to replace the Winchester/Unertl combination with a lighter rifle and a scope that would aid the sniper in getting off a "quick first round," Headquarters USMC submitted a project directive to the Weapons Training Battalion (WTB) at Quantico, Virginia, giving it a short time to come up with a suitable sniper rifle for use in Southeast Asia.

Due to the time limitations imposed for this evaluation, Weapons Training Battalion conducted comparative testing of "off the shelf" commercial weapons and telescopes, concluding that the Model 700 Remington and the Redfield 3X to 9X variable power Accu-Range telescope were "superior to items now in use."

Although the Marine Corps had stated that it was seeking a sniper rifle rather than a target rifle, there was an extremely fine line separating the characteristics of the M700 Remington and the Winchester Model 70. However, by Marine Corps definition, "A target rifle is expected to put all its shots into a very small group after some adjustments to the sights. The sniper's rifle must put the first shot of any day into the same spot as the last shot of any other day. A free-floating barrel allows this with very few adjustments. A sniper gets no sighting-in shots, and he doesn't intend to put ten shots into the same target."

Consequently, on 7 April 1966, the Model 700 Remington and the Redfield telescope were adopted for Marine Corps sniper use in Vietnam. Officially designated (Rifle, 7.62mm Sniper, M40), the new issue utilized regular production components and, as the Marine Corps put it, "there were no unique specifications, just the right combination of parts."

Essentially the M40 sniper rifle was a standard production action fitted with a tapered, free-

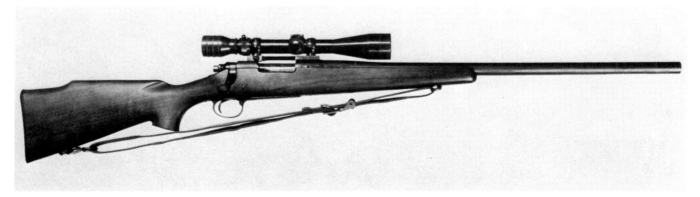

Adopted by the USMC in April 1966, the Model 700 Remington was designated Rifle 7.62mm, Sniper M40 in its original form. Photo Credit: Remington Arms Company.

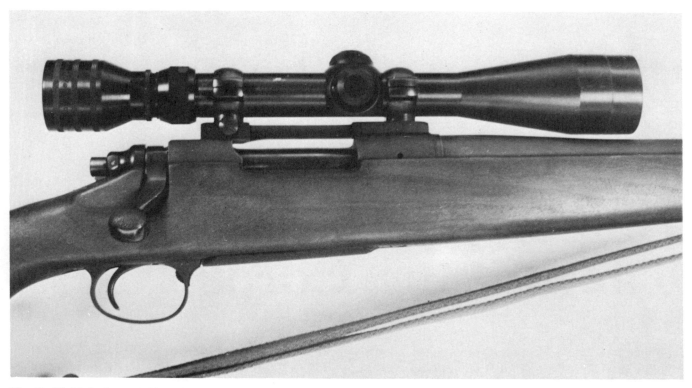

The Redfield 3x-9x variable power scope employed with the USMC M40 also served as the basis for the ART system used with the Army's XM21 sniper rifle. Photo Credit: Peter R. Senich.

A close view of the Redfield 3x-9x variable power scope in use with the M40 rifle. Photo Credit: U.S. Marine Corps.

The business end of an M40 rifle—a view seldom seen or survived. Photo Credit: U.S. Marine Corps.

Ammunition within easy reach, an M40-equipped Marine sniper takes careful aim during the battle for the Imperial City of Hue in February 1968. Redfield "Supreme" lens covers provided a water- and dust-tight seal but popped open instantly. Photo Credit: U.S. Marine Corps.

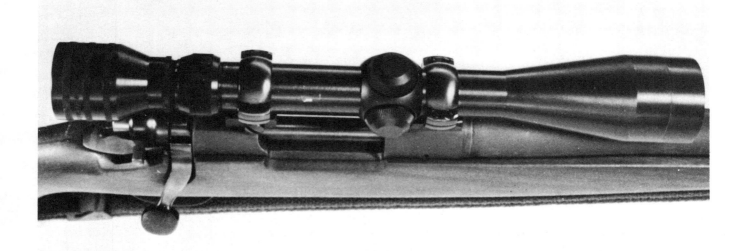

Redfield Accu-Range 3x-9x variable power telescope as originally issued with the M40 rifle. The power selector ring, located directly behind the rear mount, controlled the power of magnification and the range-finding functions of the scope. Elevation (top) and windage adjustment screws were protected by threaded caps. Scopes were furnished with a black-matte or military-olive-drab finish. Photo Credit: Peter R. Senich.

floating 24-inch-by-.830-inch diameter muzzle, medium-heavy target barrel in .308 caliber, one-in-ten inch twist, and six land rifling. The stock, a standard sporter-type with an integral cheek rest (combination), was fitted with a checkered butt plate and had an austere nonreflecting oil finish. Except for the bolt assembly, all metal, including the scope mount, was parkerized. The rifle, complete with scope and mount (Redfield Jr.), weighed about nine and one-half pounds, with an overall length of 43.5 inches. No provision was made for conventional iron sights inasmuch as the scope was mounted directly over the centerline of the receiver.

The barrel was stamped "7.62 NATO" and the left side of the receiver bore the designation "Remington Model 700" as well as "U.S.," which appeared over the six-digit serial number. Both telescope and mount were numbered to correspond with the rifle serial number to which they were matched. The M40 was topped with a Redfield Accu-Range 3x to 9x variable power telescope identical to the civilian model except for a spartan black-matte finish. Equipped with a special reticle

and range scale, which permitted accurate range estimation, the Redfield variable power sight could in effect "zoom" in on a target by lengthening its focal distance.

Technical data of the Redfield Accu-Range system was cited in the USMC Field Manual, FM I-3B, *Sniping,* dated 5 August 1969.

TABULATED DATA

Weight	12.5 ounces
Length	12 3/4 inches
Magnification (variable)	3x9 Power adjustable
Eye relief	Between 2 and 3 inches
Adjustments	Internal (1/2-minute graduations)
Reticle	Cross hairs
Lenses	Coated

The standard ammunition used with the M40 rifle was basically the same employed for National Match shooting with .308 caliber (NATO) rifles, 7.62mm M118 Match. Manufactured at Lake City Arsenal (Missouri), the M118 cartridge with a 173-grain boat-tailed bullet and velocity of 2,550 feet per second, possessed excellent ballistic char-

While deployed for sniping, the choice and mode of concealment was a matter of discretion. Elaborate camouflage was rarely used by U.S. snipers in Southeast Asia. Photo Credit: U.S. Marine Corps.

A Marine sniper team during combat in South Vietnam. The M14-equipped rifleman provides "security" for the sharpshooter. Photo Credit: U.S. Marine Corps.

A Marine marksman fires from an unorthodox position during operations in the Que Son Mountains (Vietnam), May 1970. The weapon is an M40 sniper rifle. Photo Credit: U.S. Marine Corps.

A 3rd Marine Division sniper candidate on the firing line at Quang Tri, Vietnam, July 1969. Photo Credit: U.S. Marine Corps.

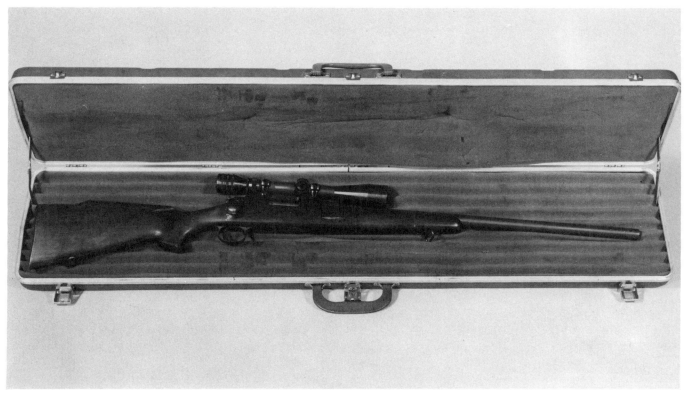

Marine Corps issue lightweight carrying case with force-fitted sponge rubber liner for holding the M40 sniper rifle with its accessories. Photo Credit: U.S. Marine Corps.

A Marine sniper at work in the Demilitarized Zone of South Vietnam, September 1968. The towel provided protection from the sun and camouflage for the rifleman's head. Photo Credit: U.S. Marine Corps.

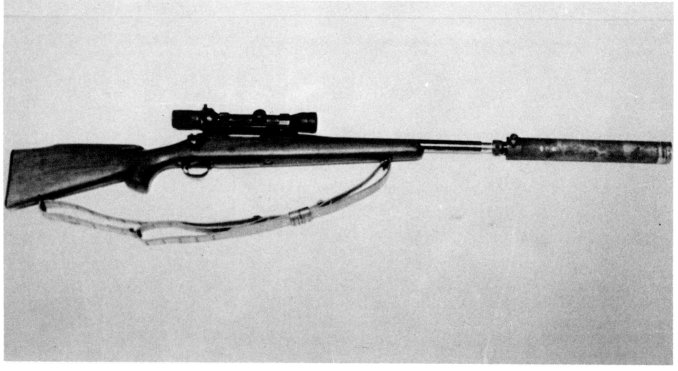

Remington sniper rifle with autoranging scope and Sionics (MAC) noise suppressor. The barrel has been machined and threaded to accommodate the suppressor. Photo Credit: Donald G. Thomas.

First Marine Division sniper-spotter during action west of Da Nang, April 1970. Even though a number of problems were experienced with the M40 system in Vietnam, a great many VC and NVA personnel were "taken out" with this weapon. Photo Credit: U.S. Marine Corps.

acteristics for long-range shooting, a fact attested to by its 1,000-yard accuracy during competitive shooting matches. Although regular issue ball ammunition could of course be utilized with this system, conclusive Army and Marine Corps studies had determined the M80 round to be unsatisfactory for sniping purposes.

Unlike the Army's XM21 sniping system, which allowed the sniper to interchange the Adjustable Ranging Telescope (ART) with a Starlight Scope for night operation, the M40 rifle possessed only a daylight capability and could only be employed between dawn and dusk. Inasmuch as there was no provision for mounting night-vision equipment, Marine snipers were limited to using the Starlight Scope with regular M14 or M16 rifles. Efforts to

broaden the M40's capability led to the introduction of a special aluminum mount developed by the Quantico-based Marksmanship Training Unit (MTU) in late 1969. The new mounting retained the telescopic sight in its original position over the bore and allowed the Starlight Scope to be placed on the left side of the M40.

Even though the M40/Redfield combination possessed the characteristics sought by the Marine Corps, the system was plagued by a number of difficulties with both the telescope and rifle. In response to this situation, in late 1969 the Marine Corps Development and Education Command (MCDEC), Quantico, Virginia, was charged with evaluating improvement recommendations and unsatisfactory equipment reports from the field.

Marine Corps sniper candidates make final sight adjustments prior to qualification at the 3rd Marine Division Sniper School (Quang Tri, Vietnam). Only outstanding marksmen with the M14 were considered for specialized sniper training. Photo Credit: U.S. Marine Corps.

A Marine marksman uses an old tombstone as a rest for his M40 rifle during an isolated encounter in RVN. Photo Credit: U.S. Marine Corps.

A 1st Marine Division sniper team operating in Vietnam, April 1968. Twenty-power observation telescopes (M49) permitted sightings well beyond the capability of 7 x 50 binoculars. Although bulky, the spotting scope was carried whenever the mission justified its use. Photo Credit: U.S. Marine Corps.

As subsequently stated by the MCDEC in its *Marine Corps Sniper Rifle and Associated Equipment Report:*

Liaison was made with Remington Arms, manufacturer of the M40, the current USMC Sniper Rifle, to discuss product improvement of the weapon. The product improved model with stainless steel, free-floating barrel, impregnated stock, stamped steel trigger guard, and bipod was designed to eliminate all UERs, in addition, MTU, Quantico, fabricated a cast aluminum mount for the M40 to accept the current ART and Starlight Scopes.

Remington M40 Product Improved Sniper Rifle

Two Product Improved M40 Sniper Rifles have been contracted for and delivery is expected at MCDEC for reliability testing in July 1970.

XM21 Sniper Rifle System

Two XM21 systems have been contracted for, and delivery is expected at MCDEC in July 1970.

Military Potential Test of Adjustable Ranging Telescope

The MPT will be conducted by the USAIB Fort Benning with distinguished shooters and is expected to begin in July 1970. Results of the test are anticipated ninety days after completion.

Upon completion of MPT, adopt the ART scope with the highest degree of reliability and potential for use with the improved M40. [Concurrent with USMC reevaluation of the M40/Redfield, Realist, Incorporated, had submitted a telescope based on the ART concept for Army consideration as well.]

Although comparative official testing was scheduled for August 1970, the results of these evaluations were never disclosed by the Marine Corps. In retrospect, acceptance of the Army's M14-based XM21 or ART scopes for the M40 rifle did not transpire.

The Marine Corps chose to retain the M40 and

The initial, improved version of the USMC M40 tested in 1970 included an Adjustable Ranging Telescope (ART) and bipod. The new aluminum mount extended down the left side of the receiver to form the same mounting area as the M14 rifle, allowing use of either the ART or Starlight Scope. Photo Credit: U.S. Marine Corps.

A 1st Marine Division sniper-spotter during action at Da Nang. Photo Credit: U.S. Marine Corps.

has continuously upgraded the system originally fielded for use in Southeast Asia to the point where it remains sniper standard, bearing the new designation, M40A1. In modified form, the M40A1 differs from the original M40 mainly in its special stainless steel barrel (furnished by H&S Precision Incorporated, of Prescott, Arizona) and glass-bedded, fiberglass stock.

Even though the Redfield 3x-9x variable power sight would continue as a part of the M40A1 system well beyond the end of Marine Corps involvement in Southeast Asia. In an effort to enhance the durability of the M40A1, the Marine Corps eventually placed a contract with the John Unertl Optical Company for a satisfactory military rifle scope.

With appropriate Marine Corps specifications serving as a guideline, the Unertl organization would design and produce an entirely new telescopic sight, a rugged instrument intended primarily for sniper use. The first scopes from an initial order of 600 were reportedly delivered to the Marine Corps beginning in 1980.

Tabulated data for the 10x power UNERTL USMC SNIPER SCOPE, as it was officially designated, was cited in the Marine Corps field manual,

FM 1-3B, SNIPING, dated 28 January 1981.

UNERTL USMC SNIPER SCOPE

Weight	2 pounds 3 ounces
Length	12 1/2 inches
Eye Relief	3 inches (fixed)
Adjustments:	
Elevation and Windage	1/2 minute
Main Elevation	Ballistic come-ups for M118 Lake City Match Ammunition (7.62mm) built-in.
Fine Tune Elevation	+ or –3 minutes to adjust for shooter's zeros, temperatures and ammunition lots.
Windage	60 minutes main adjustment; + or – 4 1/2 minutes with stops on either end to allow shooter to run windage on and off in the dark.
Reticle	Mil dot duplex for range estimation and calculating leads on moving targets.
Lenses	HELR coating (high efficiency, low reflection film), gathers in over 90 percent of available light.

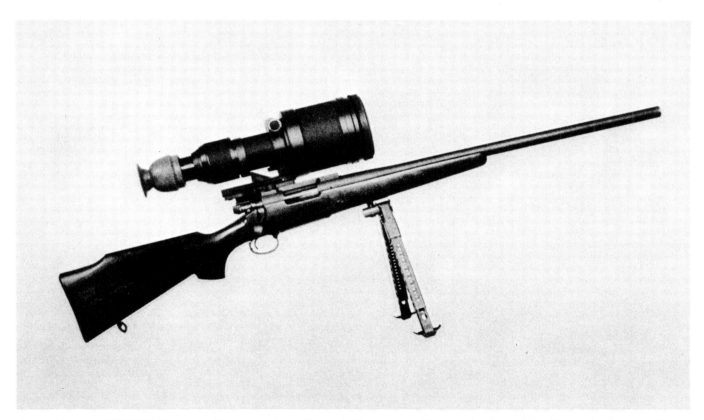

A post-Vietnam USMC M40 sniper rifle mounting a Smith & Wesson Star-Tron night-vision sight. Photo Credit: U.S. Marine Corps.

Steel tube with black chrome finish.

Capability of reading elevation and windage settings from the rear while shooting.

Scope allows shooter to shoot point of aim/point of impact back to 1000 yards.

Capability of adjusting parallax.

The principal part of the system was a hand-crafted, precision rifle produced by skilled armorers at the USMC Weapons Training Battalion (WTB) at Quantico, Virginia. According to the Marine Corps:

> The sniper rifle used by the Marine Corps is a Marine Corps designed and produced bolt-action 7.62mm rifle with a stainless steel barrel for improved accuracy. It weighs 14 pounds and has a maximum effective range of 1000 yards. The rifle is fitted with a top-mounted telescope base, to which the sniper scope can be readily attached without special tools.

Said to produce "surgical accuracy," the special sniper rifle is capable of shooting a minute of angle or better with Lake City (M118) Match Ammunition. With hand loads, it will reportedly shoot one-half (1/2) minute of angle.

Referenced as the RIFLE, SNIPER, 7.62 x 51mm NATO, M40A1, the principal characteristics for the Marine Corps sniper rifle are noted as follows.

M40A1 RIFLE

Caliber	7.62 NATO
Length	44 inches
Weight	14 pounds
Barrel Length	24 inches
Lands and Grooves	6
Twist, Right Hand	1 turn in 12 inches
Trigger Weight	3 to 5 pounds
Torque	65 inch/pound
Magazine Capacity	5 rounds
Maximum Effective Range	1000 yards

The free-floating heavy barrel, a product of the Atkinson Gun Company, is fabricated from No. 416 stainless steel, has a recessed crown, and is chemically treated to provide a dull black finish.

The heat of the M40A1 system, a Remington Model 700 (M40) action is "accurized" in accordance with Marine Corps specifications. The Remington trigger mechanism is retained and a steel trigger guard and floor plate from the Winchester Model 70 are adapted for use.

The special M40A1 stock, furnished by Gale McMillan, is made of pressure-molded fiberglass color-impregnated in an "earth red with forest green" camouflage pattern. Impervious to the effects of heat, cold, and moisture, the fiberglass stocks are considerably stronger and much lighter than wood. Machine-inletted for the Model 700

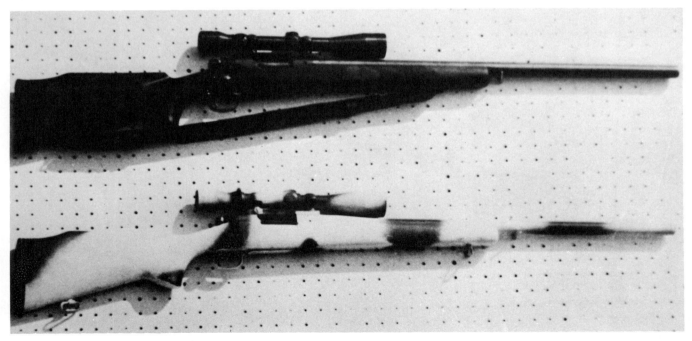

Camouflaged USMC M40A1 sniper rifles with Redfield 3x-9x variable power scopes, stainless steel barrels, and glass-bedded, fiberglass stocks. Photo Credit: U.S. Marine Corps.

The Marine Corps M40A1 sniper rifle with the Unertl 10X USMC Sniper Scope. A precision combat rifle produced by skilled armorers at the USMC Weapons Training Battalion (WTB) at Quantico, Virginia. Photo Credit: U.S. Marine Corps.

A camouflaged sniper team is shown during a training exercise. The radio-equipped team leader is calling in support. According to the Marine Corps, a two-man team is the basic operational organization for the employment of snipers. Both members are trained scout-snipers; either member can fill the function of the sniper. Photo Credit: U.S. Marine Corps.

Students on the firing line at the USMC Scout-Sniper Instructor School (Quantico, Virginia). Marine snipers are trained to operate in two-man teams, one acting as an observer, the other as the sharpshooter (both are sniper qualified). Photo Credit: U.S. Marine Corps.

A close view of the 10x Unertl USMC Sniper Scope. A rugged instrument made of steel, the optics are thick, strong, precision hand-ground lenses coated with a light transmitting substance known as HELR (high efficiency, low reflection film), a feature that allows over 90 percent of the ambient light to pass through the scope thereby providing better target definition at longer ranges in marginal light. The scope is set on 600 yards with 2 minutes down + 2 minutes left windage. Photo Credit: U.S. Marine Corps.

A winter field experiment intended to reduce lens glare. Medical gauze and a "tape slot" were found effective in bright light. The M40A1 rifle is camouflaged with medical tape. Photo Credit: U.S. Marine Corps.

action, epoxy steel resin is used for bedding the receiver in the stock. Sling swivels are provided and a brown rubber butt plate from the Pachmayr Gun Works is also used. For transportation purposes, a lightweight fiberglass carrying case with a force-fitted sponge rubber liner is furnished for the M40A1 and its accessories.

An accurate, reliable weapon, the Marine Corps sniper rifle has proven to be an intelligent blend of uncomplicated, durable components.

Marine Corps sniper candidates on the firing line at Quantico. The observer records pertinent information in the firing data book. Today's Marine sniper is trained during an all-encompassing course of instruction lasting eight weeks. Photo Credit: U.S. Marine Corps.

A camouflage "Ghillie Suit" currently in vogue among Army and Marine Corps snipers. Designed primarily for stalking purposes, a uniform or smock is covered with irregular patterns of garnish of blending color to give the suit the appearance of vegetation. Photo Credit: U.S. Marine Corps.

An essential part of the USMC Scout-Sniper School syllabus. Students receive thorough marksmanship training in all aspects of sighting, firing positions, trigger control, sight adjustment, weather effects, and zeroing. By Marine Corps definition: "Rifle marksmanship must be practiced constantly in order for a shooter to deliver accurate hits on a target, to effectively provide support for his rifle, to correctly align his sights, and finally, to fire without disturbing his sight alignment." Photo Credit: U.S. Marine Corps.

A refined version of the Marine Corps sniper rifle, a "second generation M40A2" produced by the Gale McMillan Company. A respected arms manufacturer, the McMillan organization has developed a variety of sophisticated sniping systems for military use. Photo Credit: Gale McMillan.

McMillan M86 Sniper Rifle with Leupold & Stevens 10x telescopic sight, fiberglass stock and folding bipod. A state of the art system employed by U.S. Navy SEAL teams. According to the manufacturer, "The McMillan Sniper Rifle is employed by more elite military and law enforcement units than any other rifle." Photo Credit: Gale McMillan.

Chapter 16 ◆◆

The Army M21– 900 Meter Kills

The period between the Korea and Vietnam conflicts saw little advancement in sniper equipment or training other than a myriad of concepts and objectives formulated under or stemming from the Army's marksmanship training program known as "Trainfire."

As a matter of course, studies were conducted and training manuals periodically amended but, as in the past, sniper training was not compulsory. Excepting the rare occasion when a sniper program was set up under the aegis of a division or regimental commander during their tenure, few snipers were fielded.

Even though the M1's successor, the M14 (adopted in 1957), had a groove and screw recess on the left side of the receiver, ostensibly for mounting night-vision equipment and telescopic sights, no telescope mounting was adopted for this weapon. The first notable application of telescopic sights to the M14 took place in 1958 when LTC Frank Conway (Ret), while serving as an Ordnance Captain with the U.S. Army Marksmanship Training Unit (USAMTU), mounted commercial Weaver K-6 scopes on two M14s by means of special bases. The front base was mounted on the barrel with the rear handguard clip removed and the handguard cut to fit. The rear base in turn was affixed to the receiver in place of the conventional sight. In order to compensate for the difference in height between the rear of the receiver and the barrel, a "high" Weaver mount was used in front and a "low" mount at the rear to bring the scope in line with the bore.

As such, these rifles were fired by Captain Richard Wentworth at the Running Deer World Championships held at Moscow with excellent results.

Nevertheless, the task of convincing higher echelons that a sniper system was necessary during peacetime remained formidable. With no requirements for such equipment, sniping developments not only lagged, but were, in fact, virtually non-existent. Consequently, along with the realization that combat personnel were being "taken out" by VC and NVA snipers during the early days in South Vietnam, the Army found itself in a familiar posture, i.e., no satisfactory sniping equipment was available for immediate use. As a result, a flurry of both official and quasiofficial efforts to field sniper weapons commenced in earnest.

In 1966, in an attempt to satisfy the urgent requirement for a telescope-equipped sniper rifle, Army Weapons Command (USA-WECOM) developed a hinged-telescope mount to accommodate the M84 sight. On 19 October 1966, the United States Infantry Board (USAIB) was directed to test this mount with the M14 rifle to determine its suitability for use in Southeast Asia. Accordingly, the following materiel was received for test:

(1) Four each of the Rifle, 7.62mm M14 with hinged-telescope mount and Telescope M84.

    (A) Serial numbers of the rifles were as follows: 676743, 1300588, 1299278, and 1292367. They were issued with reinforced fiberglass stocks. All rifles except

With a day and night capability, the Vietnam-era XM21 mounting the ART, or Starlight Scope, in combination with a Sionics M14SS-1 suppressor wrought havoc among VC and NVA personnel in Southeast Asia. Photo Credit: <u>Infantry</u> magazine.

Weaver commercial mounts as adapted to the M14 for shooting matches held in Moscow in 1958. Photo Credit: Lieutenant Colonel F. B. Conway (Retired).

Close-up of the special rear base affixed to the M14 receiver in place of the conventional sight. Photo Credit: Lieutenant Colonel F. B. Conway (Retired).

one, 1300588, met National Match accuracy requirements.
(B) The same four rifles employing conventional iron sights were used for control purposes.
(2) Ammunition:
  (A) Cartridge, ball, 7.62mm, NATO, M80 (ball cartridge), Lot Number WCC 6282.
  (B) Cartridge, ball, 7.62mm, NATO, National Match M118 (match cartridge), Lot Number FA-25.

The mount assembly consisted of the mount base and a cradle support. The mount base was attached directly to the receiver of the rifle by means of a base screw. The cradle support, in turn, was attached to the mount base at the hinge point by means of a knurled collar, which caused two pivots to protrude from the hinge portion of the cradle support into the hinge cones on the mount base. The scope rested in the cradle and was held by two clamping brackets and four screws. The

scope and the cradle support attached to the mount base at the hinge point by application of thumb pressure to a knurled collar in a counterclockwise direction.

Initial alignment of the scope was accomplished by adjustment of the mount. The hinge-cone locking nuts on each end of the hinge portion of the mount base could be loosened, permitting adjustment of the hinge-cone adjusting screws (causing a nonlinear adjustment in the orientation of the scope to the rifle). When the correct alignment was effected, the hinge-cone locking nuts were tightened. Iron sights could not be employed when the scope was in position over the centerline of the bore. They could be used, however, when the scope was swung to the side (left).

Test sights were regular issue M84 Telescopes originally designed in 1945 for use as a sniper's sighting device with the .30 caliber M1C and M1D rifles. No difficulty was encountered in acclimating the personnel used in this test since all had an Army Marksmanship Qualification of Expert.

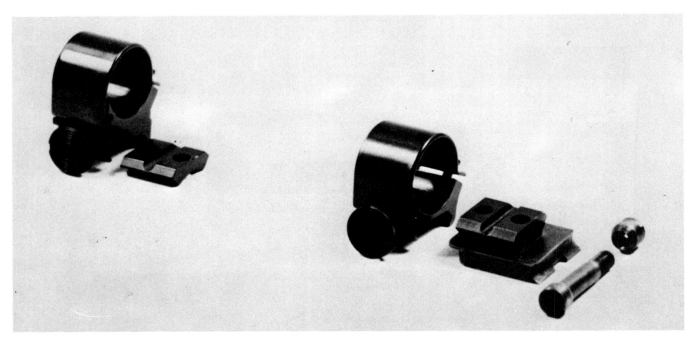

A Weaver "high" mount was used in front and a "low" mount at the rear in order to compensate for the difference in height between the receiver and M14 barrel. Photo Credit: Lieutenant Colonel F. B. Conway (Retired).

A mounting fashioned from Redfield components represents Jim Leatherwood's early efforts to develop a telescope mount for the M14. Photo Credit: Lieutenant Colonel F. B. Conway (Retired).

However, the initial exercise of aligning the scope with the rifle required over one hour for each system under ideal range conditions and proved to be beyond the capability of the average soldier in a field environment.

After confirmation of zero, each soldier fired a simulated combat exercise with telescope and iron sights using ball and match ammunition. Targets were engaged at various ranges from 115 to 800 meters during daylight hours and 400 to 800 meters at twilight. Shots were fired semi-automatically from a prone, sandbag-supported position. Neither the mount nor telescope were sufficiently durable, with a number of malfunctions and breakages experienced at various times during the testing.

The principal deficiency of the M84 scope rested with its marginal benefit in seeking and/or engaging targets at extreme ranges due to low magnification. Flakes of internal coating material appeared within the field of view of each sight at various times, distracting the shooter. The scopes also had the tendency to rust excessively under prolonged humid conditions.

Although the maximum effective range of the M84 telescope, as determined by the test, was approximately 800 meters, it was objective consensus that "pure chance" accounted for hits at this range. As a matter of interest, during subsequent combat use in Vietnam, documented hits were recorded out to 800 meters with the M84, but this was rare and two or three shots were required to get on target.

The Army Weapons Command (AWC) mounts were, in fact, similar to the Pachmayr type tested between 1951–53 by the USAIB, when a swing or

hinge mount was necessary to facilitate clip loading of the M1 rifle from above. However, since the M14 was normally loaded by magazine from beneath, the requirement for a telescope mount such as this no longer existed. Based on the results of its testing, the Army Infantry Board concluded that:

(A) The hinged-telescope mount for the M14 rifle will not be suitable for sniper use in Southeast Asia until its deficiencies are corrected.
(B) The Cartridge, 7.62mm, Ball, M80 is not sufficiently accurate for sniping purposes.
(C) The M84 Telescope is unsuitable for use, except under some conditions, and represents the least suitable element of the system furnished for test.
(D) The M14 rifle with National Match accuracy characteristics employing 7.62mm, M118 National Match Ammunition, provides sufficient system accuracy for sniper purposes.
(E) A variable power telescope or one with a minimum of 4x magnification is needed in the sniper role.

In retrospect, the most significant aspect of the USAIB evaluation was perhaps the suitability of a match-grade weapon and ammunition for sniping. This of course was unprecedented, and actually paved the way for what eventually became the first military application of accurized, semiautomatic rifles and match-grade ammunition for combat use (i.e., the XM21 system).

At this juncture, however, in order to meet the pressing need for telescopic sights in Vietnam, it was decided that "the M84 Telescope should be used as an interim item until a satisfactory variable ranging telescope could be adopted." Conse-

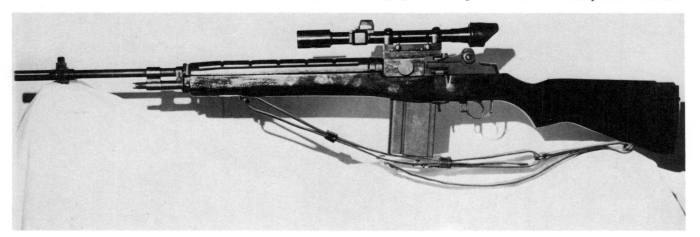

Match-grade M14s with M84 telescopes prepared by Army Weapons Command (AWC) remained in general use in RVN even after the sophisticated XM21/ART system had been fielded in quantity. Photo Credit: Lieutenant Colonel F. B. Conway (Retired).

M84 telescope, Griffin & Howe mount, and the offset receiver bracket developed by Army Weapons Command for use with match-grade M14s in Vietnam. Photo Credit: Peter R. Senich.

quently, even though the hinge mount never made it to Vietnam, the M84 on the other hand, despite acknowledged deficiencies, was employed in considerable numbers, particularly during early sniping activity.

In some quarters, including Army Weapons Command, retention of this sight with standard issue M14s and M80 ball ammunition was, for a time, considered adequate for Army snipers. The M84 was available from military stores and presented a practical choice among those having no conception of what effective sniping consisted of at the field level. However, there was still no mount to permit use of this sight with the M14, or the M16 for that matter.

As early as 1965, efforts to fill this vacuum included a number of improvisations. Among these, M/SGT Walsh, an USAMTU machinist, fashioned special aluminum mounts to adapt M84 scopes to the M14 for the Eleventh Air Assault Division following its alert for combat duty in RVN.

Shortly after this, a similar mount was fabricated at the MTU and sent to AWC at Rock Island for its consideration. In this case, use of a Weaver "long-base" enabled virtually any telescope to be used. In addition to using the standard mounting spot on the M14 receiver, this mount also attached to the clip-guide to provide increased rigidity much the same as a bridge-type mounting.

At Chu Lai early in 1967, the 196th Brigade, in addition to establishing one of the first in-country Army sniper schools, fielded a number of effective M14 sniping arms for use by its marksmen. SFC

Herbert F. Donnally designed three prototype mounts to mate the M84 to the M14, which were handmade by the ordnance section of the Brigade's 8th Spt. Bn.

After choosing the final design, duplicates were machined by the 64th Ord. Section at Cu Chi. Drawing on his experience with Army rifle teams, Sergeant Donnally "fine-tuned" the M14s and, since the scopes were offset to the left, leather cheek rests originally intended for the M1C were obtained and attached to the stocks. Innumerable measures both stateside and in Vietnam included mounting telescopic sights to the M14 and M16 by every means short of electrician's tape. The cases cited were indicative of these efforts.

With telescopic sights in short supply, commercial sights were brought from the States or procured from the PX by enterprising units and individuals. Although military regulations prohibited bringing personal weapons to Southeast Asia, rifle scopes were not included. Consequently, a number of sniping weapons were fielded under these circumstances.

A satisfactory receiver mounting bracket, developed by Army Weapons Command, emerged as the principal device utilized with the M14/M84 combination, remaining in general use in a supplementary role even after the sophisticated XM21/ART system had been fielded in quantity.

With a male dovetail virtually identical to the M1C receiver base, the AWC offset receiver bracket made use of the World War II vintage Griffin & Howe mount assemblies originally manufactured to accommodate M81 and M82 Telescopes. While it

Comparative view of an original M1C receiver base male dovetail with that of the AWC M14 receiver bracket. Photo Credit: Peter R. Senich.

Weapons Command receiver mounting brackets as utilized with M84 telescopes were either blued or parkerized and furnished with large, knurled locking knobs or small-diameter knurled knobs having a screw-driver slot. Photo Credit: Peter R. Senich.

Army Weapons Command M14 receiver mounting brackets for the M84 telescope with large and small diameter locking knobs. Photo Credit: Peter R. Senich.

did serve to adapt the M84 to the M14, this mounting was in fact nothing more than an extension of the state of the art as it existed in 1945.

Match-grade M14s were eventually prepared by Army Weapons Command utilizing this mounting with the M84 for sniper use in RVN. While these were reported to be "somewhat less accurate" than the M14s accurized in accordance with USAMTU rebuild procedures (XM21), a fair share of VC and NVA personnel were rendered *hors de combat* with this variant. For the sake of clarification, an M14 accurized by, or according to, the rigid specifications set forth by the U.S. Army Marksmanship Training Unit (USAMTU) constituted "a weapon possessing match-grade characteristics, and then some."

Although a number of evaluations were conducted by diverse organizations during the mid-1960s in quest of a satisfactory telescope for Army sniper use, the Adjustable Ranging Telescope (ART), fielded by the U.S. Army Limited Warfare Laboratory (LWL), met the necessary requirements for accurate long-range sniping in Southeast Asia. The ART, in conjunction with the M14s accurized according to USAMTU standards, (firing M118 National Match Ammunition) provided the Army with the epitome of sniping efficiency—a weapon capable of consistent first round hits.

The workings of the Adjustable Ranging Telescope were summarized in the Department of the Army Training Circular, TC 23-14, *Sniper Training and Employment,* 27 October 1969.

The ART is a lightweight, commercially procured, three to nine variable power, telescopic sight, modified for use with the sniper rifle. This scope has been improved with modified reticle and a ballistic cam mounted on the power adjusting ring.

The modified reticle utilizes vertical and horizontal stadia marks to measure size or actually the angle of an object of known size. The vertical stadia marks subtend thirty inches while viewing at three power. As the telescope incorporates a nonmagnifying reticle (i.e., the stadia mark spacing remains the same

Army sniper team in Vietnam, October 1969. The rifle being sighted is equipped with the AWC telescope mounting and M84 scope. The other M14 has the night-vision sight adapter bracket in place on the receiver. Photo Credit: U.S. Army.

regardless of power change), the sniper can then utilize the increasing power of the scope to pull any known object of thirty inches, within the scope's capability, toward him until it fits between the stadia lines. This calibration will give a ranging capacity from 300 to 900 meters, comparable to the three to nine power capability of the scope. Ranges and/or powers are inscribed on the focusing ring to give a range read-off capability. This method is considered 95 per cent accurate when applied by a trained sniper.

The ballistic cam is affixed to the power adjustment ring and is designed and ground to compensate for the trajectory of 7.62mm, M118 match ammunition. The trajectory of the 7.62mm, M118 match ammunition is much flatter than that of other 7.62mm service ammunition. The ballistic cam must be changed to match the cartridge if any degree of accuracy is to be maintained with different ammunition. The cam rests on the cam base of the scope mount and is held in position by a loading spring positioned in the mount.

As the cam is calibrated to the ranging capability of the scope, from 300 to 900 meters, any ranging accomplished is accompanied by an automatic adjustment in elevation of the scope to correct for bullet trajectory. This in effect eliminates the necessity to adjust sights manually for each range.

The scope mount is of lightweight aluminum construction and designed for low profile mounting of the scope to the rifle utilizing the mounting guide grooves and threaded hole on the left side of the receiver. The mount consists of a side mounting plate and a spring-loaded base with scope mounting rings. These are held together with a hex socket head screw and lock washer.

TABULATED DATA

(1) Scope:

Weight (with cam and lock)	16.05 ounces
Length	12 3/4 inches
Magnification (variable)	3 to 9 power
Eye relief	3–3 3/4 inches
Adjustments	Internal (1/2 minute graduations for elevation and windage)
Reticle	Cross hairs (with stadia marks)
Ballistic cam	For M118 match ammunition
Objective diameter	1.820 inches
Eyepiece diameter	1.565 inches
Finish	Black matte anodize

(2) Mount:

Weight	5.95 ounces
Material	Aluminum 7075-T6
Operation	Hand fixed, spring loaded base
Finish	Black matte anodize

As originally fielded, a Redfield "Accu-Range" three by nine variable power sight provided the basis for the Adjustable Ranging Telescope (ART). In addition to the ballistic cam, the heart of the system—the Redfield sight—was further modified by removing its interior range indicator, and the reticle pattern was changed to include marks on the horizontal cross hair subtending sixty inches at 300 meters that could be used for estimating the hold-off for wind. However, the reticle spacing of the horizontal stadia lines remained the same as in the conventional Accu-Range.

Once a target was sighted, the sniper adjusted the ballistic cam until the correct portion of the target was framed between the horizontal stadia lines (waist to top of head for a target of occidental stature—waist to top of head for a target of oriental stature), centered on cross hair, and fired.

The ART increased accuracy significantly by eliminating the guesswork of range estimation and "hold-over" shooting that had plagued riflemen through the years. One of the greatest benefits of this system rested with the "self-ranging" feature which allowed competent riflemen to be effective snipers without extensive training. An indication of the accuracy possible with this system was demonstrated during early testing when several marksmen of the USAMTU at Ft. Benning recorded ten-inch groups at 900 meters (2,952 feet) after ranging on a standard "E" silhouette target.

Originally conceived by James Leatherwood in 1964, the significance of this sighting principle was quickly recognized by the Army while Leatherwood was stationed at Ft. Benning. Following basic testing, this concept was referred to the Limited Warfare Laboratory late in 1965. As a result, a project was initiated to develop a sniper sighting system based on Leatherwood's principle.

Although a number of individuals were responsible for bringing the ART to fruition, credit must be given to Franklin Owen, who did the design work, supervised initial fabrication, and gave the ART its name, and to the man responsible for guiding the development of the new telescope, LTC Vincent Oddi.

Three variations of the ART were eventually produced by the LWL: the original P1, intended for use with the .50 caliber Browning MG as well as the M14; the P2, with mounts furnished by an outside contractor; and the P3, with mounts fabricated at Frankford Arsenal. Later efforts saw the Realist firm producing an improved version of the P3 in order to meet the demand for ARTs in Southeast Asia.

A number of the original "tool-room" versions of the ART were sent to Southeast Asia for combat evaluation under the auspices of the Army Concept Team in Vietnam (ACTIV), charged with the task of evaluating sniper operations at the field level. Although the ART mounts and ballistic cams used for these evaluations were fabricated in the LWL Technical Support machine shop, the USAMTU fabricated the original mount for the Redfield self-ranging (Leatherwood) scope, with M/SGT Walsh doing the necessary machine work. With the exception of the screws, spring, and pin, the MTU prototype mount was made of untreated aluminum. Subsequent manufacture under the control of the LWL were hard-anodized to provide strength and better wearing surfaces.

According to the Review of MTU Involvement in Sniper Rifle/Sight/Ammo Program, 18 May 1967, USAMTU support for what eventually became the XM21 system commenced when:

We were contacted by SGT Billy Willard of the Limited Warfare Laboratory to see if we could accurize ten M14 Rifles that were to be equipped with the Leatherwood scope for test in Vietnam. On first contact, we were told that standard issue M14s would be used. However, SGT Willard, a competitive shooter and coach, talked his superiors into using National Match rifles. He personally carried these rifles to Ft. Benning where we worked them over. Basically, this is what was done:

A. The rifles were disassembled down to the basic receiver.
B. Barrels were selected for straightness and uniformity with dimensions to match the lot of ammunition that would be used with them (LC 12049).
C. The barrels were installed with minimum headspace adjustment.
D. The area of contact of the operating rod guide was knurled to make splines to prohibit the guide from rotating on the barrel.
E. The gas cylinder and band were screwed together as an assembly and internally polished to reduce carbon build-up.

The U.S. Army Marksmanship Training Unit (MTU), active in development of telescope mountings for the M14, designed and fabricated various aluminum mounts for evaluation purposes prior to their involvement with the ART system. Photo Credit: Lieutenant Colonel F. B. Conway (Retired).

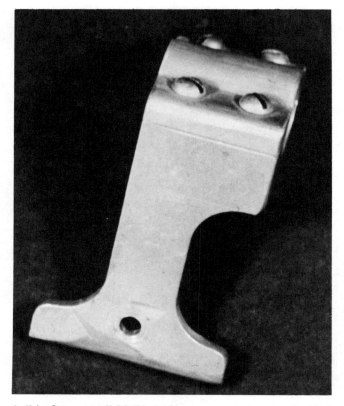

A "single-support" MTU rigid scope mounting for the M14 rifle. Photo Credit: Lieutenant Colonel F. B. Conway (Retired).

The original Adjustable Ranging Telescope (ART) proto-type mount as fabricated by the USAMTU. The aluminum mount was built around an M80 Ball ballistic cam furnished by Franklin Owens of the LWL. Photo Credit: Lieutenant Colonel F. B. Conway (Retired).

Maj. Ray Orton (Retired) and the late M/Sgt. Robert Walsh. Maj. Orton, Chief of the USAMTU Test & Evaluation Section during the XM21 period, is shown with the "first and final prototype" ART mount. Photo Credit: Tom Dunkin.

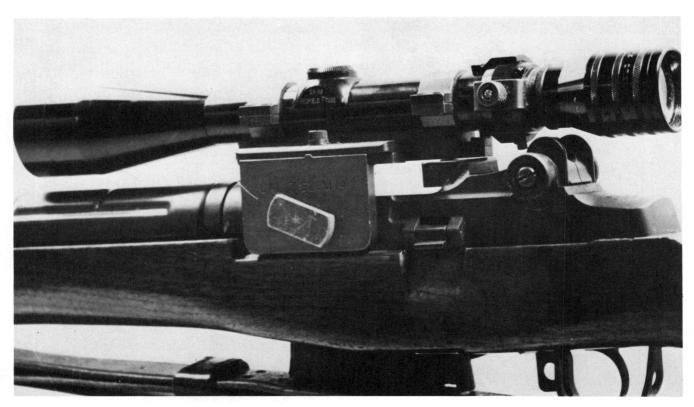

One of the original Redfield Adjustable Ranging Telescopes (ART) as furnished by the Limited Warfare Laboratory (LWL) for Army sniper use with the XM21 in Southeast Asia. Although early ART models were fielded with a blue finish and commercial markings as shown, the production version was given a parkerized finish and military markings. A recommended modification in this case, the circular locking knob was given large "flats" to provide a better grasp. Note the extremely low profile of the special USAMTU 7-round magazine. Photo Credit: Lieutenant Colonel F. B. Conway (Retired).

A close view of the 7.62mm M80 Ball and M118 Match ammunition ballistic cams developed for the Adjustable Ranging Telescope. The M33 Ball cam (right) was part of the original LWL concept of equipping .50 caliber Browning machine guns with the ART. The aluminum alloy cams were held to the magnification sleeve by one screw and could be changed by the sniper as circumstances warranted. Cams were given a Martin Hardcoat and dyed black. Photo Credit: Lieutenant Colonel F. B. Conway (Retired).

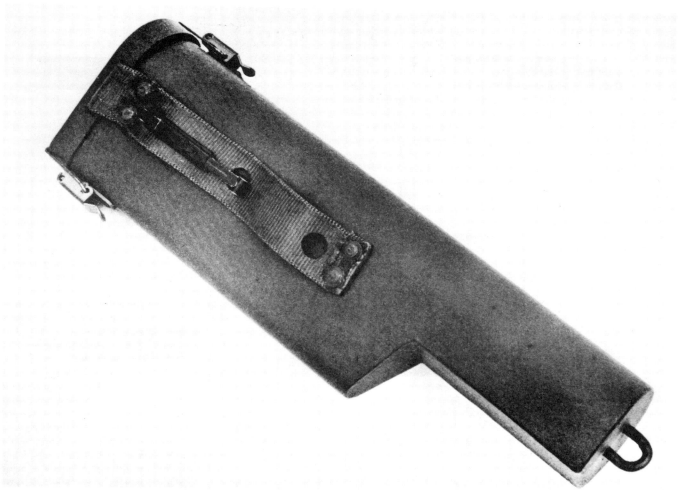

ART carrying cases were made from 6061-T aluminum alloy, coated with O.D. vinyl paint which had a tendency to peel, and weighed in at eighteen ounces empty, forty ounces with scope and mount. Photo Credit: U.S. Army.

F. The piston was polished to reduce carbon build-up.

G. The flash suppressor was reamed out internally to a diameter previously determined to give the best accuracy with NM ammunition.

H. The mating surfaces between the barrel and suppressor were matched for perfect alignment.

I. Specially treated NM stocks were used after being treated as follows:
The stocks are placed in a large container (eight feet in diameter). The lid is toggle-bolted down, the temperature raised to approximately 300 degrees, turning all moisture in the stock to steam. A vacuum pump is turned on and run for about an hour. This removes all moisture. While in the tank at this temperature, an epoxy (by Western Sealant of Conn.) is run inside in a liquid state and held at one-hundred-psi for an additional hour. The pressure is then slowly lowered and the stocks removed. They are then placed in

a curing oven where they remain for approximately three days. This sets-up the epoxy while reducing shrinkage to a minimum. The purpose of this treatment is to fill all of the sap pockets and pores with the epoxy, thereby displacing the moisture in the stock. This increases the tensile strength, completely eliminates warpage, and the expansion and contraction of the stock from moisture variations are negligible.

J. Prior to "glassing" the stock, the stock liner was removed and modified to provide one-eighth inch of bedding compound in the recoil areas.

K. The stocks were then fitted to the metal parts in two stages of glass bedding (a type of fiber-glass/epoxy used to obtain a perfect fit between wood and metal). The first stage was to provide a centering of the assembly, as looked at from above. The second stage was to provide a downward pressure (pre-loading) of the front part of the stock to uniformly dampen barrel vibrations and reduce the effect of changes in sling tension.

L. Triggers were adjusted to provide a fine pull (four and one-half to four and three-fourths pounds).

M. The hand guard was cleared of the stock and anchored to the band.

N. The gas cylinder lock was selected to index finger tight at the six o'clock position.

O. A newly manufactured operating spring guide was installed with a cylindrical cross-section to provide smoother functioning, uniform distribution and side pressure on all parts of the operating spring.

P. Certain cams, corners, and bearing surfaces throughout the mechanism were modified to provide smoother operation and uniform return of all moving parts.

These rifles were then tested by the Test Section in our machine rest (cradle) and averaged 5.3 inches vertical by 4.7 inches horizontal with the assigned match ammunition. The ART scopes were mounted and zeroed with all rifles checked to about 700 meters. Due to time limitations and range availability, shooting was not done beyond this range.

An XM21 sniper rifle in combat trim. M14s serving as the basis for this system were rebuilt from those made by the various manufacturers (Springfield Armory, Harrington & Richardson, Winchester, and Thompson Ramo Woolridge), with all regarded equally desirable, except for barrels having chromed bores which were considered unsatisfactory for precision shooting. "SAK" barrels manufactured at the Saco, Maine Ordnance Depot were reportedly used with the bulk of the Vietnam era XM21 rifles. Rifle stocks were "pattern painted" to facilitate their concealment. Photo Credit: U.S. Army.

A right view of the Redfield 3x-9x variable power ART with the XM21. A fixed pivot mounting allowed the rear of the scope to move up or down when "camming" the sight. Normal eye relief was three to three-and-one-half inches. The telescope could not be moved within the mount since it was necessary for the ballistic cam to retain its relationship with the mount. Photo Credit: U.S. Army.

Once accepted into the sniper school, students brought a Starlight Scope and mount when reporting for training. A precision M14 rifle and scope was issued and retained for subsequent operations. The marksman is sighting an XM21 mounting the Adjustable Ranging Telescope (ART). Photo Credit: U.S. Army.

In 1968, rebuilding procedures based directly on the aforementioned were put into manual form by Lt. Col. F. B. Conway (Ret.) to accommodate "individual rifle accuracy specialists and organizations within and outside the military services." As further stated therein:

> The procedures or characteristics specified here are in addition to those of Army Weapons Command for the National Match Rifle and supersede them when requirements are more specific or exacting.

As a matter of interest, these procedures served as the rebuilding standard for the XM21 system.

As such, the original "ten" mounting the "toolroom" ARTs were tested in Vietnam through the latter part of 1967. Although three of the ARTs developed internal fog (common to all sights in

Vietnam) and the mounting rings did not appear to be rigid enough, on an overall basis, the ART and the special M14s performed as well as could be expected.

However, much to the chagrin of those close to the project in the States, regular issue M80 ball ammunition was used and in many cases, average riflemen, including those who had never fired a rifle with telescopic sights before, were used for evaluative purposes. Nevertheless, a few riflemen functioning as snipers with units of the 1st and 9th Infantry Divisions recorded a number of first round hits out to 600 meters with the ART. Prior to this, these same marksmen had rarely engaged targets beyond 400 meters with their M84-equipped M14s and/or M16s mounting 3X Colt Realist scopes.

However promising and effective the new sys-

Qualification firing at 150, 300, 600, and 900 meters was conducted during the last two days of the 9th Division sniper course. Those failing to qualify were washed out with no exceptions. Photo Credit: U.S. Army.

tem was in fact, fielding it in quantity, in an undiluted state, proved to be no small task. For the first time in U.S. history, the Army had a first-class sniping system and those cognizant of this "dug-in" and prepared for the struggle to have it adopted.

In lieu of the Army's commitment to the M16 as its principal infantry arm, the M14, out of production since 1963, was destined for obsolescence. As a result, in some quarters, the M14 was considered "unsuitable for long term development" in this capacity, prompting the question as to why it was being "pushed" as the basis for a new sniping arm rather than the M16 or a bolt-action target rifle.

Contrary to most beliefs, however, the M16 did

receive due consideration for use as a sniping weapon, but could not match the long-range accuracy of the M14, as proven conclusively when the M16 was subjected to innumerable tests over an extended period. However unsuited the M16 may have been for long-range sniping in Vietnam, the right combination of marksman, rifle, ammunition, and telescope accounted for documented hits at ranges out to 700 meters. Nevertheless, results such as this were far from common.

There were, of course, a number of organizations supporting the use of accurized M14s for sniping, but credit must be given to the various agencies at Ft. Benning among which the USAMTU, under the command of Col. Robert F. Bayard, had considered the accurized M14 a prime requisite

A student sniper on the firing line at Bearcat, the site of the original 9th Infantry Division sniper school in South Vietnam. An early ART system, the telescope mount locking knob has large flats for tightening purposes. Photo Credit: U.S. Army.

from the beginning. Their position was based on the results of evaluations conducted with all military and commercial rifles available in the U.S., in combination with various ammunition and telescopes during the quest for an efficient sniping system.

The additional reasons were cited by LTC Frank Conway (Ret.), the MTU Shop Officer during the development and subsequent fielding of the XM21 system.

> We realized that it was possible to obtain acceptable accuracy with a manually operated target rifle, and that it was much easier to prepare and glass-bed a target rifle than the machinery of a self-loader. However, if acceptable accuracy could be obtained, the self-loading rifle offered the following advantages:

A. In case of target movement or errors on the part of the sniper, a second shot could be fired immediately.

B. Engaging multiple targets.

C. There was no perceptible movement with a self-loader. Consequently, the possibility of detection was reduced significantly.

D. Both semi- and full-automatic fire capability enabled the sniper to defend himself or engage the enemy as circumstances warranted.

E. The M14 possessed both day and night capability, whereas at that point, no work had been done mounting night vision equipment on bolt-action rifles.

The only real disadvantage of the self-loader, as we saw it, rested with the ejection of brass which could compromise the sniper's position. We considered

Potential snipers carefully squeezing off each round in preparation for "working the Mekong Delta." Photo Credit: Mike West.

having sniper ammunition colored dull black as was done with some dummy rounds. To my knowledge, however, nothing was done in this direction.

As for the M14's accuracy, for example, we analyzed countless score sheets by "All Army" rifle teams and determined that the percentage of first round "V" ring shots at 1000 yards between the M14 and the 30/338 Magnum rifle were not too different. Let me emphasize—when I say M14, I do not mean the regular issue rifle or even the National Match variant prepared by Army Weapons

Command, but rather those built to USAMTU specifications.

One point beyond dispute rested with the proven ruggedness of the M14. By this time, the Marine Corps M40 was simply not holding up in the field. These weapons were never intended for the rigors of combat.

There was no question in our minds. We were convinced; accurized M14s were the only way to go. Nevertheless, we had a very difficult time convincing Weapons Command that our system was a good one.

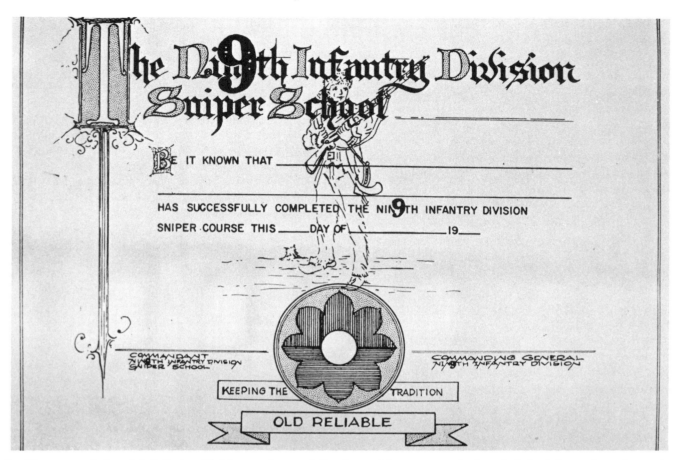

Certificate awarded to 9th Infantry Division marksmen following satisfactory completion of their eighteen-day sniper training. So demanding were the requirements that only 50 percent of the candidates successfully completed the first five classes. Photo Credit: Peter R. Senich.

Snipers reported directly to company commanders, received a briefing on proposed tactics, picked the platoon and area where they thought they could be most effective, and waited for a target. Photo Credit: U.S. Army.

We didn't claim to know all the answers, but we were getting accurate results.

Even though the USAMTU was in fact a basic infantry unit, its contributions to Army marksmanship had earned the respect of the "front office."

Following the ACTIV field evaluations of the new system, further development and refining of the ART system continued in the States. In late 1967, prior to assuming command of the 9th Infantry Division, Lt. General Julian J. Ewell contacted the MTU requesting its assistance in developing a program for training 9th Division snipers. With the 9th operating in the Mekong Delta, General Ewell envisioned an effective utilization of snipers inasmuch as large portions of this region were relatively flat, encompassing large areas of rice paddies.

In response, a sniper instruction team (the first of its type to be used in RVN), comprised of eight noncommissioned officers, a National Match armorer, and its commander, MAJ Willis K. Powell, arrived in Vietnam in June 1968. At this juncture, there were no accurized M14s with the ART in Southeast Asia.

Upon arrival, the team set about establishing a sniper training facility from scratch. During this period of organization, the MTU team served as snipers in order to gain practical experience in actual combat situations. It was reported that during the first month, two members of the team "bagged" ten VC in a night ambush, engaging the enemy at 500 meters.

The first accurized M14s mounting the Adjustable Ranging Telescope to reach the 9th Division Sniper School (approximately fifty) were built and shipped by the USAMTU later that year. Early in 1969, the MTU also tested, packaged, and shipped forty Sionics M14SS-1 noise suppressors to the 9th for combat evaluation.

The brainchild of Atlanta-based Sionics, Inc., the M14SS-1 suppressor made it next to impossible for the VC to locate the firing source at distances greater than fifty to one hundred meters ahead of the weapon. Based on initial combat use, a select 9th Infantry Division sniper related: "The suppressor is very effective; the VC just seem to mill around even after a couple of them have been dropped."

Early evaluations of the Sionics noise suppressor with the XM21 rifle were recorded as follows:

Field tests were conducted by the 9th Division Sniper School at Dong Tam in February 1969. The tests consisted of an accuracy test, noise suppression test, and muzzle flash test at night. These tests confirmed that the suppressor would function as designed.

Reports from the field told of numerous contacts indicating that the snipers were able to make multiple kills from one ambush position. The suppressor controlled the muzzle flash and noise so well that at no time did the VC actually pinpoint the direction of fire or the location of the ambush site. Field and combat test data indicate that the suppressor does the following:

A. Eliminates muzzle flash.
B. Suppresses the muzzle noise considerably and makes it virtually impossible to pinpoint the sniper's position using the "crack" and "thump" method.
C. Accuracy or range is not affected.
D. The added weight is of no consquence when the above advantages are considered.

Based on the successes of the 9th Division snipers in the field with the suppressor equipped rifle, the CG, 9th Division, desired to have at least one suppressor for each two man sniper team. It is recommended that the noise suppressor be furnished as an integral part of the sniper weapons system.

Additional test firings conducted with modified 7.62mm subsonic ammunition, although quiet, were found unacceptable due in part to its range limitations and marginal accuracy beyond eighty-five meters. Since high-velocity match grade ammunition was a prime factor in the XM21 system, it was thought that the ballistic differences between match and subsonic ammunition would create zeroing problems if used alternately. At that point, further consideration of modified ammunition on an issue basis was dropped.

An explanation of noise suppression and the principal function of the M14SS-1 suppressor was set forth in the Operation and Maintenance Manual for this unit by Sionics, Inc.:

Noise Sources

When the XM21 rifle, or any high muzzle velocity weapon is fired, the resulting noise is produced by two separate sources. Depending on the distance and direction from the weapon, the two noises may appear as one or two closely spaced different sounds. These are the muzzle noise and the ballistic crack, or sonic boom produced by the bullet.

A. The muzzle noise is generated by the blast wave created by the high velocity gases escaping into

Ninth Infantry Division sniper on patrol in the Mekong Delta region. Photo Credit: U.S. Army.

An Army sniper scanning the area for enemy activity with the ART. Vietnam, February 1970. Photo Credit: U.S. Army.

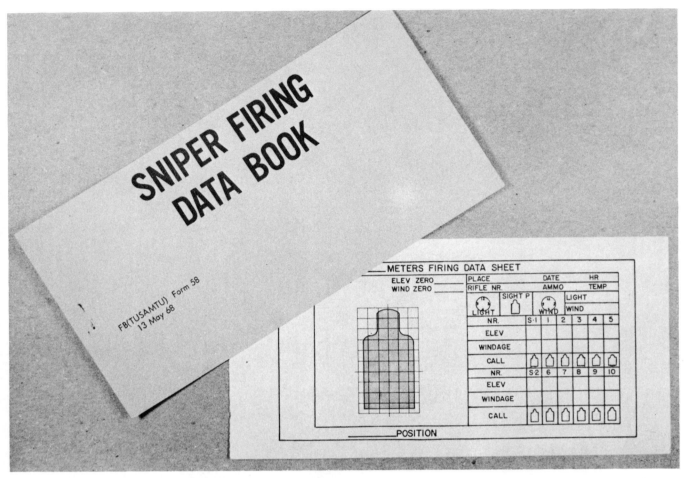

A "Sniper Firing Data Book" employed by Army marksmen in Southeast Asia. The small booklets provided an effective means of analyzing the performance of the sniper and his rifle. Photo Credit: Peter R. Senich.

the atmosphere behind the bullet. This noise is relatively easy to locate as to source, as it emanates from a fixed point.

B. Ballistic crack results from the supersonic speed of the bullet, which compresses the air ahead of it exactly in the same fashion as a supersonic jet creates a sonic boom. The only difference is that the smaller bullet produces a sharp crack rather than a large overpressure wave with its correspondingly louder shock wave. Unlike the muzzle noise which emanates from a fixed point, the ballistic crack radiates backwards in a conical shape similar to a bow wave from a boat, from a point slightly ahead of the moving bullet. Thus the sonic boom created by the supersonic bullet moves at the velocity of the bullet away from the muzzle noise and in the direction of the target. Location and identification of the initial source of the shock wave is extremely difficult because the moving wave impinges on the ear at nearly ninety degrees to the point of origin. Attention is thus drawn to the direction from which the

wave is coming rather than towards the initial source, i.e., the firing position of the weapon itself.

Action of the M14SS-1 Suppressor

A. The M14SS-1 suppressor is effective in reducing and disguising muzzle noise and has no effect on the muzzle velocity of the bullet. It does not in any way reduce or change the ballistic crack of the bullet.

B. The M14SS-1 suppressor effectively reduces muzzle noise in three ways.

First, the rapidly expanding propellent gases behind the bullet are permitted to flow into the suppressor expansion chambers, which greatly increases the space available in which the gases may expand. As the space into which the gases may flow is enlarged, the gas pressure is reduced.

Secondly, the gases entering the suppressor spiral chamber are directed, by the unique design of the suppressor rings, in a spiral path through the chamber before re-entering the bore, and may

An XM21-equipped Army sniper moves across a dike adjacent to a rice paddy. Photo Credit: U.S. Army.

Original camouflage clothing worn by a "working" 9th Infantry Division sharpshooter in South Vietnam. A cloth tab directly above the regular unit patch near the shoulder seam reads, "9th INF DIV SNIPER." The patch on the upper right pocket displays a telescopic sighted rifle.

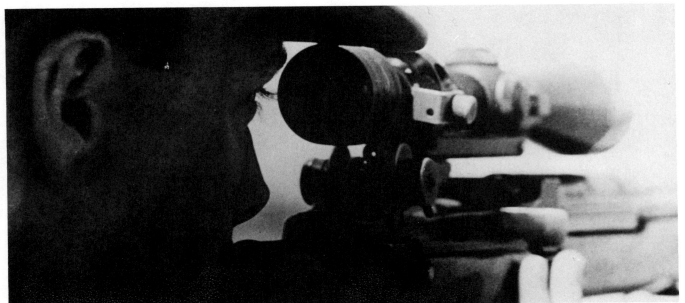

Fortunate indeed was the Army marksman who happened to claim a Viet Cong Tax Collector. As one sniper relates, "VC Tax Collectors carried large amounts of Vietnamese currency; tribute from various villages and hamlets. The recovered money was put to good use for off-duty recreation." Photo Credit: U.S. Army.

actually pass through several portions of the suppressor and bore before reaching the muzzle. This greatly increases the distance the gases must travel before being expelled into the atmosphere, which in turn, drastically reduces the velocity and the intensity of the accompanying sound wave.

Thirdly, the design and configuration of the suppressor spirals produces a series of reflections of the gas shock waves within the chamber. A large number of sound and pressure waves of various frequencies, wave lengths, and amplitudes are thus produced within the suppressor. Since the direction of the gas flow within the suppressor is alternately in opposite directions, a large percentage of the generated waves eventually get out of phase 180 degrees and thus

cancel each other out producing a sound nullifying effect and reducing the overall noise spectrum to a minimum auditory factor from a sound loudness viewpoint.

It is believed that a combination of all three of the above sound reducing methods is at least a partial explanation of the extraordinary effectiveness of the M14SS-1 suppressor.

A principal reason for the success of the Sionics suppressor rested with its "pressure relief valve" which solved several problems that had plagued the use of such devices on fully automatic and some semiautomatic weapons through the years. As experts summarized:

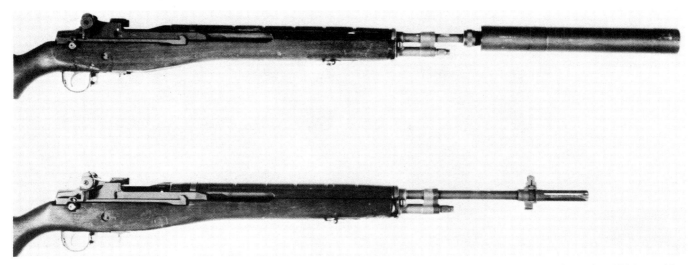

The Sionics M14SS-1 suppressor assembled and mounted on an M14 rifle. The standard muzzle area of another M14 provides a comparison. Though never officially adopted, noise suppressors were found to increase the confidence and capabilities of U.S. snipers in Southeast Asia. Photo Credit: James Alley.

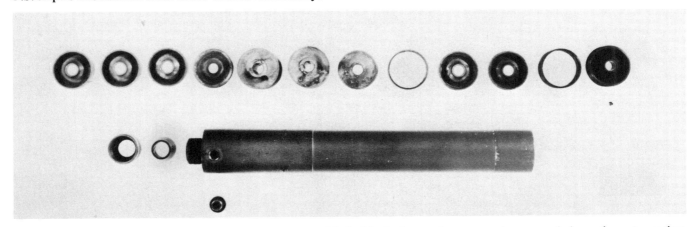

The M14SS-1 Noise and Flash Suppressor shown disassembled with the internal components arranged above the outer casing. The Sionics attachment is 12.75 inches long, extends 9 inches past the muzzle, has a diameter of 1.665 inches and weighs 1 pound 15 ounces. It is constructed of steel, aluminum, and uses a brass or teflon bushing. The finish is a black oxide coating. Photo Credit: James Alley.

The Sionics patented and exclusive gas pressure relief valve solves the following problems: it keeps the cyclic rate on fully automatic fire nearly the same rate as that without a suppressor; it prevents the serious problem of excessive gas blowback into the firer's face; it prevents excessive fouling of the gun's action; and finally, the bolt mechanism does not have to be modified on any gun because this valve handles the different pressures.

Combined use of the suppressor and Starlight Scope in night operations proved particularly advantageous to snipers for deceptive purposes, since the suppressor served to hide muzzle flash as well, thereby making auditory and visual detection equally difficult.

In early use, however, a "six-pointed star"

emitted from the pressure relief valve located at the rear of the suppressor could be observed at a distance of seventy-five to one hundred yards from the firing point. A simple solution to this problem entailed placing a cap over the relief port during night operations.

Following a period of trial and error, during which time the misuse of trained sniper personnel was cited as the greatest problem, the sniper training program employed by the 9th Division yielded extraordinary results and eventually served as the basis for a formal Program of Instruction (POI) for training Army snipers in RVN. A measure of their methods and effectiveness was summarized by MAJ Powell, Commandant, 9th Division Sniper School in February 1969.

The cover from A Sionics Operation and Maintenance Manual for the M14SS-1 Noise and Flash Suppressor Assembly (December 1969). An original copy issued with an XM21 suppressor. The attachment serial number (S.N. 10) appears on the cover. **Photo Credit: Peter R. Senich.**

Standard issue 20-round M14 magazine (left) and a special 7-round variant developed by the USAMTU for use with the XM21 rifles in Vietnam. The three-inch long magazine enabled Army snipers to maintain a lower profile when firing from a prone position. Photo Credit: Lieutenant Colonel F. B. Conway (Retired).

USAMTU personnel at the Fort Benning shop. The ART equipped XM21 has been fitted with a pistol-grip M14E2 stock assembly. Note the rubber recoil pad and raised comb. Photo Credit: Lieutenant Colonel F. B. Conway (Retired).

The 900-meter capability of the XM21 system made the everyday life of VC and NVA personnel quite hazardous. Photo Credit: U.S. Army.

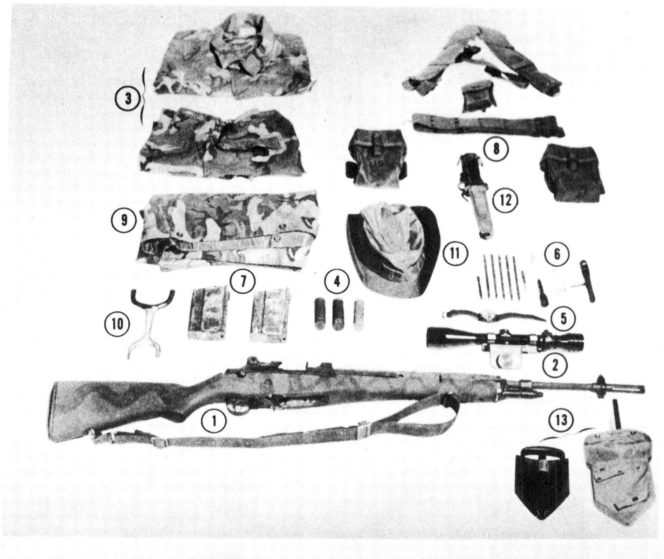

1	Sniper rifle	7	Magazines.
2	Sniperscope with mount (carrying case, protective cover caps not shown).	8	Webb equipment.
3	Camouflage clothing.	9	Camouflage poncho.
4	Camouflaging sticks.	10	Rifle fork.
5	Watch.	11	Hat.
6	Cleaning kit.	12	Bayonet with scabbard.
		13	Entrenching tool with cover.

An excerpt from Sniper Training and Employment (TC 23-14), October 1969, depicts the individual sniper equipment as issued for combat use in RVN. Photo Credit: Peter R. Senich.

Right now we are up to 148 kills and that has probably been upped since 1800 today. Most of the kills are coming at night with the Starlight Scope mounted on the M14. The VC aren't moving much in the daytime, but whenever one of our snipers gets a shot off they rarely miss.

The equipment is holding up real well, and we've had one-shot kills in daytime up to 800 meters and up to 550–600 meters at night. Most of the employment at night over here is with an ambush patrol. The snipers are given permission to engage one to five man groups and the rest of the ambush element holds their fire until needed. The snipers then maintain surveillance over any body they knock down and pick off other VC trying to recover weapons, equipment, or the body. This has worked well especially with one battalion.... Under the present set-up in the division, we will have a total of seventy-two snipers, six per battalion (equalling sixty), plus four per brigade (equalling twelve). The snipers are employed in pairs, with at least a five to eight man security element along. They are controlled and managed by the Battalion Commander and S-3, and are attached to the companies that have, or are likely to have, the most contacts.

In addition to night ambushes, they have been used on berm, roads, bridges, and firing sites as a security type mission. We have been working in conjunction with the Xenon searchlight with a pink filter. This is a very good combination when the natural light from the moon and stars is at a low level. We also coordinate flares to help out when needed. On daylight missions they are being used in numerous ways, in both elements of a cordon, and searches placed at the back of villages to pick off fleeing VC when the village search is on, and in staying behind elements when units are displacing to new objective, to pick off VC following them....

The primary consideration that must be kept in mind when planning an operation here is to put the snipers in the position with good fields of observation and long fields of fire. The units that are taking a little extra time in the planning phase of an operation are the ones racking up kills with snipers.

Although a number of outstanding feats of combat marksmanship were recorded by Army snipers serving with various divisions in Vietnam, SFC Adelbert F. Waldron (Ret.), during his tour of duty as a 9th Division sniper, was credited with 113 confirmed kills in a five-month period. Sergeant Waldron compiled this impressive score while operating during periods of day and night, armed with the XM21, mounting the ART, Starlight Scope, and noise suppressor in combination as

needed. Lt. General Ewell, commenting on the 9th's sniper program in *Sharpening the Combat Edge,* cited another mode of sniper employment:

> One of the unusual night sniper employments resulted from the 6th Battalion, 31st Infantry operations from riverine boats along the Mekong River. In this case, the snipers working in pairs positioned themselves on the helicopter landing pad of Tango boats. The Tango boats traveled at speeds of two to four knots moving about one hundred to 150 meters from and parallel to the shore. Often they would anchor for periods of a half-hour before moving to a new location. As the Viet Cong moved along the shoreline, the snipers would make positive identification of the enemy, through detection of a weapon, and would open fire. During the period 12 April to 9 May 1969, snipers of the 6th Battalion, 31st Infantry killed thirty-nine Viet Cong. About 1.7 VC were killed per engagement.

Army snipers, as one might suspect, were not the only marksmen to operate in this manner. At the request of the Navy Department, the USAMTU rebuilt, tested, and shipped forty M14 sniping rifles directly to RVN for use on patrol boats by Navy sniper personnel.

From January 1969 until the majority of the 9th Infantry Division was redeployed to the United States in August of the same year, snipers of the 9th accounted for approximately 1,300 enemy KIA with an average of 1.39 rounds expended per kill. It must be pointed out, however, that these results were obtained through combined use of the XM21 system and the National Match M14 from Army Weapons Command.

The XM21 was finally brought to fruition when *Limited Production for Sniper Rifles and Scopes* was authorized by the Department of the Army on 14 February 1969 (Msg 897570-ENSURE #240). Col. Jack Wood, Office of the Assistant Chief of Staff for Force Development, Headquarters, Department of the Army, is credited by those close to the XM21 project as having been the leading proponent in securing funds necessary for ENSURE #240.

Army Weapons Command was given the responsibility of rebuilding the M14 according to MTU procedures with the USAMTU functioning as the final inspection agency. Fifty rifles were to be shipped to Ft. Benning on a weekly basis, accuracy tested, fitted with the ART, and sighted in. Not one of the first one hundred rifles received from

Example of Vietnam-era sniper insignia (patches). The originals were usually made on a local basis as a variation of the unit patch. Left to right, 25th Infantry Division Sniper, 1st Cavalry Sniper, 9th Infantry Division Sniper. Photo Credit: John C. McPherson, Lancer Militaria.

A front and rear view of an Army sniper in camouflage clothing with the XM 21 and full field gear circa 1969. Photo Credit: Peter R. Senich.

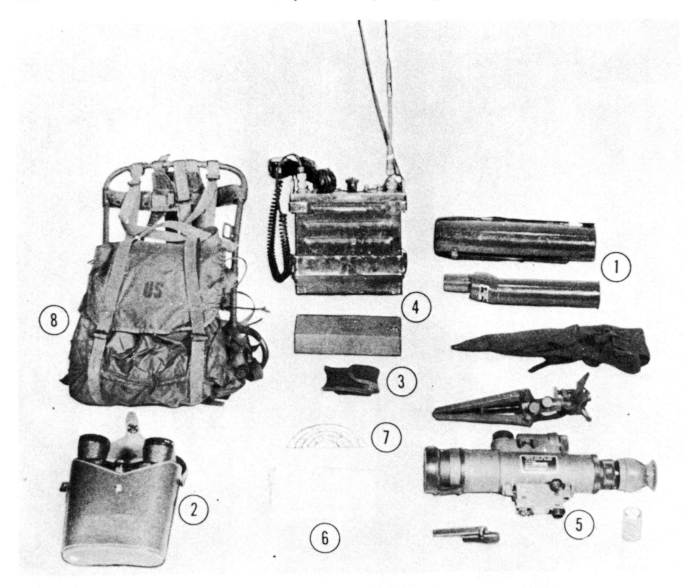

1 Observation scope w/tripod and cases.
2 Binoculars w/case.
3 Compass w/pouch
4 Radio w/batteries

5 Night vision sight w/mount, adaptor bracket and battery.
6 Maps.
7 Sector sketch/range card.
8 Rucksack.

Sniper team equipment illustration from U.S. Army training manual TC 23-14. Photo Credit: Peter R. Senich.

Vietnam-era sniper patches. Left to right, 82nd Airborne Sniper, 101st Airborne Sniper, 173rd Airborne Brigade Sniper. Sniper insignia for U.S. Navy Riverine Forces and various Marine Corps units have been noted as well. Photo Credit: John C. McPherson, Lancer Militaria.

An experimental XM21 scope base evaluated at Rock Island Arsenal in 1970. Intended to provide greater rigidity for the ART system, the "two point base" concept was later adopted in modified form. Photo Credit: U.S. Army.

An overall view of students and instructors on the firing range at the 23rd Infantry Division (American) sniper school, Chu Lai, Vietnam (September 1971). The weapons are accurized M14s (XM21). The instructors are from the U.S. Army Marksmanship Training Unit, Fort Benning, Georgia. In addition to assuming certain responsibilities in support of the XM21 system in South Vietnam. USAMTU personnel would also participate in various unit sniper training programs on an in-country basis. Photo Credit: U.S. Army.

Sniper operations were designed to harass, impede, destroy, or prevent movement of individual enemy personnel and units. When sniping was phased out in Vietnam in 1971, Army marksmen had proven the worth of first class equipment and training. Photo Credit: U.S. Army.

A measure of Army sniper effectiveness was best summarized by Lt. Gen. Julian J. Ewell. "The sniper program of the 9th Infantry Division was one of the most successful programs that we undertook. It took over a year from its inception in the States to its peak performances in Vietnam. It also took plenty of hard work and belief in the concept of our snipers. But more than anything, it restored the faith of the infantryman in his rifle and in his own capabilities." Photo Credit: U.S. Army.

RiFLE. 7.62 mm   sniper M21

In October 1970, the Department of the Army approved the Combat Developments Command "Abbreviated Performance Characteristics for a Sniper Rifle System," based on the XM21's characteristics. The XM21 was eventually adopted by the Army as its sniper standard in 1972, at which time it officially became the "Rifle, 7.62mm Sniper M21." Photo Credit: U.S. Army.

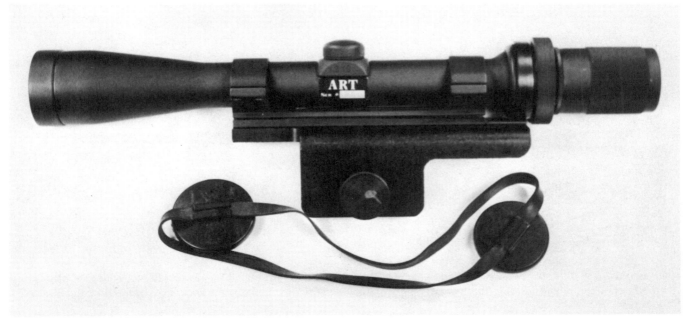

Knowledge gained from seven years of Army testing and combat use brought forth the M21 Leatherwood 3X-9X Adjustable Ranging Telescope following Vietnam. This design withstood 5,000 rounds of continuous fire during tests conducted by the U.S. Navy and erased any doubt of the ART's durability. Photo Credit: Peter R. Senich.

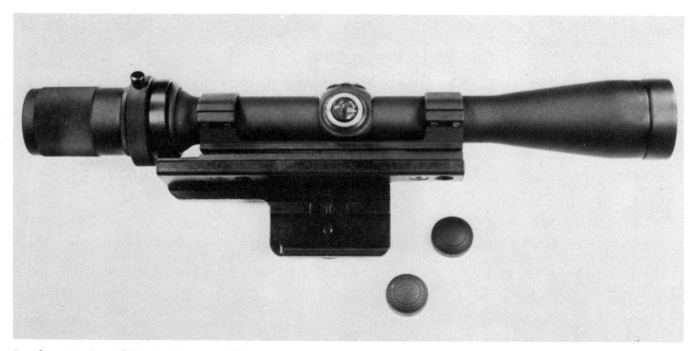

An alternate view of the Leatherwood M21 ART with elevation and windage dial caps removed. The improved mount was judged superior to the LWL-ART pivot system which had a tendency to wear, eventually making it impossible to hold zero. Photo Credit: Peter R. Senich.

Rock Island Arsenal "Product Improved" M14 Sniper Rifle circa 1975. A prototype series developed under the auspices of Army Materiel Command (AMC), the special weapons were designed to improve the accuracy potential of the M14 rifle. Photo Credit: U.S. Army.

The highly sophisticated, second-generation Leatherwood 3X-9X ART II sighting system with an M1A/M14 rifle. Photo Credit: Charles Leatherwood.

A top view of the Leatherwood ART II system. Photo Credit: Charles Leatherwood.

Designed around the proven adjustable ranging telescope concept, the Leatherwood military sight represents the ART system in its most efficient form. Photo Credit: Charles Leatherwood.

A significant part of an official post-Vietnam "product improved M14 rifle program" conducted at Rock Island Arsenal. The "Test Fixture 7.62mm Semi-Automatic Sniper Rifle" was intended to "squeeze every possible degree of performance from the M14 action." The highly modified system featured an M14 action, a massive stainless-steel barrel and gas-cylinder, laminated thumbhole stock and set trigger. Army Materiel Command, 8 December 1982. Photo Credit: U.S. Army—courtesy of R. Blake Stevens.

Weapons Command during October 1969 met the necessary accuracy requirements, and had to be rebuilt by MTU armorers before acceptance. This rejection rate eventually dropped to approximately twenty-five to thirty percent per shipment, however. Rework of both the initial and subsequent XM21 rejects from Rock Island Arsenal was directed by M/SGT Gerald "Hook" Boutin (Ret.) who was considered by his MTU associates as "one of the best in the business."

After a time, in order to facilitate their rebuilding efforts, Weapons Command requested certain changes in the MTU procedures, most of which involved a relaxation of barrel specifications. This was effected without compromising weapon accuracy. In response to the question, "Where did the XM21 title originate?", LTC Frank Conway replied, "As I recollect, I received a call from Rock Island inquiring if we had any objection to calling the system the XM21. I replied, 'I don't care what

Even though specifications for a new sniping weapon have been established, and replacement systems tested, at present, the 7.62mm M21 sniper rifle remains "the tool of the trade" for Army marksmen. Mounting early versions of the ART or ART II telescopic sights, some of the M14 based sniping rifles carried by the Army date back to the war in Vietnam. Photo Credit: U.S. Army.

you call it as long as you don't reduce the standards.'"

By Army definition, "XM followed by an Arabic numeral was used to identify an item during its development. Upon acceptance as an adopted type, the letter X was dropped, leaving the letter M followed by an Arabic numeral."

During the course of their use in Vietnam, a number of difficulties were experienced with the ART and the accurized M14s, but were duly rectified over a period of time. The XM21s were in continuous use, subjected to extremely rough handling and adverse weather conditions, but still performed as well as anticipated. One of the greatest problems rested with proper ordnance support, or rather, lack of the same. It was originally thought that the XM21 could be maintained by regular unit armorers. However, trained National

Match armorers were eventually required to render proper field support.

While tactical employment of Army snipers in Vietnam varied, so did the results. An indication of XM21 effectiveness can be derived from one report, spanning a ten-day period, as recorded by the Americal Division in May 1970.

Update Information on Sniper Program
Americal Division

1. To date, this division has 57 snipers within combat units.
2. To date, sniper actions are listed below:

Time	Sight	Terrain	Range (meters)	Rds Fired	Kill	Wounded
1630	ART	Trail	450	1	1	–

Time	Sight	Terrain	Range (meters)	Fired	Kill	Wounded
1900	Star	Trail	500	2	–	1
1930	Star	River	200	2	1	–
1200	ART	Woods	650	1	1	–
1215	ART	Jungle	75	2	1	–
1400	ART	Jungle	45	3	1	–
1715	ART	Hill Top	500	2	1	–
0815	ART	Paddy	900	1	1	–
0515	Star	River	250	1	1	–
0530	Star	River Bank	500	2	–	1
0100	Star	Paddy	100	1	1	–
1415	ART	Trail	700	5	1	–

In October 1970 the Department of the Army approved the Combat Developments Command, Abbreviated Performance Characteristics for a Sniper Rifle System, based on the XM21's characteristics. The XM21 was eventually adopted by the Army as its sniper standard in 1972, at which time it became the M21.

At the end of hostilities in RVN, there were reportedly 1,300-plus XM21 sniper rifles in the field. Despite the fact that this system had clearly demonstrated what a "first-class" sniping weapon could accomplish in a combat environment, following the general stand-down, the Army Sniper Program once again slipped into a state of lethargy until early 1976 when interest in sniper marksmanship was again rekindled under the aegis of Lieutenant General Henry Emerson, Commanding General of the XVIII Airborne Corps.

A program was launched at Fort Benning to rebuild 342 M21 sniper weapons for use by the XVIII Airborne Corps headquartered at Fort Bragg, North Carolina. During this rebuilding process, unit armorers from the 82nd Airborne Division, 101st Airborne Division, and the John F. Kennedy Special Warfare Center were trained by the MTU to support these weapons properly. Renewed interest in sniper rifles and their employment led to efforts in the Army to satisfy its current sniper needs and to consider its future sniper rifle requirements.

In line with these efforts, as noted in the *Infantry News:*

Five candidate 7.62mm sniper rifles were selected for testing by the Infantry Board. Three of the candidate rifles were bolt-action rifles, one was semiautomatic, and one was both semiautomatic and automatic. The accuracy of the candidate sniper rifles was compared with that of the M21 sniper rifle that is now classified by the Army as Standard B. The telescopes used on the candidate rifles were essentially the same as the telescope used on the M21.

During this period, six master riflemen from the Army's Marksmanship Training Unit, several of whom had been snipers in combat, fired over a modified Palma Match Course, and over a combat accuracy test course. The results of the test indicated that there were no significant differences between the test items and the standard M21 rifle from an accuracy standpoint. The test soldiers unanimously reported that they preferred a semiautomatic sniper rifle with externally loaded magazines.

According to the Army, "The candidate sniper rifles represented weapons requiring minimum development for Army use." The rifles then tested consisted of three of each of the following models:

A. AR10 rifle modified at Rock Island Arsenal with Leatherwood telescopic sight (ART) and Redfield front sight attachment.
B. Army M21 rifle.
C. Remington M40A1 (Marine Corps sniper rifle) with Leatherwood telescopic sight (ART).
D. M14 rifle modified at Rock Island Arsenal with free-floating barrel, redesigned laminated stock, Leatherwood telescopic sight (ART) and Redfield front sight attachment.
E. Parker Hale 1200 TX (Canadian C3) with Leatherwood telescopic sight (ART).
F. Winchester M70 Match rifle with Leatherwood telescopic sight (ART).

All rifles fired the M118 match cartridge.

As the state of the art progresses, and continued use of the M21 system passes well beyond the point of practicality, there can be little doubt that the venerable M14-based M21 will be replaced. However, as an MTU spokesman put it, "despite some maintenance problems, so far as accuracy is concerned, the M21 has continued to hold its own."